REGIONAL INTEGRATION AND POVERTY

The International Political Economy of New Regionalisms Series

The International Political Economy of New Regionalisms Series presents innovative analyses of a range of novel regional relations and institutions. Going beyond established, formal, interstate economic organizations, this essential series provides informed interdisciplinary and international research and debate about myriad heterogeneous intermediate level interactions.

Reflective of its cosmopolitan and creative orientation, this series is developed by an international editorial team of established and emerging scholars in both the South and North. It reinforces ongoing networks of analysts in both academia and think-tanks as well as international agencies concerned with micro-, meso- and macro-level regionalisms.

Recent Titles in the Series

Globalization and Antiglobalization
Dynamics of Change in the New World Order
Edited by Henry Veltmeyer

Twisting Arms and Flexing Muscles
Humanitarian Intervention and Peacebuilding in Perspective
Edited by Natalie Mychajlyszyn and Timothy M. Shaw

Asia Pacific and Human Rights
A Global Political Economy Perspective
Paul Close and David Askew

Latin America's Quest for Globalization
The Role of Spanish Firms
Edited by Félix E. Martín and Pablo Toral

Regional Integration and Poverty

Edited by

DIRK WILLEM TE VELDE

Routledge
Taylor & Francis Group

LONDON AND NEW YORK

First published 2006 by Ashgate Publishing

2 Park Square, Milton Park, Abingdon, Oxon OX14 4RN
711 Third Avenue, New York, NY 10017, USA

Routledge is an imprint of the Taylor & Francis Group, an informa business

First issued in paperback 2017

British Library Cataloguing in Publication Data
Regional integration and poverty. - (The international
    political economy of new regionalisms series)
    1.International economic integration 2.Poverty 3.Bolivia -
    Foreign economic relations 4.Bolivia - Economic conditions
    - 1982- 5.Bolivia - Social conditions - 1982- 6.Tanzania -
    Foreign economic relations 7.Tanzania - Economic conditions
    - 1964- 8.Tanzania - Social conditions - 1964-
    I.Velde, Dirk Willem te II.Overseas Development Institute
    (London, England)
    337.1

Library of Congress Cataloging-in-Publication Data
Regional integration and poverty / edited by Dirk Willem te Velde and Overseas
Development Institute.
        p. cm. -- (The international political economy of new regionalisms
series)
    Includes bibliographical references and index.
    ISBN 0-7546-4652-1
    1. International economic integration. 2. Regionalism. 3. Regional economics. 4.
Poverty. I. Velde, Dirk Willem te. II. Overseas Development Institute (London,
England) III. Series.

    HF1418.5.R4398 2006
    339.4'6--dc22

                                                                    2006012572

ISBN 978-0-7546-4652-5 (hbk)
ISBN 978-1-138-27821-9 (pbk)

Contents

List of Charts

List of Tables

Acknowledgments

This book resulted from a research project on Regional Integration and Poverty. The chapters in the book were presented at an ODI conference on Regional Integration and Poverty in London on 3 September 2004. I am grateful to the 60 participants and presenters for their suggestions and comments. I am also grateful to Miatta Fahnbulleh and Dirk Bezemer for valuable research inputs, to Genevieve Matthews for the layout and production of this book and to Margaret Cornell for copy-editing and indexing it, and to my co-authors Sheila Page, Oliver Morrissey, Josaphat Kweka, Osvaldo Nina, Lykke Andersen, Miatta Fahnbulleh and Phillip Mboya.

The research project on Regional Integration and Poverty is one of 23 projects funded by EC-PREP, a programme of research sponsored by the UK Department for International Development. The UK Department for International Development supports policies, programmes and projects to promote international development, and it provided funds for this study as part of that objective. The views and opinions expressed, however, are those of the authors alone. All EC-PREP research studies relate to one or more of the six focal areas of EC's development policy in the context of their link to poverty eradication. EC-PREP produces findings and policy recommendations which aim to contribute to improving the effectiveness of the EC's development assistance. For more information about EC-PREP and any of the other research studies produced under the programme, please visit the website www.ec-prep.org.

Dirk Willem te Velde

List of Contributors

Lykke E. Andersen

Lykke E. Andersen holds a Ph.D. in Economics from the University of Aarhus, Denmark, and has worked on development topics for more than ten years, living and working in Denmark, the UK, Kazakhstan, the US, Brazil, Nicaragua and Bolivia. She is the founding editor of the *Latin American Journal of Economic Development,* and is also a founding partner of the Bolivian think tank, Grupo Integral, where she currently works. She has worked as a consultant for the World Bank, the Inter-American Development Bank, the Andean Development Bank, various UN agencies (UNDP, UNFPA, UNICEF and OMS), a number of bilateral development agencies, several governmental institutions and a few NGOs. Her long list of publications on development topics includes *The Dynamics of Deforestation and Development in the Brazilian Amazon,* co-authored with the 2004 Nobel laureate in Economics, Clive W. J. Granger, (Cambridge: Cambridge University Press, 2002)

Miatta Fahnbulleh

Miatta Fahnbulleh is completing a PhD on Industrial and Economic Development in Africa at the London School of Economics. She holds an MSc in Economic History: Patterns of Development from the London School of Economics and a B.A. (Hons) in Politics, Philosophy and Economics from Oxford University. Her research interests include industrialization in Africa, the efficacy of state policy in African development, the impact of international trade and regional trade agreements on African development, economic liberalization reforms and private sector development.

Josaphat Kweka

Born in 1965 in Moshi, Tanzania, Josaphat Kweka is a graduate of the University of Dar es Salaam where he obtained an MA in economics in 1995 followed by a Ph.D. from the University of Nottingham in the UK in 2002. He has about ten years' experience in research work, and is currently a Research Fellow and Director of the Globalisation project at the Economic and Social Research Foundation (ESRF) in Dar es Salaam, having worked there previously as Research Assistant (1995-6) and an Assistant Research Fellow (1997-8). His main areas of research are trade policy and regional integration issues, tourism economics and growth and private sector development. He has published several papers in the areas of tourism economics, public finance, manufacturing and industrialization, trade and regional integration, and economic reform, and contributed the chapter 'The Form and Role of Industrial Innovativeness in Enhancing Firms' Productivity: The Case of Selected Manufacturing Firms in Tanzania' in *Industrial Experience in Tanzania* (edited by A. Szirmai and P. Lapperre, New York, 2001). Dr Kweka has also worked on several consultancy projects, among others for the ILO, the World Bank, the ICTSD, UNIDO and UNDP. His recent assignments include the Investment Climate Assessment survey of Tanzania, for the World Bank, and ODI's study on 'Identifying Linkages between Trade and Poverty in Tanzania' as part of DFID's Trade and Poverty Programme.

Phillip Gaspar Mboya

Born in 1969 in the Kilimanjaro region, Tanzania, Phillip Mboya is a graduate of the University of Dar es Salaam and also holds an MSc in Economics from the University of Zimbabwe. He has research experience with two Dar es Salaam-based NGOs, namely, Research on Poverty Alleviation (REPOA) and the Economic and Social Research Foundation (ESRF) where he worked as a Research Assistant for more than three years. He is currently working for the Bank of Tanzania, as an economist in the Department of Trade Finance and Investment Policies. His areas of expertise are corporate finance and investment issues, and monetary and environmental economics.

Oliver Morrissey

Oliver Morrissey is Professor in Development Economics and Director of CREDIT, School of Economics, University of Nottingham, UK, where he has been since 1989. In 2000-04 he was also a Research Fellow at the Overseas Development Institute (London). He has published many articles in international journals, mostly on aid policy and effectiveness, trade policy reform, conditionality and adjustment. His present research is concentrated on the economic impact of aid and capital flows; trade and non-policy barriers to export growth; and the political economy of policy reform. His major publications include *British Aid and International Trade* (with B. Smith and E. Horesh, Milton Keynes, 1992), *Evaluating Economic Liberalization* (edited with M. McGillivray, Basingstoke, 1999), *Globalization and Trade: Implications for Exports from Marginalised Economies* (edited with I. Filatotchev, London, 2001), *Economic Policy and Manufacturing Performance in Developing Countries* (edited with M. Tribe, Cheltenham, 2001), and *Foreign Aid in the New Global Economy* (edited with P. Burnell, Cheltenham, 2004).

Osvaldo Nina

Osvaldo Nina holds a Ph.D. in Economics from the University of Chile, and a M.Sc. in Economics from the Pontificia Universidad Católica in Rio de Janeiro. He is a founding partner of the Bolivian think tank, Grupo Integral, where he currently serves as Director, having previously been Director of the Institute for Socio-Economic Research at the Catholic University of Bolivia, where he coordinated the Andean Competitiveness Project for Bolivia sponsored by the Andean Development Corporation (CAF). He has worked as a consultant for a number of international organizations, including the Inter-American Development Bank, the Andean Development Corporation, the Development Research Institute, the North-South Institute, and the Overseas Development Institute, amongst others.

Sheila Page

Sheila Page is a Senior Research Associate of the Overseas Development Institute, London. From 1982 to 2005 she was a Research Fellow there. Previously she was at Queen Elizabeth House, Oxford, 1972, and the National Institute of Economic and Social Research, 1972-82. Her current research interests include how and why developing countries participate in international negotiations and trade relations between developed and developing countries, including Special and Differential treatment and EU-ACP and EU-MERCOSUR arrangements. She has also advised African and Latin American developing countries in multilateral and regional negotiations. Her publications include *Trade and Aid: Partners or Rivals in Development Policy* (2006), *Special and Differential Treatment for Developing Countries in the WTO*, with Peter Kleen (2005), *Regionalism among Developing Countries* (2000), *World Commodity Prices: Still a Problem for Developing Countries?* (2001), *How Developing Countries Trade* (1994), *World Trade Reform: do Developing Countries Gain or Lose?* (1994), Trade, *Finance and Developing Countries* (1989).

Dirk Willem te Velde (editor)

Dirk Willem te Velde has been a Research Fellow at the Overseas Development Institute, London, since 2000, specializing in trade and investment policy. He holds a PhD in Economics from the University of London. He has published around 30 journal articles and book chapters and recently completed an ODI book on *Foreign Direct Investment, Income Inequality and Poverty* (London, 2004). He advises several international organizations and governments, including DFID and the European Commission, on trade and investment policy. Before joining ODI he was a research officer at the National Institute of Economic and Social Research in London.

List of Abbreviations

ACP	African, Caribbean and Pacific countries
ACS	Association of Caribbean States
ADB	African Development Bank
AFTA	ASEAN Free Trade Agreement
AGOA	African Growth and Opportunity Act
AHSN	Animal Health Surveillance Network
AICO	ASEAN Industrial Cooperation
AIDS	Acquired Immune Deficiency Syndrome
AMU	Arab Maghreb Union
ANDEAN	Andean Community
APEC	Asia-Pacific Economic Cooperation
ASEAN	Association of South-East Asian Nations
ATPA	Andean Trade Preference Act
ATPDEA	Andean Trade Promotion and Drug Eradication Act
BIT	bilateral investment treaty
CACM	Central American Common Market
CAN	Comunidad Andina de Naciones
CARICOM	Caribbean Community and Common Market
CBI	Confederation of British Industry
CBI	Cross-border Initiative
CCIA	COMESA Common Investment Area
CEEC	Central and East European countries
CEMAC	Economic and Monetary Community of Central Africa
CEPGL	Economic Community of the Great Lakes countries
CER	closer economic relations
CET	Common External Tariff
CGE	Computable General Equilibrium
CIF	cost, insurance, and freight
CMSA	Capital Market and Securities Authority
COMESA	Common Market for Eastern and Southern Africa
CSME	Caricom Single Market and Economy
CTH	change in tariff heading
CTI	Confederation of Tanzanian Industries
CUTS	Consumer Unity and Trust Society
DC	domestic content
DFID	Department for International Development
DFIs	Development finance institutions

DRC	Democratic Republic of Congo
EAC	East African Community
EADB	East African Development Bank
EAIDSNet	East African Integrated Disease Surveillance Network
EALA	East African Legislative Assembly
EASRA	East Africa Securities and Regulatory Authority
EBA	everything but arms
EC	European Commission
ECCAS	Economic Community of Central African States
ECOWAS	Economic Community of West African States
EDB	Economic Development Board
EEC	European Economic Community
EEZ	Exclusive Economic Zone
EFTA	European Free Trade Association
EPA	Economic Partnership Agreement
ESA	Eastern and Southern African Countries
ESIPP	EU/SADC Investment Promotion Programme
EU	European Union
FAGRN	Farm Animal Genetic Resource Network (SADC)
FANR	Food Agriculture and Natural Resource Development Unit (SADC)
FAO	Food and Agriculture Organization
FDI	foreign direct investment
FOB	free on board
FTA	free trade area
FTAA	Free Trade Area of the Americas
FTZ	free trade zone
GATS	General Agreement on Trade in Services
GATT	General Agreement on Tariffs and Trade
GDP	gross domestic product
GSP	Generalized System of Preferences
GULFCOOP	Gulf Cooperation Council
HCCS	Harmonized Commodity Coding System
HDI	Human Development Index
HIV	Human Immunodeficiency Virus
IBRD	International Bank for Reconstruction and Development
ICD	Inter-Congolese dialogue
ICM	Integrated Committee of Ministers
ICSID	International Centre for Settlement of Investment Disputes
IDA	Ireland Industrial Development Agency
ILO	International Labour Organization
IMF	International Monetary Fund
IMMPA	Integrated Macroeconomic Model for Poverty Analysis
IMP	internal market programme

IOR-ARC	Indian Ocean Rim Association for Regional Cooperation
IPA	Investment Promotion Agency
IPS	Inter-Press Service
ISIC	International Standard Industrial Classification
IUU	Illegal Unregulated and Unreported fishing
LAFTA	Latin American Free Trade Association
LAIA	Latin American Integration Association
LT	long-term
LVEMP	Lake Victoria Environmental Management Project
MC	import content
MERCOSUR	Southern Common Market Agreement
MFN	most favoured nation
MIGA	Multilateral Investment Guarantee Agency
MNE	multinational enterprise
MOA	Market Opening Agreement
MRU	Mano River Union
MTS	multilateral trading systems
NAFTA	North American Free Trade Agreement
NALADISA	tariff system of the LAIA
NEP	new economic policy
NEPRU	Namibian Economic Research Unit
NT	national treatment
NTB	non-tariff barrier
OAS	Organization of American States
ODI	Overseas Development Institute
OECD	Organization for Economic Cooperation and Development
OECS	Organization of Eastern Caribbean States
PATCRA	Papua New Guinea Agreement on Trade and Commercial Relations
PRSP	Poverty Reduction Strategy Paper
PSNER	primary school net enrolment rate
PTA	Preferential Trade Area
R&D	research and development
RI	regional integration
RIA	Regional Integration Agreement
RIFF	Regional Integration Facilitation Forum
RoO	rules of origin
RTA	Regional Trade Agreement
RTP	Regional Trade Preference
SAARC	South Asian Association for Regional Cooperation
SACU	Southern African Customs Union
SADC	Southern African Development Community
SADCC	Southern African Development Coordination Conference
SAPTA	Agreement on SAARC Preferential Trading Arrangement

SDF	SADC Development Fund
SDT	special and differential treatment
SICA	Central American Integration System
SIDO	Small Industries Development Organization
SIRESE	The Sector Regulatory System in Bolivia
SMEs	small and medium-scale enterprises
SPARTECA	South Pacific Regional Trade and Economic Cooperation Agreement
SPS	sanitary and phyto-sanitary
SSA	sub-Saharan Africa
TADs	trans-boundary animal diseases
TBT	technical barriers to trade
TCCIA	Tanzania Chamber of Commerce, Industry and Agriculture
TIC	Tanzania Investment Centre
TRIMS	Trade-Related Investment Measures
UEMOA	West African Economic and Monetary Union
UNCITRAL	United Nations Commission on International Trade Law
UNCTAD	United Nations Conference on Trade and Industry
UNECA	United Nations Economic Commission for Africa
URT	United Republic of Tanzania
USA	United States of America
VAT	value-added tax
WB	World Bank
WTO	World Trade Organization

Chapter 1

Regional Integration and Poverty: Introduction

Dirk Willem te Velde

Currently there is a renewed emphasis on encouraging regional integration processes in the belief that this is good for development and poverty reduction. Unfortunately, a framework for mapping regional integration (RI) onto poverty does not exist, and this premise is therefore difficult to assess *ex ante* or even *ex post*. However, there is a lot of research that is directly relevant. For some time now (at least as far back as Viner, 1950), there have been studies examining the effect of regional integration on trade. More recently researchers have begun to extend this to RI and foreign direct investment; Ethier (1998) suggested that in the 'new' regionalism countries seek to form regions in order to attract investment. Researchers have also begun to address the effects of trade and investment on poverty (see, for example, McCulloch *et al.*, 2001; McKay *et al.*, 2000; ODI, 2002). However, the evidence has never been put together into a single framework to address the links between RI and poverty. The purpose of this book is to provide such a framework. It is hoped that such a mapping exercise will inform those responsible for regional trade policy with respect to the presence of such links and, where available, with respect to the effects of available policy options on poverty. The resultant mapping should also be useful in identifying a checklist of areas relevant to assessing the impact of regional integration on poverty in individual countries.

There are many ways in which a book on regional integration and poverty can be structured. We have opted for a relatively simple approach (Chart 1.1). Regional integration affects the movements of products and factors of production across borders – trade in goods and services and movement of people and capital – and these in turn affect poverty through various routes. Regional integration can also affect poverty directly through special initiatives and programmes (although, strictly speaking, some of this could be seen as movement of capital) and other functional cooperation. The movements of products and factors of production are related, and there may be relevant relationships here. Finally, there may be feedback from economic variables back to the regional integration processes.

The central part of this book is to develop the causal mappings in Chart 1.1 (Chapters 2–4) and test them empirically in the case of two countries (Chapters 6 and 7). The starting point is that trade, investment, migration and other regional provisions can each affect trade, investment and migration. Trade, investment and migration and complementary conditions that include public policies are causal links through which regional integration affects the poverty level of a specific country. Thus RI can affect poverty at the country level through a number of routes:

- *Route 1* through the volume and poverty focus of trade
- *Route 2* through the volume and poverty focus of investment
- *Route 3* through the volume and poverty focus of migration
- *Route 4* through other routes.

The book will essentially go through four basic steps to assess each route:

- *Step 1* Identify relevant provisions on trade, investment and migration
- *Step 2* Identify the effect on the volume and poverty focus of trade, investment and migration
- *Step 3* Identify how this change in volume and poverty focus maps onto poverty
- *Step 4* Identify how complementary conditions affect the relationship between the change in volume and poverty focus and poverty.

Regional integration can also affect poverty through other routes (including migration).

There are various reasons that further motivate us to examine the subject of RI and poverty. First, the number of regional trade agreements notified under the World Trade Organization has increased rapidly in recent years (Chart 1.2), with some regions much more advanced than others.[1] What effect does this have on development and poverty in developing countries? Secondly, (current) negotiations at the WTO are usually slow and long-drawn-out, and this has led some countries to focus on regional and bilateral trade negotiations. In the Americas, negotiations for the Free Trade Agreement of the Americas (FTAA) and others such as EU-MERCOSUR have also been underway for some time but have currently reached an impasse, and the North American Free Trade Agreement (NAFTA), now ten years old, has inspired a range of other regions. In Asia, ASEAN has recently started discussions with other Asian countries.

The formation of a region may be seen as a tool for development, but this is not always the sole, or even the main, reason for countries to come together. The development policy of the European Union (EU) is based to a large extent on

---

[1]   The European Union and Central and East European countries account for a significant number of agreements, between and amongst them.

supporting the formation of regions amongst developing countries. The European Commission is currently initiating negotiations on Economic Partnership Agreements with African, Caribbean and Pacific countries under the Cotonou Partnership Agreement before 2008. The EU appears to assume that the question is not whether a region should be formed, but rather what type of region can help to achieve development objectives such as poverty reduction.

However, there remain a number of unanswered questions related to how regional integration affects poverty. For example, there is a lack of a suitable framework for analysis. There has also been insufficient attention to the detail of regional provisions on trade, investment and other matters. Finally, there has been very little analysis of the effects of regional integration on poverty in individual countries. This book will address these issues.

There are several terms that we use frequently in this book which may need some clarification from the outset. One is regional integration. By this we mean to describe the situation where two or more countries come together to discuss common provisions to create a Regional Trade Agreement in the WTO sense of the word (see Chapter 2) with the aim to regulate or encourage cross-border trade, investment and migration. It is not geographically bound to regions or continents of the world and specifically refers to the intentional integration amongst countries. Development and poverty are other terms we use particularly in Chapter 3 and in the case studies. Both poverty, defined in section 3.1.3, and development are multi-dimensional concepts which are not easy to operationalise. In many cases we use monetised measures, such as income or growth and output measures, to describe poverty and development empirically. Thus, by operationalising the concept through mainly economic and socio-economic lenses, we may loose some of the important aspects of development, such as political development.

The book is in three parts. Part 1 deals with conceptual issues and the evidence thus far, the aim being to provide a theoretical structure or mapping of regional integration on poverty. It consists of three chapters by te Velde, Page and Morrissey. Chapter 2 discusses the upper part in Chart 1.1 – how regional provisions affect trade, foreign direct investment (FDI) and migration. Chapter 3 discusses how trade, FDI and migration affect poverty. Chapter 4 combines the main routes of these two chapters and presents the building blocks for a mapping of regional integration onto poverty.

Part 1 argues that much of the evidence is based on multi-country or multi-region studies. It deals with averages and fails to identify which provisions in which RTAs have what effect (on trade, FDI, poverty, etc.) in which countries. Studies that examine the effects of regional integration often use simple dummy variables to describe regions. This is problematic for those who want to negotiate the best possible type of region: in reality no two regions are the same, and some guidance is required on best practices in provisions in Regional Trade Agreements. For many other links we have no evidence at all.

In Part 2 (Chapter 5), therefore, te Velde and Fahnbulleh measure trade and investment provisions in several key regions and discuss how these affect

Chart 1.1 Mapping the regional integration process onto poverty

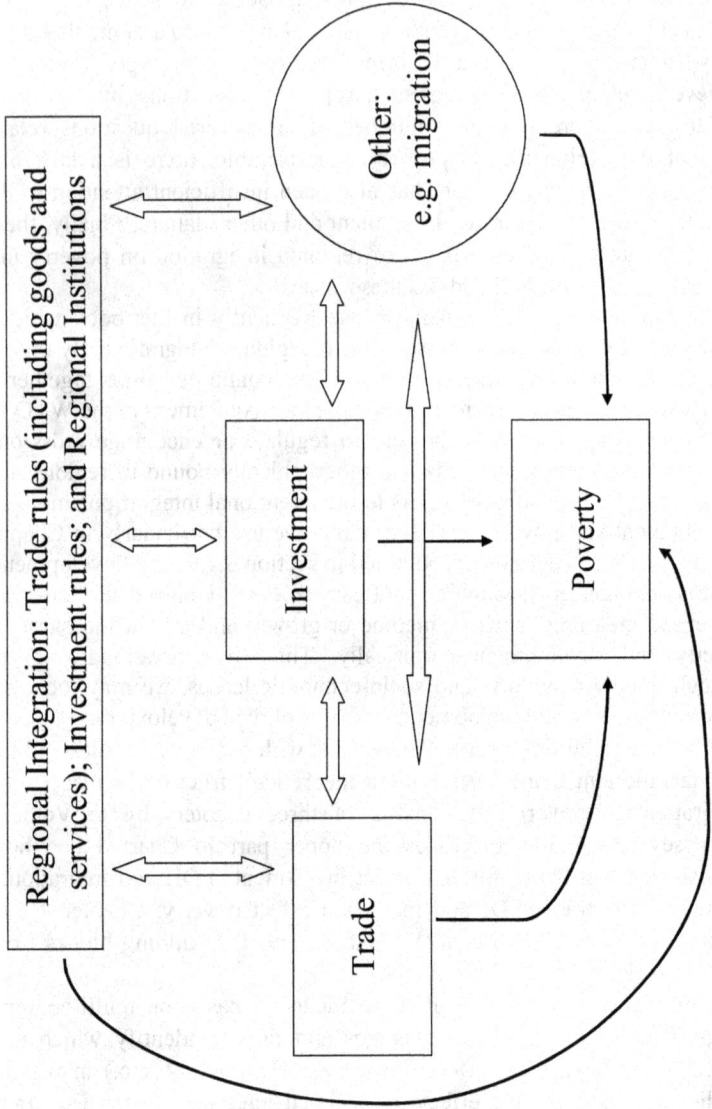

Source: Author's own.

investment. The chapter confirms and describes the fact that regional provisions related to investment differ markedly across RTAs and across time. The chapter focuses on how regional integration provisions affect FDI. In principle, there are two other types of empirical studies that would help to provide a balanced Part 2. First, it would be useful to include a detailed study on the effects of regional integration provision on trade, but as we explain in Part 1 some of this literature is only beginning to emerge and we refer to these studies in Part 1 rather than present our own, new evidence. Second, it would be useful to include a detailed study on the effects of regional integration provision on migration. This book does not include such a study, in part because the data on bilateral migration flows are even weaker than for bilateral investment flows and the necessary data has only recently begun to be developed. Thus, this is left for further research.

Most analyses of regions are carried out at the regional and not the country level. Part 3 addresses the effects of regional integration on poverty in two individual countries; this provides a good test of the mapping structure set out in Part 1. There are various countries that would be relevant for this exercise and Part 3 will discuss the experience of two countries, Bolivia by Nina and Andersen in Chapter 6 and Tanzania by Kweka and Mboya in Chapter 7. Bolivia is part of the Andean Community, is an associate member of the Southern Common Market (MERCOSUR) and a member of other regional groupings, and has been included in the EU and US Generalised Systems of Preferences. It has also one of worst poverty records in Latin America. Tanzania is a member of regions such as the East African Community (old and new) and the Southern African Development Community, and is also part of other groupings such as the GSP systems and the Cotonou Agreement, but it has withdrawn from the Common Market for Eastern and Southern Africa. While the implementation of regional trade provisions has been slow in Tanzania, it does not appear to have been much slower than in comparable countries. Chapter 8 provides a brief conclusion

Chart 1.2   The number of GATT/WTO notified RTAs in force

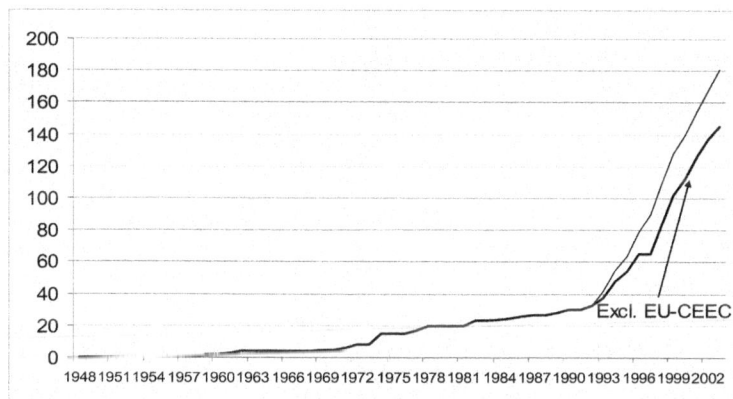

Source: WTO.

References

Ethier, W.J., 'Regionalism in a Multilateral World', *Journal of Political Economy*, 106 (1998): 1214-45.

McCulloch, N., Winters, L.A, and Cirera, X., *Trade Liberalization and Poverty; A Handbook* (London: Centre for Economic Policy Research, 2001).

McKay, A., Winters, L.A. and Kedir, A.M., 'A Review of Empirical Evidence on Trade, Trade Policy and Poverty', a report for DFID prepared as a background document for the Second Development White Paper (London: DFID, 2000).

ODI, *Foreign Direct Investment. Who Gains?* (London: Overseas Development Institute, 2002).

Viner J., *The Customs Union Issue* (New York: Carnegie Endowment for International Peace, 1950).

PART 1
Regional Integration and Poverty: Conceptual Issues and Evidence So Far

Chapter 2

Regional Integration, Trade, Foreign Direct Investment and Migration

Dirk Willem te Velde, Sheila Page and Oliver Morrissey

As discussed in the Introduction, there was a remarkable proliferation of Regional Trade Agreements in the second half of the twentieth century, with more than 100 different agreements being ratified. The first wave of regionalism in the 1950s to 1970s did not include many provisions beyond trade in goods. The second wave started in the 1990s (Ethier, 1998), and is often referred to as 'the new regionalism', since it has a number of distinctive characteristics. First, whilst the old regionalism of the 1950s/1960s typically involved RTAs that were 'North–North' or 'South–South', the new regionalism has been typified by several 'North–South' arrangements such as the North American Free Trade Agreement (NAFTA), Asia-Pacific Economic Cooperation (APEC) and the arrangements of the European Union with North African and Latin American countries. Second, many recent arrangements have been intercontinental. Third, there are more and more cases of multiple membership. Finally, many recent agreements have aspired to deep integration with commitments to the harmonization of regulatory measures and freeing up of factor movements with provisions for services and investment.

There are various ways in which RTAs or regional integration efforts affect national economies. We can distinguish between competition and scale effects, and trade and location effects. Competition and scale effects arise because national economies become more closely integrated, with a larger market permitting economies of scale to be achieved and bringing producers in closer contact, thus leading to gains in efficiency. Trade and location effects arise when the regional integration changes the pattern of trade and the location of production.

The most direct effects of RI work on member and non-members through trade (Section 2.1), FDI (Section 2.2) and migration (Section 2.3). Other effects of RI, such as dynamic efficiency gains, may be harder to capture and can be indirect. We return to these issues in Chapter 4.

2.1 Regional integration and trade

The literature on regional integration and trade is an old one, dating back, as noted in Chapter 1, at least to Viner (1950). The theoretical literature was often concerned with the question of whether regional integration was welfare enhancing. We shall not attempt to discuss this theoretical literature in any depth; a brief review, with an emphasis on empirical evidence, is, however, needed for the framework to analyze RI and poverty.

   Viner (1950) suggested that the effects of regional integration can be either *trade-creating,* when trade replaces domestic production, or *trade-diverting,* when partner country production replaces trade from the rest of the world. This implies that RI can lead to further trade, but that this is not always welfare enhancing. Reflecting this, RI is not always revenue enhancing, and could in fact reduce national welfare in the case of trade diversion and loss of tax revenues.

2.1.1 Trade in goods

In the past decade there have been various attempts to address the relationship between RI and trade. Some studies distinguish between the effects on intra-regional and extra-regional trade. One example, Frankel (1997), found that the regional integration raised intra-regional trade by 65 per cent in the European Union and 150 per cent in the Southern Common Market Agreement (MERCOSUR) and the Andean Community (ANDEAN). Table 2.1 quotes selected studies on the effect of RTAs on trade, in particular on intra-regional trade. Frankel and Rose (2001) demonstrate that RTAs have a big average effect on intra-regional trade. Soloaga and Winters (2001) show that the effects can differ amongst RTAs, with some having positive and others negative effects. They reveal that the new wave of regionalism in the 1990s (with the creation of new blocks and the revamping of old blocks) has not led to further intra-regional trade. They also show that only the EU and European Free Trade Area (EFTA) may have led to trade diversion, with the other blocks leading to trade creation.

   There are many ways in which an RTA can affect intra- and extra-regional trade. The previous studies account for this simply by including a dummy, but a more detailed account would examine how trade rules within RTAs, such as tariff liberalization and rules of origin, would affect trade.

Table 2.1   Regional trade agreements and merchandise trade: selected studies

Study	Type of equation	RTAs included	Effect RTA on trade
Frankel and Rose (2001)	Gravity equation explaining log of bilateral trade volumes using control variables such as distance, language, currency boards, income and others.	Dummies for EEC/EC; the Canada–US FTA; EFTA; the Australia/New Zealand closer economic relationship; the Israeli/US FTA; ASEAN; CACM; PATCRA; CARICOM; SPARTECA; and the Cartagena Agreement.	1.1 (Coefficient) 0.10 – (standard error)
Soloaga and Winters (2001)	Gravity equation explaining log of bilateral import values using control variables such as distance, language, income and others.	Dummies for EU; EFTA; ASEAN; MERCOSUR; CACM; LAIA; ANDEAN; GULFCOOP.	Negative and significant dummies for EU, EFTA, ASEAN. Positive and significant dummies for GULFCOOP, NAFTA, CACM, LAIA, ANDEAN, MERCOSUR. However, no significant difference in dummies before and after new wave of regionalism. Trade diversion in EU and EFTA.
Estevadeordal and Robertson (2004)	Gravity equation explaining log of bilateral import values using control variables such as distance, language, income and others.	LAIA; NAFTA; and US–Latin America and EU–Latin America under GSP. Includes preferential tariff.	Tariff elasticity significant at between -0.8 and -1.7.

Regional tariff preferences

The key negotiations on market access within RTAs focus on tariff reduction, particularly the degree to which parties to RTAs grant each other regional trade preferences. Tariff preferences can be set at a fixed level or a percentage deviation from most favoured nation (MFN) tariffs. Table 2.2 shows differences between MFN and regional tariffs. Unilateral and multilateral tariff reductions will erode the absolute level of regional trade preferences.

Estevadeordal and Robertson (2004) review existing studies and provide new empirical work showing that preferential tariffs do have a large and significant effect on bilateral trade (see also Table 2.1).

Rules of origin

Rules of origin constitute another trade rule that can affect location decisions. Rules of origin differentiate trade regimes, to ensure that goods entering a country receive the correct import treatment. Proof that the imported product was produced in a country party to the regional agreement would be sufficient to obtain preferential treatment as applied in the region. However, this may become complicated if products are produced and processed partly in a member of the region and partly outside the region. Rules of origin provisions govern when such products can benefit from preferential treatment, and when products are likely to be treated as originating from outside the region.

There are three main methods determining where a substantial transformation takes place (WTO official document WT/REG/W/45, 2002). First, the *change in tariff heading* (CTH) method; origin is granted when a processed good falls under a different tariff classification (for example, harmonized system usually at 4-digit level) from the imported good used for processing. Second, the *percentage criterion method*: this determines that a substantial transformation has taken place on the basis of a minimum percentage of the total value that must have been added in the exporting country (domestic content or DC) or a maximum percentage of value due to imports (import content or MC). Third, the *technical test method*: this stipulates certain production or sourcing requirements in the processing operations. There are advantages and disadvantages for different parties to an agreement in all three rules, which is why regions often decide to adopt more than one rule, especially if there is a dominant partner country, as in NAFTA or the Southern African Development Community (SADC).

Table 2.2   MFN tariffs and regional preferential rates: selected examples

	Average applied MFN	Average applied regional	*Absolute preferential tariff reduction (as % of price)*
SAPTA (1996)/ SAARC			
Bangladesh	17.5	15.8	1.4
India	33.5	24.1	7.0
Nepal	20.7	18.1	2.2
Pakistan	21.7	19	2.2
Sri Lanka	21.9	15.3	5.4
South Asia	26.4	20.3	4.8
AFTA (2001)/ ASEAN			
Brunei	2.6	1.0	1.6
Indonesia	7.2 (2002)	4.4	2.6
Laos	-	5.0	-
Malaysia	7.3	2.4	4.6
Myanmar	5.6 (1996)	3.3	2.2
Philippines	7.3	4.8	2.3
Singapore	0	0	0.0
Thailand	16.8 (1999)	7.4	8.0
Vietnam	16.0	3.0	11.2
ASEAN region	-	3.5	-
MERCOSUR (2001)			
Argentina	12.7	0.4 (1996)	10.9
Brazil	14.6	0.0 (1996)	12.7
Paraguay	13.2 (2000)	0.8 (1996)	11.0
Uruguay	13.8	0.9 (1996)	11.3
NAFTA			
Canada	7.7	1	6.2
Mexico	16.5	1	13.3
US	5.5	1	4.3
ANDEAN (2001)/ CAN			
Bolivia	9.6	0	8.8
Colombia	11.6	0	10.4
Ecuador	11.2	0	10.1
Peru	11.6	0	10.4
Venezuela	11.9	0	10.6

Source: Authors' own calculations.

Rules of origin can include provisions for cumulation. Such provisions describe the conditions under which imported inputs can be regarded as domestic content in the exporting country so that final products will more often benefit from preferential tariffs. Some RTAs allow for bilateral cumulation, where inputs from importers and exporters are regarded as domestic content. Diagonal cumulation allows inputs from non-parties to be regarded as domestic under certain conditions. Full cumulation allows all processing in the entire RTA area to be regarded as domestic. This would be more generous than bilateral cumulation when the domestic content of the exporting county is low, but the regional content is high.

Other concepts discussed in more detail elsewhere include tolerance and absorption levels (see WTO official document WT/REG/W/45, 2002, and Estevadeordal and Suominen, 2003). The *tolerance* rule allows a certain percentage of inputs not originating in the exporting country to be used without affecting the origin of the final product, which can make it easier for products with non-originating inputs to qualify for preferences. The *absorption* rule allows parts or materials that under the relevant rules of origin are regarded as not originating to be treated as domestic in any further processing operation.

Empirical evidence on the effects of rules of origin on trade is scarce. The evidence that has attempted to address the issue shows that RoO can prevent growth in (intra-regional) trade flows and divert resources from their most efficient source. In other words, RoO can be so stringent that importers do not use the tariff preferences due to them. Estevadeordal and Suominen (2003) summarize evidence that utilization rates of preferential trade agreements can be low.

Non-tariff barriers
There are non-tariff barriers to trade ranging from administrative requirements such as customs control procedures to labour and environmental standards, and these can have important effects on investment. Technical barriers to trade (TBT) and sanitary and phyto-sanitary (SPS) measures can also affect trade. For instance, Barrell and te Velde (2002) examined the EU's Single Market Programme, which began in 1986 with the removal of technical barriers to trade and the harmonization of standards, and showed that this has affected trade in varying degrees.

One barrier, which is not normally included in 'NTBs', is the use of anti-dumping which is consistent with WTO provisions. Not only developed countries, but increasingly also developing countries, use these provisions. Well known are the voluntary export restraints and (threats of) using quotas and anti-dumping by the EU, which have in part motivated the Japanese to set up operations inside the European Union.

2.1.2 Trade in services

Little is known about the effects of RTAs on trade in services. At the multilateral level, the General Agreement on Trade in Services (GATS) governs liberalization in this trade. However, developing countries have also begun to design RTA provisions in addressing trade in services, and some argue that the inclusion of such new provisions is part of the new regionalism (Dee and Gali, 2003). Article V of the GATS requires RTAs to be more liberalizing than the GATS itself. RTAs should have substantial sectoral coverage in services and provide for the 'absence or elimination of substantially all discrimination' through the elimination of existing discriminatory measures and/or the prohibition of new or more discriminatory measures either at the entry into force of the agreement or on the basis of a reasonable timeframe. The substantial sectoral coverage refers to the number of sectors, the volume of trade affected and the modes of supply. No mode of supply should be excluded beforehand.[1]

Stephenson and Prieto (2002) define the components often found in regional (Western Hemispheric) service agreements on the basis of three elements: coverage, liberalizing principles and depth of commitments:

- *Coverage* describes the four modes of supply (as in the GATS: cross-border delivery, consumption abroad, commercial presence, and movement of people), and whether the agreement takes a negative list approach in which all the services sectors are included subject to exceptions (called non-conforming measures), or a positive list approach specifying the type of access offered to service suppliers in scheduled sectors.
- *Liberalizing principles* include the fundamental principles of national treatment (NT – no discrimination between foreign and domestic suppliers), most favoured nation treatment (MFN – no discriminations amongst sources of foreign suppliers), local presence requirement (a local presence is required to supply the service), and quantitative non-discriminatory restrictions (for example, on the number of television frequencies).
- *Depth of commitments* includes transparency (informing members of existing restrictions on services trade), ceiling binding, freeze or standstill on non-conforming measures (no return to less liberalization), ratcheting, list or lose (non-conforming measures can be maintained only when they are listed in appendices) and future liberalization.

---

[1] There are four modes covering cross-border supply and returns to cross-border movement of factors in multilateral and regional agreements on services:
- Mode 1 Cross-border supply: when a service crosses a national border. An example is the purchase of insurance or software by a consumer from a producer abroad.
- Mode 2 Consumption abroad: when a consumer travels abroad to consume from the service supplier, such as in tourism, education, or health services.
- Mode 3 Commercial presence: when a foreign-owned company sells services (e.g. foreign branches of banks).
- Mode 4 Temporary movement of natural persons: when independent service providers or employees of a multinational firm temporarily move to another country.

Table 2.3 compares RTAs in the area of services recently concluded by countries in the Western Hemisphere and ASEAN. The following points emerge:

- Western Hemispheric RTAs, except MERCOSUR, are based on a negative list approach. The Association of South-East Asian Nations (ASEAN) is based on a positive list approach.
- RTAs offer MFN, with the exception of the Caribbean Community and Common Market (CARICOM).
- ANDEAN, NAFTA and CARICOM require transparency, while ASEAN and MERCOSUR do not have such provisions. Transparency is required when changing measures related to trade in services.
- Many (NAFTA) of the above agreements have separate rules governing investment in services (mode 3 of services), though MERCOSUR regards investment in services as mode 3 of services supplies.
- ASEAN does not have a special chapter on monopoly practices, unlike ANDEAN, NAFTA and MERCOSUR which do. CARICOM has a separate agreement on competition
- MERCOSUR and NAFTA (and CARICOM) *require* member states to encourage recognizing the titles of other member states, while in ASEAN titles *may* be recognized.
- NAFTA includes provisions on government procurement of services. Negotiations on this are ongoing in MERCOSUR.
- Treatment of mode 4 (temporary movement of people) varies considerably. In MERCOSUR it depends on the scheduled commitments, and in NAFTA there are limited provisions related to business services providers only. CARICOM is in an advanced stage, allowing movement of people based on foreign establishments and (when the protocol is ratified) free movement of 'skilled nationals'.
- ASEAN and MERCOSUR do not have rules regarding non-conforming measures, while ANDEAN, CARICOM and NAFTA are not allowed to schedule any new non-conforming measures.
- Most RTAs are quite ambitious, aiming to reduce all restrictions on trade in services within the next two decades.

Nikomboriak and Stephenson (2001) discuss differences amongst RTAs. In particular, they highlight the different approaches taken in ASEAN and in the Western Hemisphere. The latter are based (mostly) on a negative list approach with commitments being 'GATS-plus'. ASEAN's approach, on the other hand, is based on a positive list approach and so far with similar commitments to those in the GATS.

Table 2.3 Services components in selected RTAs

	ASEAN (1995)	ANDEAN (1998)	MERCOSUR (1994, to be ratified)	NAFTA (1994)	CARICOM (1997, to be ratified)
Sectoral coverage	According to schedules	Universal	According to schedules, all sectors by 2010	Universal	Not determined
Negotiating modality	Gradual, positive list	Negative list	Gradual, positive list	Negative list	Negative list
Most favoured nation	Subject to sectoral exemptions	Unconditional	Subject to sectoral exemptions	Unconditional	No
National treatment	Scheduled sectors subject to bound commitments	General obligation	Scheduled sectors subject to bound commitments	General obligation	Yes
Transparency	Not included	Each Party will promptly publish all measures of general application	Each party will publish all measures	Procedures to be established to notify restrictions	No, but when ratified the protocol requires notification of existing restrictions and provisions on services providers

Table 2.3 (continued)

	ASEAN (1995)	ANDEAN (1998)	MERCOSUR (1994, to be ratified)	NAFTA (1994)	CARICOM (1997, to be ratified)
Treatment of investment	Commercial presence covered by specific sectoral commitments; separate investment disciplines	Right of establishment guaranteed for service providers; separate investment disciplines	Commercial presence covered by specific sectoral commitments; separate investment disciplines	No local presence required, investment rules in separate chapter	While no national treatment is provided, it does establish that members shall not introduce in their territories any new restrictions relating to the right of establishment of nationals of other member states
Safeguards	Provisions exist for Emergency Safeguard Measures and Restrictions to Safeguard the Balance of Payments	Provisions exist for Restrictions to Safeguard the Balance of Payments	Provisions exist for Emergency Safeguard Measures and Restrictions to Safeguard the Balance of Payments	No provision for safeguard action in services, but provisions in case of balance of payment difficulties (different for trade in financial services)	Provisions to safeguard the Balance of Payments
Monopoly practices	No	Disciplines to be developed for monopoly practices and exclusive service suppliers	Disciplines to be developed for monopoly practices and exclusive service suppliers	Yes, for monopolies and state enterprises	Monopolies not specified, but agreement on competition

Table 2.3 (continued)

	ASEAN (1995)	ANDEAN (1998)	MERCOSUR (1994, to be ratified)	NAFTA (1994)	CARICOM (1997, to be ratified)
Recognition of titles	Each Member State may recognize the education or experience obtained, requirements met, or licences or certifications granted in another Member State	Each Party shall recognize the licences, certifications, titles of professions, and diplomas, accorded by other Member States, which activity of services requires of such instruments, according to the criteria established in a Decision dealing with the matter	Each state shall encourage its competent authorities to develop, together with those of the other Parties, mutually acceptable standards or criteria regarding the exercise of professional activities related to trade in services	Annex on professional services which requires members to encourage the relevant bodies in their respective territories to develop mutually acceptable standards and criteria for the licensing and certification of professional service providers, to provide recommendations on mutual recognition to the parties and to develop procedures for the temporary licensing of professional service providers of another party	Provision to establish common standards and measures for accreditation or, when necessary, for the mutual recognition of diplomas, certificates and other evidence of qualifications of nationals of CARICOM members

Table 2.3 (continued)

	ASEAN (1995)	ANDEAN (1998)	MERCOSUR (1994, to be ratified)	NAFTA (1994)	CARICOM (1997, to be ratified)
RoO	Benefits are denied to a service supplier who is a natural person of a non-Member State	Benefits of the protocol can be denied to a service provider from another member party, given notification and consultation, when this party demonstrates that the services are provided by a person or country not part of MERCOSUR	Benefits of the protocol can be denied to a service provider from another member party	Subject to prior notification, a Party may deny the benefits to a service provider of another party	It seems possible to deny the benefits of the protocol to a service provider from member and non-member parties
Government procurement	No	Government procurement disciplines to be applied to services, once developed	To be developed, but to be applied to services	Includes government procurement of services in separate chapter on government procurement	Not mentioned

Table 2.3 (continued)

	ASEAN (1995)	ANDEAN (1998)	MERCOSUR (1994, to be ratified)	NAFTA (1994)	CARICOM (1997, to be ratified)
Movement of natural persons	No	Freedom of temporary movement guaranteed	No, depends on scheduled commitments	Commitment regarding temporary movement of business services providers	Temporary movement of persons as services providers in connection with foreign establishment, incl. (family of) management, supervisions and technical staff; CARICOM skilled nationals act to be ratified before 2005 by all members
Dispute settlement	A specific dispute settlement mechanism may be established	Provisions provide for procedures in the case of rules of origin dispute, including consultation	Disputes are to be settled according to the dispute mechanisms of MERCOSUR	Access to investor-state dispute mechanisms under chapter 11 on investment, see e.g. financial services chapter	No mention of this in the chapter on services
Exceptions	No	Yes	Yes	Yes	Yes

Table 2.3 (continued)

	ASEAN (1995)	ANDEAN (1998)	MERCOSUR (1994, to be ratified)	NAFTA (1994)	CARICOM (1997, to be ratified)
Restricting Non-conforming measures	No	No party will increase the number of existing non-conforming measures	No	Parties need to make reference to law when scheduling commitments	Members will not introduce any new restrictions on the provision of services in the Community (standstill)
Special provisions	Financial services, basic telecommunications, maritime transport, movement of natural persons, and audio-visual	Financial services, basic telecommunications, and professional services will be elaborated in the near future	Financial services, basic telecommunications, maritime transport, movement of natural persons, and audio-visual	Financial services, air services, land transport, telecommunications, professional services, Temporary Entry for Business Persons	Professional services, air transport
Future liberalization of trade in services	Gradual liberalization through exchange of lists of commitments	Progressive liberalization of a list of commitments through negotiations within a period of 5 years (by 2005)	Progressive liberalization of a list of commitments through negotiations within a period of 10 years (by 2007)	To remove restrictions but allow for exceptions and reservations	To achieve a complete elimination of the identified restrictions to the movement of people and capital throughout the region by 2005

Sources: OAS website and RTA chapters/protocols related to services.

Table 2.4 Coverage of services in selected African RTAs

Region	*Coverage of services*
ECOWAS	Article 27 of 1975 Treaty on Community Citizenship Protocol on Free Movement of Persons and the Right of Residence and Establishment (1979) 1992 revised ECOWAS treaty affirmed right of entry, residence and settlement
SADC	Sectoral protocols (1996) on: • Energy • Tourism • Transport, communications and meteorology. SADC Draft Annex on Trade in services under discussion
EAC	Chapter 15 of 2001 EAC Treaty on cooperation in infrastructure and services
COMESA	Chapter 11 of 1993 COMESA Treaty on cooperation in the development of transport and communications Chapter 28, article 164, is on free movement of persons, labour, services, right of establishment and residence

Source: Original text of agreements and protocols.

RTAs clearly differ with respect to services agreements for various reasons. It appears that Latin American RTAs are the most liberalized, followed by ASEAN in Asia, while African RTAs have only just started to consider or implement provisions on services. Table 2.4 shows the services provisions in selected African RTAs.

An important question is whether RTAs in services can provide a boost to (intra-regional) trade in services, as has been the case for trade in goods, and if so, what strategies, or what elements, can help to achieve this. The first part of the question depends on whether an RTA can provide a credible margin of preference for regional services providers, on the one hand, and the extent of commitments, on the other. The Latin American RTAs seem to have achieved a credible margin of preference over the GATS, by including more transparency and stability for services providers through a negative list approach and a list of non-conforming measures, and also by following more liberal schedules. In principle, therefore, RTAs will be able to provide a credible margin. However, not all regions in fact do this. The second part of the question, in terms of optimal strategy, is difficult to answer, as there is little evidence as to whether developing country RTAs (do not) boost trade in services, let alone on what type of RTAs are most effective.

2.2 Regional integration and foreign direct investment

There are various ways whereby RTAs can influence foreign direct investment (FDI) and vice versa. We can distinguish between investment rules, trade rules and other links.

2.2.1 Investment rules

Investment rules are rules governing cross-border investment within the region and usually consist of rules on the treatment and protection of FDI which contribute to the 'investment climate'. Investment rules do exist in a handful of RTAs,[2] although they are not as common as trade rules, particularly amongst the poorer developing countries. Some regions include voluntary principles (for example, APEC's voluntary principles), while other regions have rules with effective dispute settlement procedures. We discuss below a number of investment provisions in regional treaties (scope, standard of treatment, performance requirements, expropriation and dispute settlement mechanisms) and their expected effects on the volume of FDI.

Scope
The scope of an investment treaty deals with the definition of investments and investors and the extent to which the treaty applies to member and non-members. Sometimes investment in general is included, while other agreements cover FDI only. Some RTAs have provisions which also apply to non-member states when they invest in the region from another location in the region (for example, performance requirements in NAFTA). The scope can also be used to determine whether the investment rules apply to listed sectors only (positive approach) or to all sectors in principle, with listed exceptions (negative approach).

Standard of treatment
While many RTAs would include fair and equitable treatment, the more contentious issue is whether the investment rules provide national or MFN treatment to post-establishment operations or to pre-establishment issues. The most liberal are those RTAs that include national treatment to members with respect to pre-establishment matters, subject to exceptions, since investors would have the right to establish a subsidiary anywhere within the region, and would be treated the same as national investors. The fewer the restrictions on establishment, the easier it is to invest and so the more investment would be possible (though the actual attraction of the investment depends on there being profitable economic opportunities). Such enhanced market access can be important, and regional arrangements may include this and thus be more liberal than the provisions in most

---

[2]   Investment rules also occur in bilateral trade arrangements (e.g. Singapore–Japan), but appear more often in bilateral investment treaties.

multilateral and investment treaties, apart perhaps from those of the US (see www.unctad.org for coverage and number of bilateral investment treaties). National treatment of foreign firms post-establishment usually refers to issues such as (abolition of) performance requirements.

Performance requirements
The more elaborate RTAs often include a section on performance requirements and the extent to which they can not be applied to new and/or existing investment. Performance requirements are requirements imposed on the operations of multinational enterprises (MNEs) and traditionally include export and domestic content (local sourcing) rules related to foreign goods producers. However, they can include more extensive requirements (for example, on employment) or deal with the service sectors in addition to the goods sector (for example, NAFTA).

Performance requirements affect investment in a number of ways. First, they may impose the requirement on foreign investors to use inefficient inputs or inefficient production processes, which, if severe, can lower the volume (and profitability) of the investment. The potential benefit of performance requirements would be less costly for countries or regions that have built up a minimum supply capacity. It may be difficult to identify the effects of performance requirements on locational decisions in practice. Few sectors are covered by performance requirements. The automobile assembly sector is one sector that is often affected, and it is a sector where local content requirements can be effective because of its dependence on component parts. Sectors that are less dependent on inputs from outside the company would be less affected. Secondly, performance requirements may influence the type of investment, because they could affect the quality of the inputs used (and hence the profitability of the investment).

Expropriation and nationalization
Expropriation is a potential threat to the interests of foreign investors if governments decide to nationalize subsidiaries of MNEs, though this seemed more likely to occur in the past in Latin America and Africa.[3] International law and regulations normally allow expropriation only when it is in the public interest, and is carried out on a non-discriminatory basis and against adequate compensation. RTAs can contain provisions that allow expropriation of property by the state on a non-discriminatory basis (national treatment and MFN). Such provisions give some comfort and diminish the non-commercial risks of an investment. Without other good reasons to invest, they would not attract FDI on their own, but they could help to create a favourable investment climate when offered as a package with other conditions.

---

[3]   Some cases take a considerable time to resolve. For instance, in January 2003, Nestlé settled an expropriation claim with the Ethiopian government dating back to the Ethiopian nationalization programme of 1975.

Dispute settlement

Investment rules, including those on expropriation, are likely to be more effective when backed by some sort of dispute settlement mechanism. There are various procedures, ranging from government-to-government to (foreign) investor-state dispute settlement procedures. In the event of an investment dispute, the more advanced regions allow for a consultation process leading to a panel review either between governments or between investors and governments. In some cases there are regional courts of justice, and in many cases disputes can be reviewed in the host country or by some independent arbitrator (when countries are members) such as the International Centre for the Settlement of Investment Disputes (ICSID) or the United Nations Commission on International Trade Law (UNCITRAL). There is much debate about the ultimate effect of such settlements on development, but it is likely that investors find some comfort in having them as they may reduce non-commercial risks. The presence of (access to) dispute settlement procedures may also form the basis for home countries offering investment guarantees against political risks in the context of bilateral treaties.

There is heated discussion on how investment rules (bilateral, regional and multilateral) affect investment decisions. In general, a predictable investment climate can be in the interest of investors who were previously disadvantaged. It is not clear whether this would lead to *additional* FDI or simply provide more comfort for the investor. Surveys clearly reveal, however, that investors want a predictable investment climate (see, for example, the Confederation of British Industry's position paper for the WTO negotiations, the EU's survey of MNEs – EC, 2000), although not necessarily at the cost of other policy liberalization (for example, further trade liberalization). The predictability of the investment climate may be enhanced when domestic policies are enshrined or locked into regional treaties. However, it remains unclear under what circumstances which investment rules would lead to additional FDI. Much will also depend on the existing treatment. If the treatment of existing foreign investors is in practice already good or better than that of domestic investors, new (regional) rules may do little to generate fresh investment or a better investment climate, other than offering a little more long-run security. There seems to be no empirical evidence that addresses the effects of individual investment provisions on FDI; this is therefore an area for further research.

2.2.2 Trade rules

There are three types of regional trade rules that may affect investment: regional tariff preferences, rules of origin and non-tariff barriers (which are not taken to include rules of origin). We discuss these with respect to the effects on intra- and extra-regional FDI.

Regional tariff preferences

The elimination of intra-regional tariffs will affect trade vis-à-vis the level of sales by multinational subsidiaries, depending on the importance of transport (including tariff) costs and the plant-level and firm-level costs to set up such subsidiaries (Markusen and Venables, 1997; Brainard, 1997; Carr *et al.*, 2001). Hence, the type of investment and the motive for it play an important role. To reflect this, the analysis will need to distinguish between intra- and extra-regional FDI and between horizontal (market-seeking: subsidiaries selling similar products) and vertical (efficiency- and natural resource-seeking: subsidiaries exploiting efficiencies or wanting control over input markets) FDI.[4]

Regional tariff preferences are likely to reduce *horizontal* (tariff-jumping) intra-regional FDI because it may now become cheaper to serve the partner country by trade rather than to establish a subsidiary and incur firm-level costs once and plant-level costs more than once. Of course, if firm-level and plant-level fixed costs are zero, there will be no trade and no concentrated production facility or FDI – just national production. However, on the other hand, regional tariff preferences encourage *vertically-motivated* intra-regional FDI, because lower trade costs will provide incentives to establish international production networks and set up an efficiency-seeking subsidiary in a partner country which can process imports for re-export. An example is the increase in US-owned production in Mexico partly as a response to NAFTA (not through *maquiladoras* which were in operation before NAFTA, see, for example, Gruben and Kiser, 2001), although domestic Mexican regulation has also played a role.

Extra-regional FDI can also be affected by declining regional tariff preferences in different ways. First, by lowering tariffs amongst parties to the RTA, it may

---

[4]   In recent decades, trade economists have begun to broaden trade theory, and the 'new trade theory' now embraces increasing returns, imperfect competition and product differentiation in addition to the traditional comparative advantage paradigm, with multinationals having been incorporated and made endogenous. The first attempts were by Helpman (1984) who integrated vertical multinationals and Markusen (1984) who integrated horizontal multinationals into the trade theory. Horizontal multinationals are multi-plant firms selling similar products in different locations; vertical multinationals separate production geographically into different plants from intra-industry trade (in practice multinationals include both horizontal and vertical features). Markusen (1997) presents a unified approach to vertical and horizontal multinationals. Horizontal MNEs dominate if nations are similar in size and relative endowments and if transport costs are high. Vertical MNEs appear with headquarters in the skilled labour-abundant country, provided that transport costs are high enough. National firms dominate if both trade costs are small and the home market is large enough: in this situation it makes sense to incur the fixed costs of setting up only one plant, from which to export. Within this framework it can be shown that trade and investment liberalization are not substitutes for each other and the two taken together may lead to a reversal in the direction of trade. Carr *et al.* (1998) provides a good empirical test of the framework, clearly showing the complexity and non-linearities affecting FDI and hence the relationship between trade and FDI.

become profitable for an extra-regional investor to avail himself of an effectively larger market (horizontal market-seeking FDI) from one or more locations in the region (export platforms). If individual countries in a region were previously served by trade, this may then raise inward FDI (export platforms or beachhead locations, see also Ethier, 1998). However, if the member countries of a region were already served through sales from a multinational subsidiary, concentration of production may occur in one or a few countries in the region, with ambiguous or negative effects for the volume of extra-regional FDI in each country. The combination of lower internal tariffs and significant plant fixed costs would lead to the consolidation of several plants in a number of countries in the region into one plant, to be used by the parent to serve the region as a whole. This may also induce FDI inflows to the most cost-efficient location (usually nearest to the largest market), possibly at the cost of FDI to other members in the same region. This could be the case for market-seeking multinationals. An example could be Unilever, which has traditionally invested in many developing countries including Bolivia, Argentina and Brazil. When confronted with lower trade (including tariffs) costs between the three countries, it may decide to rationalize production in fewer countries in order to exploit economies of scale or some other locational advantage (such a process of rationalization has recently taken place). The effects of regional trade preferences for extra-regional vertical (or efficiency-seeking) FDI are likely to be small, though lower regional preferences may reduce costs and increase efficiency in the vertically motivated subsidiary when it uses inputs from more than one country in the region (for example, the possibility of regional enterprises in the ASEAN, ANDEAN or SAARC contexts).

Regional tariff preferences have various affects on inward FDI. However, in the context of developing country regions, where most inward FDI is even more inter-regional than in developed country regions,[5] the market-size argument would be the most important, and apart from other factors regional tariff preferences would tend to increase inward FDI. It should be noted, however, that the strength of this argument depends on the difference between the tariffs applied regionally and

---

[5]   Intra-regional inward FDI makes up 6% of total FDI in ASEAN and 1% in SAARC.

Table: Intra-regional FDI flows as % of total FDI

	EU (outward)	NAFTA (outward)	ASEAN (outward)	ASEAN (inward)	SAARC (inward)
1986	36	30			
1997	49	21		12	
1999	46	18	15	6 (2001)	1

Source: ASEAN Secretariat, UNCTAD, Rugman and Brain (2002).

According to Businessmap, even though South Africa is a major and growing investor in other SADC countries, it seems to count for only 25% of total FDI inflows. The FDI stock of non-SADC origin in South Africa is also greater than the stock of South African outward FDI.

those applied to others (MFN treatment). With large regional markets but low tariff preferences, the effect is likely to be small. Table 2.2 provides data on this for selected countries.

Rules of origin
Rules of origin constitute another trade rule that can affect location decisions. The effects of RoO on investment can vary, depending on the type of investment as well as the interaction with regional tariff preferences. The RoO can encourage the use of intra-regional inputs which divert away from extra-regional inputs even if the latter are more efficient. However, stricter and more costly RoO would stifle intra-regional trade, favouring extra-regional imports (which are likely to be subject to the MFN tariff). The larger the difference between MFN and regional tariffs, the greater the incentive to comply with the RoO by importing regionally using goods certificates. This has effects for intra- and extra-regional FDI. For instance, it may encourage extra-regional FDI by setting up subsidiaries in the region to satisfy the RoO, possibly diverting investment made outside the region in the direction of the RTA. For instance, regional RoO applied to Mexico (under NAFTA) would require many *maquiladoras*, such as Japanese and South Korean electronics manufacturers, to switch away from Asian sources of components to find new suppliers in the US, Canada or Mexico, or would encourage Asian suppliers to relocate to Mexico, creating further extra-regional inward FDI.

We should distinguish between market-seeking and efficiency-seeking FDI (see Dunning, 1993) and extra- and intra- regional FDI. MNEs based outside the region are more inclined to set up a subsidiary in the region to serve the regional market particularly when the difference between MFN and regional tariffs is great, and when the RoO are strict. *Extra-regional* investors need to set up all their manufacturing and processing operations in one or a few countries in the region to serve that market if they want to satisfy strict RoO (see, for example, NAFTA). Such action would not be worthwhile if either the difference between MFN and regional tariffs is small or it is too costly/difficult to comply with the strict RoO. Efficiency-seeking extra-regional FDI would not be particularly affected, since products produced in the RTA are likely to be (re-) exported to outside the region irrespective of the RoO or the regional tariff preferences in the RTA. Such re-exports to outside the region may often go to big developed country markets such as the EU, the US or Japan, and for these exports preferential RoO are relevant (under the Cotonou, EBA, AGOA, GSP arrangements, etc.) rather than the RTA RoO.[6] On the other hand, some big developed countries have begun to form RTAs with developing countries (for example, the. EU with individual East European and African countries) which include RoO, but in this case we are speaking of *intra-regional* FDI.

---

[6]   Exceptions apply; for example, Japanese efficiency-seeking investors in Mexico producing for the NAFTA market.

The effect on intra-regional FDI can be complex, and would also depend on the type of operations. For instance, high fixed-cost, market-seeking operations would favour establishment in one of the countries when tariffs are low, as opposed to establishments in every member of the RTA. This is because the region can be served more cheaply through exports from a single (or a few) establishments in the region, thereby realizing economies of scale. Low fixed-cost operations could be expected to set up more efficiency-seeking establishments in other members of the RTA when intra-regional tariffs are decreasing, since it becomes cheaper to re-export regionally produced products. There is likely to be more intra-regional FDI in countries with few manufacturing capacities when RoOs are less strict, for example, allowing for diagonal or full cumulation so that others including non-members can supply the country that attracts intra-regional FDI, rather than when the RoO are stricter, when operations can use inputs only from one partner country.

Strict RoO can distort investment decisions when there is no common external tariff (CET) and MFN rates vary considerably, as in the case of NAFTA. Taking this example, strict RoO could prohibit some extra-regional imports (or intra-regional production) into Mexico for processing and re-export to the US market, leaving investors to choose the US even though this may be an inefficient production location. A lower MFN tariff in the US as compared with Mexico would only reinforce this trend. Another distortion can arise when using RoO provisions such as minimum domestic content, which can be more easily satisfied when production costs are high (Estevadeordal and Suominen, 2003).

Non-tariff barriers

Just as non-tariff barriers to trade have affected trade in varying degrees, they can also affect investment. NTBs include voluntary export restraints, and the threat of imposing EU quotas and using anti-dumping against Japanese exports motivated the Japanese to set up operations inside the EU. Barrel and Pain (1999) found that, after controlling for relative labour costs and market size, Japanese investment flows to European Community countries over the period 1980–91 were significantly influenced by anti-dumping measures taken in the Community.

Summary and further discussion

Table 2.5 provides a summary of possible links between trade rules and FDI. On balance, it appears that RTAs should lead to increased extra-regional FDI, but with more ambiguous results for intra-regional FDI. An important reason for the ambiguity of these effects is that MNEs are motivated by exploiting firm-specific assets (for example, firm-specific fixed costs) and hence want to enjoy economies of scale and scope, in addition to jumping trade barriers.

The table includes simple predictions as to how trade rules in RTAs affect FDI, and these compare well with the general literature on FDI and integration in developed countries, though some refinement is usually needed. For example, both Blomström and Kokko (1997) and Dunning (1997a) acknowledge that the effects of regional integration (trade rules) and FDI further depend on pre-existing rules in the region and the extent to which the regional rules will actually change such rules. Countries and industries that are already integrated prior to regional integration, due to geographical and historical reasons, can expect to see more limited effects than other countries and sectors. A stronger actual change to the investment climate, in other words whether national policies are changed dramatically and locked into a regional framework, will reinforce these effects. On the other hand, this could also increase the risks of policy reversal and instable regions.

Dunning (1997a) offers four hypotheses related to the impact of the single economic market (SEM) in the EU on EU inward FDI. First, the SEM will have a positive impact on intra-EU trade and an ambivalent effect on intra-EU FDI. Extra-EU defensive FDI could increase depending on the external tariff, and efficiency-seeking FDI may increase, due to the competitive-enhancing effects of integration, with possible investment diversion away from several investment locations towards the most suitable export platforms for the region. The SEM may diminish the importance of market size and growth and increase the importance of country-specific strategic assets or location factors.

Second, the SEM will have an ambivalent effect on the geographical distribution of FDI. There are, however, suggestions that economic integration will lead to a more concentrated geographical distribution of economic activity. Markusen (1995) argues that when countries are similar in size and become wealthier, MNEs (reaping economies of scale) will come to dominate exports, provided that transport costs are sufficiently high. The FDI/trade ratio will be higher in developed than in developing regions.

Third, depending on both country- and sector-specific factors, the SEM will have an ambivalent effect on the ownership of production in the EU. MNEs are likely to dominate sectors where there are significant firm-level economies relative to plant-level economies and intra-firm coordination costs. Fourth, the consequences of the SEM will be sector-specific and FDI will concentrate in those sectors that have characteristics conducive to MNEs, for example, FDI-intensive services, including banking and insurance and trade enhancing services.

When analyzing hypotheses and empirical findings regarding the effects of the formation of the SEM in Europe, Dunning (1997b) makes several observations. First, the main dynamic impact of the SEM is through the effects on other determinants of FDI such as market size, income levels, structure of activity and agglomeration economies. Secondly, the SEM as an independent variable has not raised extra- and intra- (less than extra-) regional FDI as much as other variables have increased FDI. Thirdly, the effects of the SEM are industry-specific, with extra-EU FDI increasing more in FDI-sensitive sectors. Fourth, there was limited evidence that economic activity has become geographically concentrated as a result of the SEM, although high value-added activities remain clustered and lower-value

Table 2.5 Summary of possible links between trade rules and FDI

		Extra-regional FDI inflows	
		Market-seeking	*Efficiency-seeking*
RoO loose	*Low intra/ extra tariff difference*	negligible	negligible
	High intra/ extra tariff difference	+	negligible[f]
RoO strict	*Low intra/ extra tariff difference*	negligible	negligible
	High intra/ extra tariff difference	++[b]	+[a]

		Intra-regional FDI flows			
		Market-seeking		*Efficiency-seeking*[c]	
		High fixed costs	*Low fixed costs*	*High fixed costs*	*Low fixed costs*
RoO loose	*Lower intra-regional tariffs*	-[d]	?	?[e]	++
RoO strict	*Lower intra-regional tariffs*	-[d]	?	?[e]	+

Notes: a) It may be easier for investors to locate an efficiency-seeking plant in one country of the region: cheaper imports processed for exports. This effect is more positive the more countries in a region supply the plant.

b) Possibly Japanese in Mexico to serve US market (while for NAFTA it was market-seeking, for Mexico it was efficiency-seeking); the more strict the RoO, the higher the share of the production process in the market

c) Relevant especially for mixed developed and developing regions

d) Concentration of investment in one country: more trade and fewer individual plants

e) Depends on trade-off between lower tariffs/transport costs and fixed costs

f) This could be positive, for example, in the case of Japanese efficiency-seeking investors in Mexico that happen to service the rest of NAFTA.

Source: Authors' own calculation.

activities have become more dispersed. Finally, there is complementarity between trade and FDI.

There is no standard for a region, so it is obvious that regions differ. Chapter 5 of this study documents how regions differ in two fundamental respects with regard to investment-related provisions:

- *over time* when regions change or add investment-related provisions
- *across regions* when investment-related provisions differ at one single point in time.

The chapter also shows that there are significant differences with respect to investment-related provisions in key areas including:

- the extent of regional tariff preferences
- the restrictiveness of rules of origin
- the investment rules, including national treatment for pre- and post-establishment and the presence of effective dispute settlement mechanisms
- regional coordination of investment, and
- type of membership: North–North, South–South, North–South, South–South–North.

Regions (with an economic motive) that desire to formulate new investment-related provisions or change existing ones might be helped by an analysis of their effects. Experience over the past three decades shows that regions can be subdivided into four categories with respect to investment provisions: (i) regions that do not have investment-related provisions, except for trade rules (most RTAs); (ii) regions that impose a common policy towards investment (ANDEAN in the early 1970s) that is more restrictive than individual member policies were; (iii) regions that choose to develop a common approach gradually over time, introducing provisions that stimulate regional investment cooperation and promotion and (begin to) grant national and MFN treatment (pre- and post-establishment) to foreign firms (for example, ASEAN); and (iv) regions that include comprehensive investment provisions from the beginning, including pre-establishment national treatment and effective investor-state dispute mechanisms (for example, NAFTA).

In understanding the effects of RTAs on FDI, particularly in developing countries, the existing variation in investment-related provisions across regions and over time has not yet been fully exploited. Existing empirical evidence has recently begun to address the links between RTAs and FDI. Table 2.6 gives a simple review of a few studies showing the tentative finding that RTAs in most cases boost extra-regional FDI and in some cases intra-regional FDI. Levy *et al.,* (2002) address the issue of regional integration and FDI at a basic level, using dummies for regions and applying the analysis to the OECD databases, thus excluding many developing countries. The market-size effect is used but it is not a true market potential function, as allowances for RoO and regional preferences have not been made. Other researchers have examined individual regions; Waldkirch (2003) and

Monge-Naranjo (2002) for NAFTA, Chudnovsky and Lopez (2001) for MERCOSUR. UNCTAD (2003) includes a useful overview of several regions but does not provide new empirical research.

Only one recent study, Dee and Gali (2003), examines how 'new' trade provisions in Preferential Trade Agreements affect the patterns of trade and investment flows. It uses gravity models of trade and investment between pairs of countries over the period 1988–97, and includes two types of indices: (i) covering 'traditional' trade provisions regarding agriculture and (ii) covering industrial products and 'new age' provisions covering services and other provisions such as investment rules. The indices are unweighted averages of scores on sub-categories. They also control for the usual control variables in gravity equations and include three dummies for each RTA provision to measure intra-regional effects, extra-regional effects on inward FDI and extra-regional effects on outward FDI.

The traditional trade provisions affected both intra- and extra-regional inward FDI stocks in the South Pacific Regional Agreement SPARTECA (investment creation), but only extra-regional outward FDI in the EU and US–Israel RTA (investment diversion). The new age provisions led to net investment creation in EFTA, the EU, NAFTA, MERCOSUR and SPARTECA, CER, and net investment diversion in the Asian FTA (AFTA), and had no impact in ANDEAN and the US–Israel agreement (Tables 4–7 in Dee and Gali, 2003).

While this study has gone some way in explaining the effects of different provisions on trade and investment flows, many questions remain unanswered. For instance, it does not address all RTAs or any with African member countries; it excludes a great many developing countries, focusing its attention on RTAs relevant for Australia; it does not compare provisions over time – and provisions can change over time (as, for example, in ASEAN); it lumps all 'new' trade provisions together; and finally, it does not make clear which types of countries within regions gain (most).

2.3 Regional integration and migration

There are various ways in which RTAs deal with migration. OECD (2002) distinguishes between:

- RTAs that provide for full mobility for people. For instance, the EU covers free mobility of workers and non-workers, and COMESA foresees free movement of labour by 2025. Such agreements provide for full access to labour markets (in the case of the EU there is currently some controversy about the effects of enlargement on intra-regional migration, and most of the old member states have imposed temporary controls on migration from the new members).

Table 2.6   RTAs and FDI inflows, selected examples

Study	Research question; Region, countries and years; Methodology	Explanatory variables	Findings
Levy, Stein and Daude (2002)	How do RTAs affect the location of FDI? FDI from 20 OECD countries to 60 OECD/non-OECD countries, 1982–98.	RTA membership, extended market host, extended market source, capital/worker distance, market size, bilateral trade, inflation trade/GDP, privatization capital/worker, investment environment, common border, common language.	• RTA membership doubles FDI stocks on average FDI increases upon joining a FTA with: • more trade/GDP (openness) • more similar capital/worker • better investment environment • larger market.
Mody and Srinivasan (1997)	Which factors determine US and Japanese FDI? 35 OECD and non-OECD countries, 1997–92, split into groups of low–middle, high income countries; and EEC, Latin America, East Asia.	Market size, labour costs, capital costs, previous FDI infrastructure (telephone, electricity), country risk openness.	• When split by periods (1977–81; 1982–86; 1987–92), no evidence that IMP increased US and Japanese FDI (but we should bear in mind that IMP was completed only in 1993).
Brenton *et al.* (1998)	Does European integration increase FDI? Does it divert FDI? Are trade and FDI substitutes or complements? FDI in- and outflows, imports, exports for EU and CEEC countries.	Population, distance, trade/FDI agreement dummies, host country economic freedom dummies, CEE dummies, host country EU membership dummy, FDI residual (in trade regression).	• Single European Act (1992) and Iberian enlargement: more FDI but no observed FDI diversion.
Pain and Lansbury (1996)	How has intra- and extra- EC FDI by UK and German firms in different sectors changed with the introduction of the Internal Market Programme? UK and German outward FDI for seven sectors, 1980/81–92.	Sector output, factor costs, currency volatility, corporate finance conditions, non-tariff barriers (1–3 scale), IMP dummy, sector dummies.	• FDI determinants differ over sectors • IMP introduction boosted FDI • IMP redirected UK FDI from US to EC.

- RTAs that provide for mobility of certain types of people. A prime example is CARICOM which has a separate agreement on the movement of skilled nationals, allowing movement of natural persons based on foreign establishments, and (when the protocol is ratified) free movement for 'skilled nationals' plus access to labour markets.
- Other RTAs that use provisions under the GATS (mode 4) with some elements. Table 2.3 on provisions on services includes a row dealing with temporary movement of people which some agreements facilitate. In particular, APEC has introduced an APEC business travel card facilitating visa procedures.

There are marked differences in provisions on migration or temporary movement of people. Hence, there can be different effects on the movement of labour within a region, although the evidence tends to show minor effects. At one extreme when full mobility of labour is granted (as in the EU's Treaty of Rome), this has not led to significant labour mobility; intra-region mobility covers 0.2 per cent of the total EU population according to the World Bank (2003). At the other extreme, GATS-type commitments in regions do allow for the temporary movement of people, but even in this situation movement is severely limited by qualification requirements, economic needs tests and residence requirements (and is thus dependent on FDI regimes).

There are not many studies that examine the effects of RTAs on labour mobility. Those that are available find that there is little effect (for example, Fuchs and Straubhaar, 2003). As noted above, intra-regional mobility for the EU is estimated to be much less than 1 per cent, despite large wealth gaps between Southern and Northern European members, and persistently high unemployment differentials across countries. There also appears to be no effect of the Nordic Common Labour Market (Denmark, Finland, Sweden and Norway).

2.4 Regional integration and cross-border investment: other links

There are various other links between RTAs and FDI. Provisions other than the trade and investment rules include free movement of people (CARICOM) and free transfers of profits, all of which can facilitate the establishment of intra-regional FDI. Many other provisions are region-specific and cannot easily be categorized.

For instance, some regions (ANDEAN, ASEAN, MERCOSUR) have cooperation schemes which occasionally aim to establish regional enterprises by promoting joint ventures. The ASEAN region seems to be one of the most advanced in this field. The ASEAN Industrial Cooperation scheme (AICO scheme) seeks to promote joint manufacturing and industrial activities between ASEAN-based companies, more than 100 projects have been selected for special tax and tariff incentives. The initiation of these schemes may also help to foster the process of regional integration, as opposed to being the result of it.

Some argue that the effects of RTAs on FDI are not so much concerned with trade and investment rules, but with the increased predictability of the investment climate by locking-in general reforms (regulation, competition policies, property rights, contract enforcement, guaranteed access to members' markets and stable trade policies) in a wider context. The fact that national policies are 'locked' into regional treaties should give investors additional security that policy reversals are less likely, thus reducing non-commercial risk. In practice, this argument would depend on how strong the region is vis-à-vis the individual members. The argument is also related to signalling, namely, that signing an RTA signals an intention which can be regarded as favourable to investors.

Many argue that the important effects of RTAs on FDI are dynamic, with competition creating a more efficient industry and greater growth, which in turn can affect FDI. Neary (2001) includes dynamic effects in a theoretical model describing MNEs. First, there is the tariff-jumping motive, as discussed earlier: FDI is favoured over exporting, the higher the external tariff and the lower the fixed costs of a new plant. Second, the export platform motive could affect FDI, as lower intra-regional tariffs would favour the establishment of a single plant in the region. Finally, lower intra-regional tariffs would lead to increased competition from stronger domestic firms and hence less FDI. On the other hand, a more efficient private sector can also increase efficiency-seeking investment by regional suppliers becoming efficient, as well as raising strategic asset-seeking investment.

Blomström and Kokko (1997) also argue that regional integration leads to efficiency gains and higher growth, and thus further FDI. FDI can actually be such a catalyst through spillovers in terms of technology transfer and other linkages with local firms. There can thus be long-lasting effects on growth and productivity, as opposed to a one-off effect based on a more efficient allocation of resources.

While regional integration can lead to more extra-regional investment for the region as a whole, this may not lead to more FDI in each individual member country. As discussed briefly earlier, the extent to which polarization or uneven distribution takes place depends on the level of external MFN tariffs, the strictness of RoO, market size and the agglomeration effects in individual member countries. If polarization takes place, this could lead to a conflict of interest amongst member states in maintaining the region and in facilitating regional efforts to address investment. While increased intra-regional FDI could be expected to enhance the integration process, competition for FDI between member states can result in the opposite. The attempt to reduce such competition is thought to be one of the reasons why MERCOSUR has begun further talks on investment issues (Chudnovsky and Lopez, 2003) and why the EU and NAFTA have included provisions on capping incentives. The annual report of the UN Economic Commission for Africa on regional integration shows that there is an expectation that cross-border investment and trade could lead to closer integration. If regional integration leads to further FDI with equal benefits, this could start a virtuous circle. If, however, FDI benefits member states unequally, this may actually put the region in jeopardy.

Despite competition amongst RTA member states for the same FDI, which, according to Oman (2000), increased during the 1990s, it is possible to think of cooperation when competition has become too fierce or too costly, or when joint promotion of investment may bring benefits shared across the region. ASEAN has organized ministerial-level joint investment promotion activities in major developed country markets, with the aim of conveying a strong regional image. The ASEAN Secretariat has also begun various activities in the area of investment facilitation, by providing information through portals, databases, publications and statistics. It can thus be argued that a region can do much more to try to promote investment than just designing and implementing trade and investment rules. It can put in place regional infrastructures (legal, institutional, etc.) to deal with investment issues at a regional level.

Apart from trade and investment rules and regional institutions, regions can also decide to harmonize their fiscal and monetary policies. For instance, the Euro area (within the EU), the West African Economic and Monetary Union and four of the Southern African Customs Union members (within SADC) have common currencies. This reduces intra-regional exchange-rate variability and may reduce cross-border transaction costs, which are amongst the factors contributing to investment. Because the EU and SACU are incomplete currency areas, there should be implications with regard to which parts of the region are influenced.

2.5 Conclusions

This chapter has shown that regional integration affects trade, FDI and migration in a number of different ways. It found that regional integration is associated with increased intra-regional trade (and in several cases trade creation), as well as with increased FDI from outside the region. The chapter emphasized that there are many different regional provisions which can have different effects. It is therefore important to understand the peculiarities of each region.

References

Barrell, R. and Pain, N., 'Trade Restraints and Japanese Direct Investment Flows', *European Economic Review*, 43, (1999): 29–45.

Barrell, R. and te Velde, D.W., 'European Integration and Manufactures Import Demand', *German Economic Review*, 3 (2002): 263–93.

Blomström, M. and Kokko, A., *Regional Integration and Foreign Direct Investment,* NBER Working Paper 6019 (Cambridge, MA: National Bureau of Economic Research, 1997).

Brainard, S.L., 'An Empirical Assessment of the Proximity–Concentration Trade-Off between Multinational Sales and Trade', *American Economic Review*, 87, (4) (1997): 520–44.

Brenton, P., Di Mauro, F. and Luecke, M., 'Economic Integration and FDI: An Empirical Analysis of Foreign Direct Investment in the EU and in Central and Eastern Europe', Kiel Working Paper No. 890 (Kiel: Kiel Institute of World Economics, 1998).

Carr, D.L., Markusen, J.R. and Maskus, K., 'Estimating the Knowledge-capital Model of the Multinational Enterprise', *American Economic Review*, 91, (2001): 693–708.

Chudnovsky, D. and Lopez, A., 'La inversion extranjera directa en el Mercosur: un análisis comparativo', in Chudnovsky, D. (ed.), *El Boom de Inversión Directa en el Mercosur* (Madrid: Siglo XXI Editoria Iberoamericana, 2001): 1–50.

Dee, P. and Gali, J., 'The Trade and Investment Effects of Preferential Trading Arrangements', NBER Working Paper No. 10160 (Cambridge, MA: National Bureau of Economic Research, 2003).

Dunning, J., 'The European Internal Market Programme and Inbound Foreign Direct Investment', *Journal of Common Market Studies*, 35, (1997a): 1–30.

Dunning, J., 'The European Internal Market Programme and Inbound Foreign Direct Investment', *Journal of Common Market Studies*, 35, (1997b): 189–223.

Dunning, J., *Multinational Enterprises and the Global Economy* (Boston, MA: Addison–Wesley Publishing Company, 1993).

Estevadeordal, A. and Suominen, K., 'Rules of Origin: A World Map', Draft IADB Paper (2003).

Estevadeordal, A. and Robertson, R., 'Do Preferential Trade Agreements Matter for Trade?' in A. Estevadeordal, D. Rodrik, A.M. Taylor and A. Velasc (eds), *Integrating the Americas: FTAA and Beyond* (Cambridge, MA: Harvard University Press, 2004).

Ethier, W.J., 'Regionalism in a Multilateral World' *Journal of Political Economy*, PO6 (1998): 1214–45.

European Commission, *Survey of the Attitudes of European Business to International Investment Rules*, by T.N. Sofres S.A., for DG Trade of the EC (Brussels: European Commission, 2000).

Frankel, J., *Regional Trading Blocs in the World Trading System* (Washington, DC: Institute for International Economics, 1997).

Frankel, J. and Rose, A., 'An Estimate of the Effect of Common Currencies on Trade and Income,' *Quarterly Journal of Economics* (2001), May.

Fuchs, D. and Straubhaar, T., 'Economic Integration in the Caribbean: The Development towards a Common Labour Market', International Migration Papers 61(2003), http://www.ilo.org.

Gruben, W.C. and Kiser, S.L., *NAFTA and Maquiladoras. Is the Growth Connected?* (Federal Reserve Bank of Dallas, June 2001).

Helpman, E., 'A Simple Theory of Trade with Multinational Corporations', *Journal of Political Economy*, 92, (1984): 451-471.

Levy, Y.E., Stein, E. and Daude, C., 'Regional Integration and the Location of FDI' (IADB Draft, 2002).

Markusen, J.R., 'Multinationals, Multi-plant Economies, and the Gains from Trade', *Journal of International Economics*, 16 (1984): 205–26.

Markusen, J.R., 'The Boundaries of Multinational Enterprises and the Theory of International Trade', *Journal of Economic Perspectives*, 9, (1995): 169–89.

Markusen, J.R. and Venables, A.T., 'The Role of Multinational Firms in the Wage-Gap Debate', *Review of International Economics*, 5, (4), (1997): 435–51.

McCulloch, N., Winters, L.A. and Cirera, X., *Trade Liberalization and Poverty; A Handbook* (London: Centre for Economic Policy Research, 2001).

McKay, A., 'Methodological Issues in Assessing the Impact of Economic Reform on Poverty', in M. McGillivray and O. Morrissey (eds), *Evaluating Economic Liberalization* (Basingstoke: Macmillan, 1999).

Mody, A. and Srinivasan, K., 'Japanese and US firms as foreign investors: Do they march to the same tune?', *Canadian Journal of Economics*, 31 (1998): 778–99.

Monge-Naranjo, A., 'The Impact of NAFTA on Foreign Direct Investment Flows in Mexico and the Excluded Countries' (Draft paper, Northwestern University: 2002).

Neary, J.P., 'Foreign Direct Investment and the Single Market', Draft paper CEPR and University College Dublin (Dublin: University College, Dublin, 2001).

Nikomboriak, D. and Stephenson, S.M., 'Liberalization of Trade in Services: East Asia and the Western Hemisphere' (Draft report, 2001).

ODI, *Foreign Direct Investment. Who Gains?* ODI Briefing Paper (London: Overseas Development Institute, May 2002).

OECD, 'The Relationship between Regional Trade Agreements and the Multilateral Trading System: Services', TD/TC/WP(2002)27/FINAL(Paris: OECD, 2002).

Oman, C., *Policy Competition for Foreign Direct Investment: A Study of Competition among Governments to Attract FDI* (Paris: OECD Development Centre, 2000).

Pain, N. and Lansbury, M., 'The Impact of the Internal Market on the Evaluation of European Direct Investment' (London: NIESR, 1996) mimeo.

Rugman, A. and Brain, C., 'Intra-regional Trade and Foreign Direct Investment in North America' Draft paper (Indiana University, 2002) mimeo.

Soloaga, I. and Winters, A., 'Regionalism in the Nineties: What Effect on Trade?', *North American Journal of Economics and Finance,* 12 (1) (2001).

Stephenson, S.M. and Prieto, F.J., 'Evaluating Approaches to the Liberalization of Trade in Services: Insights from Regional Experience in the Americas' (Draft report, 2002).

UNCTAD, *World Investment Report 1993* (Geneva: UNCTAD, 1993).

UNCTAD, *World Investment Report 2003* (Geneva: UNCTAD, 2003).

Viner, J., *The Customs Union Issue* (New York: Carnegie Endowment for International Peace, 1950).

Waldkirch, A., '"The New Regionalism" and Foreign Direct Investment: The Case of Mexico', *Journal of International Trade & Economic Development*, 12, (2003): 151–84.

World Bank, *Global Economic Prospects 2004* (Washington, DC: World Bank, 2003)

Chapter 3

Trade, FDI, Migration and Poverty

Dirk Willem te Velde, Sheila Page and Oliver Morrissey

3.1 Trade and poverty

Examination of the relationships between trade, trade policy and poverty (see Page, 2001; Bird, 2003 for an extensive discussion and bibliography) shows that trade can have significant effects on total income and its distribution, and therefore on poverty. Both the macroeconomic and the sectoral and distributional effects are now well studied (and sometimes even exaggerated, Freeman, 2003). The direct impact on poverty of particular changes in trade can be traced, through price, employment and fiscal effects on incomes, and then through household analysis, to the income and asset aspects of poverty. If policy such as a regional agreement or its cessation (unlike normal trend changes in trade) creates abrupt changes (loss of a whole sector), the effects may be more severe. If opening to trade increases or decreases the vulnerability of an economy to large variance in income, this may have important impacts on poverty as the poor are less able to adjust to changes. More opportunities in trade (through imports or access for exports) are likely to increase national income and may increase efficiency sufficiently to raise growth. Any of these income effects may have direct effects on poverty (the evidence is that they are likely, but not inevitable), and clearly will have effects on the potential to reduce poverty. This, however, depends on the policy response of government.

If we assume that countries have the objective of reducing poverty and that they possess the administrative skills and institutions to redistribute income, then we need look only at the first-round effects of a change in trade: if this increases income, then poverty can be reduced. If we take the more reasonable approach in a development context – that countries face problems with regard to the skills and institutions needed to implement policies – then we must look at where the initial benefits from trade come from: do they reduce the prices of the goods purchased or produced by the poor? Are any negative changes impossible to reverse through policy? If we assume that, even if governments do not have poverty reduction as an objective, other governments (donors or trading partners) have some internationally given 'right' to impose this target on them, then we can look only at the first-round effects (and even this requires an assumption that governments are unable to redistribute for administrative reasons).

3.1.1 Output and growth effects

In traditional terms, opening to trade (or to more trade) should raise a country's income (its potential welfare) by permitting it to change the composition of its output to a more efficient structure, that is, permitting it to specialize according to its comparative advantage. This produces a one-off increase in total national income and may, through the effect of an increase in output on investment, cause some further increase in output.[1] This assumes that prices are operating as correct signals (or that they are altered to remove distortions as part of the opening up of the economy) so that transmission effects work, and that there are no binding obstacles to growth. If, instead, the economy (or at least those elements which are opened to trade) is assumed to be operating under other constraints, of inefficiency for example, then greater integration will not necessarily increase output (but equally it is unlikely to have a negative effect). The traditional efficiency gain is problematic when faced with increasing evidence that external openness is not necessarily associated with reduced distortion in domestic prices, but at a minimum it can contribute to reduced price distortion and therefore to some increase in efficiency. Transmission effects may not function as directly (or as smoothly and fast) as the analysis would suggest, because the country's economy is not fully integrated or because of policy interventions insulating individuals from either good or bad effects, or postponing or attenuating them.

Trade does not raise all incomes, and may lower some. One obvious example is if a change in trade policy shifts from protecting some sectors, either by restricting imports or subsidizing exports, towards opening. Total income will normally rise, but it is clear that some in the protected sector will lose, unless there is immediate and perfect mobility out of it. And if some institutions have depended on the subsidies, for example marketing arrangements (Winters, 1999: 4), then the losers may not be confined to the sector which is liberalized; all those who used the marketing boards will lose a service. Normally, it is not the poorest (which are, probably, politically the weakest) sectors which are protected; normally, therefore, a shift of income away from a protected sector to other sectors is more likely to improve the poverty situation or income distribution, rather than to worsen them, but this is not certain.

---

[1]   While there is a lot of evidence on trade, trade policy and growth regarding the goods sector, there is comparatively less on trade in services. Surveys of recent work (OECD, 2003) indicate that liberalization of services trade offers benefits particularly in three sectors. Efficient financial services contribute to investment and growth, and foreign providers offer potential gains. Efficient transport services can reduce the costs of trade substantially. Telecom services are an important element in effective communications and dissemination of information. The problem is ensuring competitive provision in relatively small markets; there is a need for safeguards that protect consumers as well as foreign investors.

Fields (2001: 101) notes that 'it has proved far easier to generate economic growth than to change the Gini Coefficient. In the developing world, GDP per capita grew by 26 percent between 1985 and 1995. . .while Gini coefficients in the world barely changed over the same period.' What is not clear from this observation is what 'easier' means in this context: growth has been the objective of most developing countries during this period, not inequality, so it may indicate no more than that countries had more success in what they were trying to do than in something which was at most a secondary objective. A detailed analysis of projections of possible growth and/or inequality paths, in an attempt to determine whether the development targets for reducing poverty by 2015 are feasible, found that, except for the very poorest countries, policies which spread the gains from growth more evenly will lift people out of extreme poverty more effectively than plausible increases in the overall rate of growth (Hanmer and Wilmshurst, 2000: 9). And, although the precise elasticities depend on the shape of the inequality curves, in general the more unequal a population, the smaller the effect of growth on poverty.[2]

Fields also (2001: 190) finds that examples are quite common of growth leading to all distinguishable income groups seeing an increase in income (and, in the reverse: all suffering from a fall), when looking at the experience of the Asian, but also some Latin American, countries. Inequality has increased, however, in many of the cases, so that if inequality as well as levels of income are part of the welfare function, the results are not unambiguously good or bad.

3.1.2 Distribution of trade effects

The most common area in which to look for explanations of how growth affects poverty or income is in its composition effects: 'The composition of economic growth and the inequality of a society have a significant effect on the relationship between growth and poverty reduction' (Weiss, 2000), justifying the analysis of poverty in terms of sources of income. While the direction of effects from individual elements of trade or other international integration or from growth to the economic variables is normally clear, or subject to known influences, even if difficult to quantify in particular cases, the interaction of all the effects can only be analyzed under strict assumptions about the general equilibrium of an economy,

---

[2]   Because of differences in the degree of inequality, general conclusions that on average reductions in poverty are closely correlated with increases in average income are not helpful. Gallup, Radelet and Warner 1998, cited in McKay *et al.*, 2000 find 'that some cases show less than proportionate growth. . . , but argue that these are balanced by cases where the poor have done better than average' (p 28). It is not clear in what sense the fact that the poor in some countries have done well 'balances' the fact that they have done badly in others: it seems more logical to rephrase this as that the effects depend on the policies and the existing distribution of income rather than to attempt to draw generalizations which do not answer the specific question (see also Dollar and Kraay, 2000).

and assuming either no policy or very specific policy changes. As well as the obvious practical difficulties of modelling and analyzing economies which are in the process of major structural change (from development, even if there is no change in their integration), the policies themselves will react to the changes, and the analysis therefore becomes undetermined. Here, we shall look at the direct, partial effects.

Increased specialization makes the characteristics of the sectors in which a country has a comparative advantage a particularly important determinant of the direct impact of trade on the economy. In developing countries, this is often initially a primary product, either agricultural or mineral, but later it can become a specialized manufacture or service. If it is a product also consumed (or used as an input) in the country, growing specialization in its production may lower consumption costs, and increase the return to output in the country, as well as the income from exports. If it is not directly used in the country, and if the income from production is not distributed appropriately, there will be more pressure on the country's institutions to redistribute the income both to support other development and to increase the income of poor households. Thus the nature of the export helps to determine how important it is to have effective fiscal and social institutions in order to obtain the optimum effects on poverty.

Trade theory argues that increasing the openness of an economy improves the return to factors which are less scarce in the country than in those to which it opens up (it moves their price, and therefore their return, nearer to the other levels). For countries with abundant labour, this is likely to mean an improvement in the distribution towards wages, but for those where natural resources, whether agricultural, mineral, or scenic (in the case of tourism) are the principal advantage, it may instead shift the distribution towards returns to the holders of these resources, that is, towards profits and rents. Where the move is towards labour, it is likely (for a developing country) to be towards labour that is unskilled relative to world levels, so that there is 'mixed evidence on the effects of greater openness on relative skilled-unskilled wages' (McKay *et al.*, 2000: 19), made more uncertain by different countries' definitions of the boundary.

The labour which gains may not be the lowest skill level by national standards. Producing internationally competitive products requires some habituation of labour, if not what would be defined as training, to 'skilled' level. It is, however, likely to increase total employment. This may increase the employment of the less skilled through the substitution at various levels of untraded and already traded activities, as the more skilled move into the new traded sectors. Thus, where labour is a country's main advantage in international trade, there is likely to be an improvement in the distribution of income at least to the less well off, and probably to some previously unemployed. This is likely to include some defined as poor. But, as discussed above, if a country had protected its manufacturing industry before liberalizing and increasing its trade (McKay *et al.*, 2000), then removing this distortion may counterbalance some or all of the potential gains to labour income. The potential opening up of trade in services would increase this bias of positive trade effects on labour-intensive countries.

The greater specialization encouraged by trade may make individual producers/households more vulnerable to shocks, and if neither the economic unit (because it is too small or lacks access to capital markets) nor the country (because it is poor or administratively lacking) has a suitable income-protection or insurance scheme, then small producers who decide to specialize may be more vulnerable to income shocks and poverty following an opening to trade. It could be argued that they have made a choice; to go for the more risky but higher income path of specialization rather than sticking to a still feasible joint production strategy, but they may also lack information about the nature of more specialized markets. The policy question is whether the implication of this is that there should be less openness to trade to encourage small producers or fewer small producers, to allow the country to have the advantages of greater trade. Providing income support may be particularly difficult and costly for a poor developing country. It may be better to shift to larger trading units (it is notable that in all developed countries most trade is done by large companies).

But if mobility of labour among different types of work or different sectors is high, then any increase in income will come through more strongly and losses from any falls will be reduced, as people shift from losing to rising sectors. And in practice, especially in poorer households engaged in informal or agricultural activities, many of these separate interests are actually the same people or companies. All are consumers. Many producers of exports use imports. Many people and companies may be involved in the production of a variety of products, including both import substitutes which may lose, and exports and potential exports which may gain. Therefore it cannot be assumed that all losses correspond to or allow us to identify 'losers' from trade.

3.1.3 What poverty is to be measured?

There are differences in the concept, in the quantification, and in the approach to analyzing poverty. The simplest economic definitions depend on income or capital, expressed and measured in money terms. Most quantification based on this measures income-type concepts, not capital. The income may include imputed non-monetary income (subsistence, public services). But when the definition is modified to include either additional economic or new non-economic elements, these are normally expressed and measured as forms of asset or capital: health characteristics, education levels, access to financial capital, perhaps plus measures of non-economic assets like empowerment or exclusion. Although much empirical discussion of the impact of trade on poverty finds significant effects from wealth distribution factors, in particular land distribution, capital is not normally found in the analysis of trade's effects on poverty.

Current research emphasizes the time dimension of poverty. Adjustments downwards (reductions in output, employment, and therefore income) can normally be very rapid. New activities, investing in capital and labour resources, producing and marketing new products, require adjustment time. Fluctuations in income have more effect on those who are poor than on others. Researchers are now trying to distinguish between the chronically poor and the transitorily (perhaps in response to a shock) or even seasonally poor. Trade can increase the probability of some types of shock, but would normally be expected to reduce the size and frequency of shocks (by increasing the range of possible markets and sources of consumption goods).

Definitions which start from either analysis or surveys of what 'the poor' want are also based on income (if only to identify the 'poor' whose wants are to be measured). Such surveys suggest that the poor would add elements such as health or education characteristics, but also other, apparently non-economic, needs: 'a sense of insecurity or vulnerability; lack of a sense of voice vis-à-vis other members of their household, community, or government' (Farrington et al., 1999). These may be related to income or relative income, but cannot be directly 'purchased' by reallocation of spending as education or health can potentially be. They may suggest a need for institutions as well as income or market redistribution to equalize outcomes.

For both conventional income or capital and power/vulnerability measures, it would be desirable, but is normally impossible, for the unit of analysis to be the individual. In most countries, this is the unit on which power and voice in government are based (subject to exclusions such as children), and it is the normal base for welfare analysis in economics. The existence of different distributions of power in households is paralleled by different effective access to income (and capital). But there are rarely data on intra-household stocks or flows or relationships, and in practice most analysis of the impact of policy on poverty has tended to go in the opposite direction, of treating the household as the unit, and assuming that households take a collective 'livelihood' approach to all the different types of income and expenditure found within the unit. Another approach would carry the emphasis on sources of income to the extreme, to look at 'classes' of those dependent (entirely or predominantly) on particular types of income, and assume that these can be treated together as having the same interests (a definition of a Marxist approach, Cogneau and Robilliard, 2000: 7).[3]

---

[3]   The 'livelihood' approach is a mixture of capital and income measures (of assets and activities). It is an extended version of the income plus other economic elements approach, based on the total capital available: financial, human, natural, and social (Farrington et al., 1999). Further additions, like 'clean water and other services which are required to prevent people from falling into poverty' (Farrington et al., 1999) can be made, but to be consistent these would need to be based on an analysis of rigidities either in the economy or in the public provision of services which would prevent individuals from obtaining these by using the 'income' or capital included in the basic measure, or on rigidities in utility functions. If each of 'a range of livelihood outcomes (health, income, reduced vulnerability, etc.)' is to be considered an end in itself, not a component of aggregate utility or welfare, this would not

3.1.4 Policy responses

While most effects of trade unambiguously lead (eventually) to an increase in national income, the direct consequences for the distribution of this among (and within) households are not necessarily the most favourable for reducing poverty, and may have temporary or permanent effects that increase it for some people. Therefore, the principal determinant of the effect of trade on poverty is likely to be not any of the factors determining the initial distribution of effects, but the policies followed (or not followed) by the government to redistribute income or assets, through taxes, support for incomes, and provision of public goods, temporarily through safety nets or permanently. The increase in national income permits increased spending (whether public or through redistribution of income to households) on education and health, seen both as components of welfare in their own right and as contributing to future welfare by increasing productivity. It also permits increased investment, on infrastructure (water provision, transport, basic financial and marketing services) and directly productive activities, and any effects on growth (as discussed under the output effects) will also stimulate increased demand for investment. Over time, the increase in the size of the economy and the increased availability of specialized resources from abroad enhance the efficiency of the structure of the economy, by providing the scale necessary for basic commercial and financial services to operate.

If this pattern of short-term losses and long-term gains holds, it raises a basic policy question: whether it is better to try to reduce poverty in the short run by increasing or preserving production in the traditional sector (which may be difficult: the possibilities of production increase may be limited, so that productivity and income can only be increased by transferring labour out), and thus increasing or stabilizing the income of the poorest in the short run, or to encourage the modern sector in order to accelerate the transfer. The decision requires choosing among different targets (poverty, distribution, total income).

---

accept the trade-offs basic to normal utility analysis. It is not clear whether they should be considered additional or merely a component of the minimum basket of goods on which poverty lines or other income measures can be based. To the extent that they are based on 'other streams of analysis, relating for instance to households, gender, governance and farming systems', this may imply findings of rigidities, and the emphasis on structures, processes, and institutions is a useful way of conceptualizing the rigidities which may require looking at multiple impacts and objectives. As its proponents point out, 'it is essentially an integrating device, helping to form and bring together the perspectives which contribute to a people-centred. . .approach. . .[It] does not replace other approaches but builds on them.' It uses detailed quantified analysis for variables for which this is possible. By starting from the population on which effects are to be measured, it also avoids omission of negative indirect effects (if the impact of one effect is to alter that of another) (Ashley, 2000: 19).

Whether governments can redistribute any addition to national income and whether they will do so will depend initially on the share of any increase going to the government in taxes or easily available to it in taxable sectors, and then fundamentally on its social objectives, political will, and administrative competence. Any increase in income can be captured by appropriate taxation, but for increases in trade there are also direct effects. For many poor countries, tariff revenue is a major source of revenue, and administratively one of the easiest and cheapest to collect. Trade taxes are particularly important for small countries (where trade is a high share of total income and output) and for many least developed countries (McKay *et al.*, 2000: 2 cite an IMF result that for 36 it is 'nearly one third of total tax revenue or around 5 percent of GDP'). For this reason, tariff reform is normally assumed to require simultaneous increases (or introduction) of other taxes. The least market-distorting practical tax is normally an indirect tax (value added tax), but if the government wants to 'distort' incomes in favour of the poor, either an income tax or a discriminatory sales tax, combined with subsidized or free provision of the desired social services, will be more appropriate. The important point to note is that, unless specific action is taken to alter other taxes, lower tariffs may reduce the share of government revenue, at a time when the risk that the increase in national income may go, under some conditions, more to the high-income than to the poor requires the share to increase.

3.2 FDI and poverty

3.2.1 FDI and development

There are many areas in which foreign direct investment affects development, namely:

- employment and incomes
- capital formation, market access
- structure of markets
- technology and skills
- fiscal revenues, and
- political, cultural and social issues.

We can distinguish between static and dynamic effects and FDI can have positive and negative dynamic effects on development in all of these areas. While FDI was traditionally seen as an additional source of capital, vital for the development of countries with insufficient economic capacity and infrastructure and where domestic saving rates are low, the view that FDI can also bring new techniques and skills is also important. This can lead to growth and eventually to poverty reduction.

As FDI is associated with direct as well as indirect costs and benefits, a simple quantitative measure (FDI flows, direct employment, wage levels, etc.) is not sufficient as a means of assessing the impact of FDI on development. There are three alternatives:

- detailed econometric studies assessing one aspect of the investment, for example productivity spillover effects
- cost-benefit analyses, valuing the costs and benefits of all aspects of an investment, and
- qualitative accounts comparing outcomes in similar situations but with alternative policies in place.

While the first two approaches are criticized for not being able to construct a 'strategic counterfactual', the qualitative approach may not address cause and effect adequately. Outcomes of all the approaches may further depend on the time framework and the sector of analysis.

There is heated discussion about the impact of FDI on development, and at least a significant part of it derives from the observation that (foreign) multinationals are different from local (non-multinational) firms. Foreign multinationals tend to be larger, to pay higher wages, to be more capital- and skill-intensive and to introduce more up-to-date technology (see, for example, Dunning, 1993; Caves, 1996). Some of the characteristics of multinationals relate simply to the size of the firm, which itself is often related to higher pay, more training and usage of the latest technologies. However, while controlling for factors such as size, foreign ownership is still related to better performance.

3.2.2 Output and growth effect

When discussing the econometric evidence of FDI on growth and productivity, there are different types of econometric studies. Macro and meso studies usually find positive and significant correlations between FDI and GDP per capita or productivity. This may come as no surprise, as FDI tends to locate in higher value-added industries. It is often not clear whether productivity increases at the macro level are driven by spillovers to and learning effects in local firms, or are only due to a composition effect. It is therefore important to understand *whether* and *how* positive spillovers to local firms occur, because FDI associated with positive spillovers has long-lasting effects for development whereas FDI without spillovers may have only one-off effects which may disappear when the foreign investor leaves the country.

Microeconometric studies can account for the composition effect testing whether local firms can improve their productivity as a result of foreign presence. It should be noted, however, that spillover studies are usually confined to manufacturing industry. A significant body of evidence (for example, Haddad and Harrison, 1993; Aitken and Harrison, 1999; Djankov and Hoekman, 2000) finds that the productivity level of foreign firms is higher than that of domestic firms (but with some exceptions, see Matsuoka, 2001, for Thailand), but that the effects on productivity levels and growth in domestic firms are mixed. As a result of the presence of foreign firms, domestic firms in the same sector could be better off as (foreign) competition forces them to upgrade technologies (as in the case of Indonesia, see Blomström and Sjöholm, 1999). They could be worse off when foreign firms take the market of existing local firms (as in Venezuela, suggested by Aitken and Harrison, 1999). Or they could not learn at all, as the productivity gap is too large to learn anything (as in Mexico, see Blomström, 1986). In Morocco, Venezuela and the Czech Republic, the presence of foreign firms reduces productivity *growth* in domestic firms.

While useful in themselves, the above econometric studies do not specify how spillovers occur (Mortimore, 2004). Various authors have tried to set the literature on FDI and development in the framework of learning by local firms. Narula and Lall (2004) argue that FDI *per se* does not provide growth opportunities unless a domestic industry exists which has the technological capacity to profit from the externalities from MNE activity. Thus an understanding of how technological knowledge is acquired is relevant to how FDI affects development. There are widely varying experiences, with some countries having used FDI to upgrade domestic firms, while others have been less successful. Countries are most successful if they use policies to maximize the impact on learning in local firms. The long-run effect on growth will also be greater when the domestic sector benefits. One such effect works through linkages, and learning through linkages is greatest when domestic firms have built up an absorptive capacity.

3.2.3 Distribution of investment effects

The links between FDI and income inequality are complex. We can distinguish between the effects on wage inequality and on non-wage income inequality. The following general effects play a role:

- *Skill-specific technological change.* In addition to initial efficiency differences, FDI could induce faster productivity growth of labour in both foreign (technology transfer) and domestic firms (spillover effects). If such productivity growth is skill-biased (for example, information technology), FDI may increase skill-biased technological change (Berman and Machin, 2000).
- *Skill-specific wage bargaining.* Skilled workers are usually in a stronger bargaining position than less skilled workers because they possess key skills which are in relatively scarce supply, and may also have better skills to negotiate higher wages.
- *Composition effect.* Foreign firms tend to locate in skill-intensive sectors or skill-intensive segments within sectors. If FDI causes a relative expansion of skill-intensive sectors, this will improve the relative position of skilled workers and increase wage inequality (Feenstra and Hanson, 1995).

- *Training and education.* FDI may affect the supply of skills through firm-specific and general training and through contributions to general education. While foreign firms generally train more than their local counterparts, after controlling for other factors that are positively related to training such as size, much training benefits skilled workers.

The above points demonstrate that FDI can be expected to increase wage inequality, in contrast to predictions by traditional trade theory (in the 2 by 2 skilled/unskilled labour variant of the Heckscher Ohlin model) that FDI reduces wage inequality in developing countries because it allows them to specialize in less skill-intensive activities. However, because there are many possibly opposing effects, empirical testing is required.

In addition to the effects of FDI on wage inequality, there can be effects on non-wage income. For instance, FDI may increase profits and the return to capital, relative to other types of income such as that of the self-employed and employees. Real wages have fallen over the past two decades in many Latin American countries, implying that owners of capital have benefited more from the economic reforms. This could have helped to increase income inequality. Other effects on income inequality could be indirect, for instance through the effects on fiscal revenues and expenditures. These could nonetheless be very significant or the main link to inequality for certain types of investment (for example, natural resource-based FDI).

ODI (2002) summarizes the recent evidence so far. Most evidence on the relationship between inward FDI and wage inequality at the macro level is concerned with developed countries. Blonigen and Slaughter (2001) find that multinational activity was not significantly correlated with skill upgrading within US manufacturing sectors over the period 1977–94, but te Velde (2001) finds evidence for a sector bias towards using skilled workers. Figini and Görg (1999) find that FDI was associated, up to a point, with skill upgrading and increased wage dispersion in Irish manufacturing over the period 1979–95, while Taylor and Driffield (2000) find significant effects of FDI on wage dispersion in UK manufacturing.

With regard to the evidence for developing countries and Latin America in particular, Feenstra and Hanson (1995) find that inward FDI increased the relative demand for skilled labour in Mexican manufacturing over the period 1975–98. In some localized regions, FDI can account for over 50 per cent of the increase in the labour wage share in the late 1980s.

Studies that include a wide range of countries tend to find little systematic effect of FDI on inequality. Freeman *et al.*, (2001) find no evidence of a consistent relationship between FDI and wage inequality in a large sample of developing countries. Lee and Vivarelli (2004) find a neutral impact in 45 developing countries in the 1990s, but the analysis is based on the more general Gini measures of inequality (which include wage and other inequalities).

However, this does not mean that FDI has no effect on (wage) inequality in individual countries. Te Velde and Morrissey (2004) provide macro evidence of the effects of FDI on wages and wage inequality in five East Asian countries (Korea, Singapore, Hong Kong, Thailand and Philippines). Wage inequality has been low and decreasing in some but not all East Asian countries. Using ILO data for wages and employment by occupation, they failed to find strong evidence that FDI reduced wage inequality in five East Asian countries over the period 1985–98. Controlling for domestic influences (wage setting, supply of skills), they found that FDI has raised wage inequality in Thailand, and also that FDI raises the wages for both skilled and low-skilled workers. Te Velde (2003) provides further evidence for Latin America, arguing that FDI increased wage inequality in Bolivia and Chile, while having very little to no effect in most other Latin American countries. The macro evidence thus shows that FDI does not tend to reduce wage inequality but may increase it in some cases.

The empirical evidence on foreign ownership and wages at the micro level shows that:

- foreign-owned firms pay their workers more than local firms. Wage differentials can be up to 60 per cent, but are often more modest;
- studies that do not control fully for other effects (size, location, industry, etc.) overstate the effect of foreign ownership on wages; and
- studies that distinguish between average wages in two separate skill categories find that wage differentials are greater for non-production (relatively skilled) workers than for production (less skilled) workers.

An issue of current interest is whether FDI can contribute to the objective of reducing poverty (ODI, 2002). This will depend on how the gains from FDI are distributed among sectors, workers and households. Systematic evidence on the effects of FDI on income distribution and poverty in developing countries was discussed earlier. In principle, there is no direct link between FDI and poverty reduction – this does not include 'socially responsible' investment which may directly benefit the poor– but there are three possible indirect links:

- If FDI contributes to export growth, productivity growth and finance for the balance of payments, it supports increases in national income that offer the potential to benefit the poor. In this case FDI does not reduce poverty directly, but it helps to create an enabling economic environment.
- If FDI increases employment it may help some to move out of poverty. With the exception of investment in textiles, a lot of FDI in manufacturing is likely to employ labour that is relatively skilled (in terms of the local market), and does not directly benefit the poor. Well-developed linkages with local suppliers may increase the employment of various skill groups.
- Foreign firms may pay higher wages than local firms for workers with similar qualifications. Because of the skill bias of FDI, this will not directly affect the

poor and is likely to increase inequality of wage incomes, raising the skilled/unskilled wage differential, and to increase urban/rural income differentials. However, establishing a higher paid labour force and developing better skilled effects depend on the country, sector and time framework of interest.

In Lee and Vivarelli's (2004) book on globalization, education and poverty, Sanjaya Lall argued that the effects of globalization on employment are content-specific and depend on specific circumstances as well as active policy interventions. Indeed, in general little is known about the impact of FDI on employment. Most authors tend to examine the effects on income distribution rather than on employment generation or income growth. Spiezia argues that FDI has more positive employment effects in richer rather than in poorer developing countries. So while the FDI-employment link is potentially important in reducing poverty, the relationship is not always positive or negative, and it is not the only route to poverty reduction.

3.2.4 Policy responses

Most econometric work on the effects of FDI on development tends to ignore economic and policy factors affecting the link between them. It is often shown that FDI is correlated with growth and productivity, but this masks the fact that different countries with different policies and economic factors tend to derive different benefits and costs of FDI. Whether the positive effects of FDI outweigh the negative effects will depend on the economic and policy factors in the host country as well as the sector and the strategies of multinational affiliates. Recently, researchers have begun to stress the importance of local capabilities (an educated and trainable workforce, see, for example, Borensztein *et al.*, 1998), investment in R&D (see, for example, te Velde, 2001), and the ability to conduct an outward-oriented trade policy (see, for example, Balasubramanyam *et al.*, 1996) in deriving benefits for the local economy. One implication could be that countries with relatively few local capabilities are less able to derive benefits from FDI. On the other hand, however, researchers have also suggested that countries have more to gain, the further they have to catch up.

With respect to the effects of policy on the distribution of investment effects, there are potentially ways in which government and business can coordinate their actions or form partnerships in order to improve the impact of MNEs on the development of the poorest workers. Such opportunities are most likely to arise when government and business activities interact. The following areas, where the business and development cases are linked, deserve further attention (te Velde, 2003):

- *Education and training.* MNEs will train their workers more when workers have a good and appropriate basic education. Governments could therefore consider whether the quantity and quality of basic education are sufficiently geared towards areas of economic expansion and the needs of MNEs. They may also consider providing incentives (public–private partnerships in training, subsidies, taxes, standardization) for more training of less-skilled workers, particularly in larger firms.

- *Health.* A healthy workforce is in the (business) interest of the MNE and a healthy population is a government priority. In the case of epidemics, MNEs and less wealthy governments may combine to fight the disease, as witnessed in Southern Africa. Neither partner would be able to fight the epidemic on its own. The government may have limited funds, but the provision of health care for (future) employees can make economic sense.
- *Supplier development.* MNEs will source locally when local quality suppliers are present. There may be a role for the government to provide an enabling environment for private sector development and to actively support linkages between MNEs and local firms in a market-led way. This would involve matching local suppliers with MNEs and upgrading the basic capabilities of local firms. Well-developed Investment Promotion Agencies (such as IDA Ireland and the Singapore Economic Development Board) already perform such tasks through national linkage-support programmes. MNEs may then develop their suppliers further. An example of supplier development in Latin America relates to the Intel plant which has more than 100 suppliers. The Costa Rican government is helping local suppliers to become more competitive (see Larrain *et al.*, 2000).
- *Infrastructure.* It may be in the interest of both the MNE and local communities to provide local infrastructure. A combination of MNE activities and government funds may maximize the benefits to the development of infrastructure in host countries.

3.3 Migration and poverty

3.3.1 Output and growth effects

The literature on migration is emerging and this chapter will deal only briefly with the subject. The static gains from migration can be shown on the basis of a variation of the 2 by 2 Heckscher Ohlin model. If neither trade in goods nor capital flows are permitted, labour flows would also achieve factor price equalization in a situation where labour is optimally allocated. Simulations using general equilibrium models, based on a number of assumptions, provide estimates of the static gains from migration. If developed countries permitted movement of labour up to 3 per cent of the total labour force, world incomes would rise by $156 billion (Winters, 2002). Developing countries would be the main gainers and the net welfare for the home region, Africa, would be $14 billion. While most of such gains are clearly related to developed–developing migration, there may also be some (but obviously lower) benefits for developing country regions.

But there are static and dynamic effects. It is useful to distinguish between the effects on labour-sending and labour-receiving countries (World Bank, 2003). The benefits for the sending country are threefold. Labour emigration reduces unemployment and raises wages. Once they have emigrated, workers send home remittances which are an important source of external capital flows for developing countries. Table 3.1 shows that remittances to developing countries amount to $80 billion, about 50 per cent more than aid flows. For sub-Saharan Africa remittances constitute about a third of FDI flows. The emigrant worker can also acquire skills abroad, which can be useful once he/she returns. Obviously, emigrant labour will initially translate into a loss of human capital for the sending country, or a brain-drain cost. The receiving country will initially gain by importing labour that can be put to work in areas of labour shortage.

Table 3.1 Worker remittances to developing world (2002)

	$ bn	% GDP
Total	80	1.3
East Asia and Pacific	11	0.6
Europe and Central Asia	10	1.0
Latin America and Caribbean	25	1.5
Middle East and North Africa	14	2.2
South Asia	16	2.5
Sub-Saharan Africa	4	1.3

Source: World Bank (2003).

3.3.2 Distribution of migration effects

North–South migration is usually undertaken by skilled workers, while there appears to be some evidence that the poor migrate less (for example, there is a poverty constraint, see Clark *et al.*, 2003; Hatton and Williamson, 2001). This may relate to the migration of medium to highly skilled workers in education, information technology and health to developed countries. However, this may be less so for South–South migration, for example, migration to the South African mines. Thus (North–South) migration is likely to benefit the relatively skilled workers directly. However, indirectly remittances may also benefit the poorest countries and workers. The type of migration may also affect income inequality. If migration takes place in those skill groups that are relatively unskilled for the receiving country, this may increase inequality, but if immigration is in skilled categories this may lead to an increased supply of relative skills and hence reduced inequality.

3.3.3 Policy responses

There are various types of responses to migration, and different appropriate responses depending on whether it relates to temporary or long-term migration. The sending country may want to limit permanent emigration in favour of temporary emigration and maximize the productive use of remittances. The receiving country may also want to react to the labour market consequences, especially when income inequality is increasing.

3.4 Conclusion

This chapter has provided a number of important building blocks relevant for the book as a whole. Whilst regional integration may affect trade, FDI and migration, each of these variables will affect poverty differently. The main message is that the impact of trade, FDI and migration depends on the complementary conditions in place, many of which can be influenced by appropriate policies.

References

Aitken, B.J. and Harrison, A.E., 'Do Domestic Firms Benefit from Direct Foreign Investment? Evidence from Venezuela', *American Economic Review*, 89 (1999): 605–18.

Ashley, C., *Applying Livelihood Approaches to Natural Resource Management Initiatives: Experiences in Namibia and Kenya*, Working Paper No. 134 (London: Overseas Development Institute, 2000).

Balasubramanyam, V.N., Salisu, M. and Sapsford, D., 'Foreign Direct Investment and Growth in EP and IS countries', *Economic Journal*, 106, (1996): 92–105.

Berman, E. and Machin, S., 'Skilled-Biased Technology Transfer: Evidence of Factor-Biased Technological Change in Developing Countries', (Boston, MA: Department of Economics, Boston University, 2000).

Bird, K., 'A Framework to Analyse Linkages between Trade Policy, Poverty Reduction and Sustainable Development' (First Draft, 2003).

Blomström, M., 'Foreign investment and productive efficiency: the case of Mexico', *Journal of Industrial Economics*, 35 (1986): 97-110.

Blomström, M. and Sjöholm, F., 'Technology Transfer and Spillovers: Does Local Participation with Multinationals Matter?', *European Economic Review*, 43 (1999): 915–23.

Blonigen, B.A and Slaughter, M., *Foreign-Affiliate Activity and US Skill Upgrading*, NBER Working Paper 7040, in *Review of Economics and Statistics* (2001).

Borensztein, E., De Gregorio, J., and Lee, J-W., 'How Does Foreign Direct Investment Affect Economic Growth?' *Journal of International Economics,* 45 (1998): 115–35.

Caves, R.E., *Multinational Enterprise and Economic Analysis,* 2nd edition, (Cambridge: Cambridge University Press, 1996).

Clark, X., Hatton, T. and Williamson, J.G., 'What explains cross-border migration in Latin America?' (Draft paper revised June 2003).

Cogneau, D. and Robilliard, A-S., *Growth, Distribution and Poverty in Madagascar: Learning from a Microsimulation Model in a General Equilibrium Framework,* TMD Discussion Paper No. 61 (Washington, DC: IFPRI, 2000).

Djankov, S. and Hoekman, B., 'Foreign Investment and productivity Growth in Czech Enterprises', *World Bank Economic Review,* 14 (2000): 49-64.

Dollar, D. and Kraay, A., 'Growth is Good for the Poor' (Washington, DC: World Bank, 2000) mimeo.

Dunning, J. *Multinational Enterprises and the Global Economy* (Boston, MA: Addison–Wesley Publishing Company, 1993).

Farrington, John, Carney, D., Ashley C. and Turton C., *'Sustainable Livelihoods in Practice: Early Applications of Concepts in Rural Areas',* Natural Resources Perspectives No. 42 (London: Overseas Development Institute, June 1999).

Feenstra, R.C. and Hanson, G.H., *Foreign Direct Investment and Relative Wages: Evidence from Mexico's Maquiladoras,* NBER Working Paper No. 5122 (Cambridge, MA: National Bureau of Economic Research, 1995).

Fields, G.S., *Distribution and Development: A New Look at the Developing World* (New York: Russell Sage Foundation and Cambridge, MA: MIT Press, 2001).

Figini, P. and Görg, H., 'Multinational Companies and Wage Inequality in the Host Country: The Case of Ireland', *Weltwirtschaftliches Archiv,* 135, (1999): 594–612.

Freeman, R.B., *Trade Wars: the Exaggerated Impact of Trade in Economic Debate,* Working Paper 10000 (Cambridge, MA: National Bureau of Economic Research, 2003). http://www.nber.org/papers/w10000

Freeman, R.B., Oostendorp, R. and Rama, M., 'Globalization and Wages', work in progress quoted in M. Rama (ed.) 'Globalization and Workers in Developing Countries' (Washington, DC: World Bank, 2001), mimeo.

Gallup, J.L., Radelet, S. and Warner, A., 'Economic Growth and the Income of the Poor' (Cambridge, MA: Harvard Institute for Economic Development, 1998) mimeo.

Haddad, M. and Harrison, A., 'Are There Positive Spillovers from Direct Foreign Investment? Evidence from Panel Data for Morocco', *Journal of Development Economics,* 42, (1993): 51-74.

Hanmer, L. and Wilmshurst, J., 'Are the International Development Targets Attainable? An Overview', *Development Policy Review,* 18, (1) (2000): 5–10.

Hatton, T. and Williamson, J., *Demographic and Economic Pressure on Emigration out of Africa,* NBER Working Paper 8128 (Cambridge, MA: National Bureau of Economic Research, 2001).

Larrain, F.B., Lopez-Calva, L.F. and Rodriquez-Clare, A., *Intel: A Case Study of Foreign Direct Investment in Central America*, CID working paper 58 (2000).

Lee, E. and Vivarelli, M. (eds), *Understanding Globalization, Employment and Poverty Reduction* (Basingstoke and New York: Palgrave Macmillan, 2004).

Matsuoka, A., *Wage Differentials among Local Plants and Foreign Multinationals by Foreign Ownership Share and Nationality in Thai Manufacturing* (ICSEAD Working Paper Series 2001-25, 2001).

McKay, A., Winters, L.A. and Kedir, A.M., 'A Review of Empirical Evidence on Trade, Trade Policy and Poverty' (A report to DFID prepared as a background document for the Second Development White Paper, 2000).

Mortimore, M., 'The Impact of TNC Strategies on Development in Latin America and the Caribbean', in D.W. te Velde (ed.) *Foreign Direct Investment, Inequality and Poverty: Experiences and Policy Implications* (London: Overseas Development Institute, 2004).

Narula, R. and Lall, S., *Understanding FDI-assisted Economic Development*, special issue of the *European Journal of Development Research*, 16, (3) (2004).

OECD, 'Services Trade Liberalization: Identifying Opportunities and Gains. Key Findings' TD/TC/WP(2003)25/FINAL (Paris: OECD, 2003).

ODI, *Foreign Direct Investment. Who Gains?*, ODI Briefing Paper (London: Overseas Development Institute, 2002).

Page, S., *Trade and Climate Change: Implications for Poverty and Poverty Policy* (London: Overseas Development Institute, March 2001).

Taylor, K. and Driffield, N., 'Wage Dispersion and the Role of Multinationals: Evidence from UK Panel Data', Paper presented at the International Economic Association conference on Globalization and Labour Markets, (University of Nottingham, July 2000), see http://www.nottingham.ac.uk/economics/iea

Velde, D.W. te, 'Foreign Direct Investment and Factor Prices in US Manufacturing', *Weltwirtschaftliches Archiv* 137(4) (2001): 622–43.

Velde, D.W. te, *Foreign Direct Investment and Income Inequality in Latin America. Experiences and Policy Implications*, ODI Working Paper (London: Overseas Development Institute, 2003).

Velde, D.W. te and Morrissey, O., 'Foreign Direct Investment, Skills and Wage Inequality in East Asia', *Journal of Asia and Pacific Economies* (October 2004).

Weiss, J., *Poverty in the ASEAN Region* (Background Paper, Development and Project Planning Centre, University of Bradford, 2000).

Winters, L.A., *Trade Liberalization and Poverty* (Brighton: School of Social Sciences, University of Sussex, 1999).

Winters, L.A., 'The Economic Implications of Liberalizing Mode 4 Trade', Paper prepared for the joint WTO–World Bank symposium on 'The movement of natural persons (mode 4) under the GATS', WTO, Geneva, 11–12 April 2002.

World Bank, *Global Economic Prospects* 2004, (Washington, DC: World Bank, 2003).

Chapter 4

Regional Integration and Poverty: Towards a Conceptual Framework

Dirk Willem te Velde, Sheila Page and Oliver Morrissey

In this chapter we develop a framework to identify and assess the various ways in which RTAs can affect poverty, in particular the effects that operate via the volume of trade and investment. Whereas Chapter 2 discussed the circumstances under which RTAs lead to more trade (investment and/or migration), and Chapter 3 discussed how such increases in trade (investment and/or migration) can affect poverty, this chapter aims to provide the links from RTAs to poverty impacts.

Section 4.1 outlines the three basic ways in which RTAs can have effects on poverty – through the level of activity (volume), prices and the share of the poor in economic activity ('slice' effects). We then consider whether features of integration can alter the poverty focus (or impact) of RTAs through differences with respect to the regional versus global composition of trade, investment and migration in Sections 4.2, 4.3 and 4.4 respectively. Is it possible for two identical countries with the same volume of trade, investment and migration to have different poverty reduction profiles because of RI? Section 4.5 considers a variety of ways that RTAs can affect poverty other than through trade, investment and migration. Section 4.6 then presents a conceptual framework for mapping the effects of RTAs on the poor and poverty reduction, while Section 4.7 concludes with some implications for future research.

4.1 RTAs and poverty: volume, price and slice effects

As it supports increased trade and investment, at least in principle, integration would be expected to expand the level of economic activity. Given the prevailing pattern of distribution, the poor can expect to benefit from this level or volume effect. The 'volume' effects on poverty reduction are greatest when RTAs are trade (and investment) creating, because the poor are better off if they can get the same share of a larger trade (and therefore income) cake. On the other hand, when RTAs are trade diverting through lower internal tariffs, the reduction in tax revenues can offset any positive 'volume' effects. Volume effects are likely to be greatest if integration involves relatively large and rich countries with diversified and complementary patterns of production and trade. Where integration is between low-income and structurally similar countries, it is likely that the volume effects and hence the poverty reduction impacts will be relatively small.

Another important link with poverty is the 'price' effects of an RTA. Trade policy liberalization (for example, tariff reductions) can lead to lower prices, which will benefit consumers (although there is a cost in terms of lost tax revenue). To the extent that tariffs are reduced on products that are consumed proportionately more by the poor, for example, staple foods, and the tariff reduction is passed on to the consumers, this will benefit the poor proportionately more. This effect is relevant even in the absence of changes in volumes. However, if the poor tend not to consume imported goods, then they are least affected by import liberalization. Furthermore, if the propensity to consume imports is lowest for the poor, the poor will derive the least proportional benefit from lower import prices.

There are also more general price effects in addition to those on imports, as the level effect on domestic and export production can generate price effects. In terms of the poverty impact, the important issue is the effect on the prices of goods that matter most to the poor, whether because they are a large share of the consumption basket or because the poor are engaged in their production (perhaps as employees). Integration would have the greatest benefit for the poor if it can be shown to reduce the price of the goods they consume (necessities and basic foods) and increase the price of the goods they produce, or at least increase demand for what they produce. As the volume effect can increase the demand for informal sector services, this can also benefit the poor.

There are ways in which RTAs can affect poverty by altering distribution or the share of economic activity involving the poor. The pro-poor price effects outlined above are one example; another is where the RTA has a particular benefit for a sector especially important to the poor. There can be a 'slice' effect if the slice of the same cake would be bigger for the poor as a result of signing an RTA, for example, if the RTA changes the poverty focus of trade, investment and migration (compared with multilateral integration). We discuss this in Section 4.2. Another type of slice effect could arise if government spending is targeted on the poor, or is at least redistributive. In this case, the effect of integration on tax revenue may be very important, and is likely to have negative impacts on the poor (since a fall in tax revenue is likely).

4.2 Does regional integration change the poverty focus of trade?

Trade policy reforms have economic effects on (a) prices of traded products, (b) output, wages and employment opportunities in the affected sectors, and (c) the government's fiscal position (see for example, McCulloch *et al.*, 2001; McKay *et al.*, 2000). Research could focus on import prices and consumers to address (a), and export performance to address (b), although one should also consider whether any sectors have evidently suffered from competition from cheaper imports. Most of the literature is concerned with international trade at a global level. RI is a policy reform that affects trade at the relevant regional level. Vis-à-vis each of the three issues, we consider how RI may affect trade and poverty in a manner that is different from the way global trade affects poverty:

a. *Prices of traded goods.* Open international trade implies that domestic prices of traded goods should tend (downwards in nearly all cases) towards world prices. In the case of RI, there is only convergence of regional prices, which will tend to be above world prices. If there is a common external tariff lower than pre-RI tariffs, then regional (domestic) prices will fall. Thus, the principal effect of RI will be to reduce prices of goods traded within the region. This will benefit consumers, and would be expected to benefit producers in some countries in the region (those able to expand exports) at the expense of others (those with relatively high initial protection who face increased competition from regional imports). The overall effect on poverty will depend on which products are traded regionally and how prices are affected, but consumers overall gain. In this context, it would be worth asking whether poor people consume relatively more products traded intra-regionally than products traded extra-regionally. There is another issue related to the pattern of tariff liberalization. In RTAs, tariff liberalization will be uniform across all products, eventually reducing all tariffs to zero (possibly with some exceptions). However, due to pressure groups, multilateral negotiations may reduce tariffs in a way that disproportionately benefits the non-poor.

b. *Static and dynamic output effects.* In principle countries should raise their output as they specialize on the basis of comparative advantage (static effect). But not all countries may benefit to the same extent. Often, the bigger members of a developing country RTA will have a competitive advantage (typically in basic manufactures) and will benefit the most. The smaller members are likely to face increased competition from imports, and production will not therefore increase as much. *Ceteris paribus*, the poverty impact is beneficial in large countries and adverse in small countries. The small countries may benefit if they can export food within the region, and growth in agriculture typically benefits the poor.

RTAs can affect poverty through dynamic output and productivity effects, such as through competition and scale. Many argue that the important effects of RTAs are dynamic, with competition creating a more efficient industry and higher growth. Lower intra-regional tariffs would lead to increased competition (Neary, 2001). The new trade theory emphasizes the long-run productivity effects of trade (Grossman and Helpman, 1991). Productivity spillovers can occur via importing and exporting (Coe and Helpman, 1995; Coe *et al.,* 1997). Not only does a country's efficiency increase due to allocation effects: trade also helps actors to learn from each other and appropriate R&D spillovers, and these learning effects can be translated into long-run efficiency gains.

Unfortunately, there is little evidence of these dynamic effects. Schiff and Wang (2003) find no empirical evidence of the dynamic effects of Regional Integration Agreements (RIAs) based on technology diffusion. They go on to show that NAFTA imports have raised productivity (between 5.5 and 7.5 per cent) in Mexico through imported foreign knowledge stocks, while extra-regional imports had no effects (but this may be due to the specifics of NAFTA). These are long-lasting effects that can in the long run benefit the poor. There can also be long-lasting effects on productivity through learning by exporting. Such effects may be appropriate particularly when dealing with more developed partners, and they tend to be extra-regional.

c. *The effect on tax revenue* depends on the pre- and post- RI pattern of trade and tariffs. Import liberalization might be expected to reduce government revenue, as tariffs are typically an important source of tax revenue. This effect is reinforced when RI leads to trade diversion (Viner, 1950). There are a number of reasons why import liberalization may not be associated with lower tariff revenues. First, the lower tariff rates discourage evasion and avoidance so collection efficiency improves. Second, quantitative restrictions may be converted into tariffs. Third, the remaining tariffs may apply to an increasing value of imports. This may arise either because demand is elastic or because there has also been devaluation (which increases the domestic price of imports). If tariff revenue declines, as it typically does, the fall can in principle be compensated by increased revenue from other taxes (mostly domestic sales). In practice, however, tax revenues have tended to decline.

The presence of import barriers or restrictions creates an anti-export bias by raising the prices of importable goods relative to exportable goods. Removal of this anti-export bias through trade liberalization would induce a shift of resources from the production of import substitutes to the production of exports. The factors used intensively in the production of exports – land and rural and/or unskilled labour in poor countries – should benefit most. On the other hand, factors employed in the production of import-competing goods – mostly urban capital and labour – may suffer losses. Typically, import supply from the rest of the world responds more rapidly than domestic export supply, so liberalization imposes adjustment costs (losses tend to be immediate, whereas export gains can take time). As RI does not involve exposure to imports from the rest of the world, but only from the region, adjustment costs (hence adverse poverty effects) are lower, but so are the possible gains.

There is another effect of trade on poverty in RTAs, but this is based on the distribution of the benefits. The benefits of regional integration may not be evenly spread amongst the members of a region. Venables (1999) argued that South–South agreements will tend to lead to divergence of income levels of member states, while North–North agreements may lead to convergence of income levels. The explanation of this is based on the position of countries within a region compared with those outside the region. Countries with a comparative advantage (for example, in manufacturing) closer to the world average do better in a region than do countries that are at the extremes, since the latter are more likely to switch import suppliers (of manufactures) and face trade diversion costs. This explanation is based on manufacturing, but it is less clear when other sectors are also included. Nevertheless, possible divergence due to relocation effects may actually put RIAs under strain, as may have been the case in the East African Community. While peripheral countries in the EU such as Ireland have caught up with other member states in terms of productivity levels apparently through trade and FDI spillovers, there was a degree of divergence and agglomeration in developing regions such as the East African Community and the Central American Common Market (CACM) both of which date back to the 1950s and '60s. This also brings home the fact that the distribution of gains among member states may affect further regional integration processes.

In general, as intra-regional trade among low-income countries tends to be lower than for high-income countries[1] and limited to fairly simple products (basic manufactures and perhaps food), the overall trade impact may not be great. However, the level and the share of intra-regional trade appear to be on the increase, although this may not be happening in all regions in all years, with several regions (MERCOSUR, the EU, for example) experiencing a decline in the intra-regional share of trade over the last five years. Furthermore, we should realize that trade is probably more under-recorded in low-income countries than in high-income countries.

Table 4.1   Share of intra-regional trade in total exports and imports

	Exports			*Imports*		
	1990	1995	2002	1990	1995	2002
EU (15)		64.0	61.6		65.2	61.9
NAFTA (3)	42.6	46.0	56.5		37.7	38.1
ASEAN FTA (10)	20.1	25.5	24.0	16.2	18.8	23.6
MERCOSUR	8.9	20.5	11.5	14.5	18.1	17.0
ANDEAN	4.3	12.3	10.2	7.7	12.9	13.9
CARICOM	9.5	9.8		12.3	16.4	

Source: WTO, *International Trade Statistics.*

---

[1]   See, for example, Page, 2000: Table 7.1 for 1996, which shows it ranging from more than 50 per cent of total trade in EU15, less in NAFTA, MERCOSUR, ASEAN, 13 per cent in ANDEAN and CACM, 12 per cent in SADC to just 4 per cent in SAARC.

In some regions, there will be one large member (measured in terms of economic market size[2]) that is likely to derive the most benefit because it has a comparative advantage in regional manufactures (for example, Kenya in the EAC, Nigeria in ECOWAS). The smaller countries are only likely to benefit if they produce niche products, for example if they are able to expand food exports to the large member. This distributional effect implies that the large member may have to compensate the smaller members (a similar argument applies to distributing revenue from a common external tariff). Failure to agree compensation is one reason why RTAs among low-income countries have often failed in the past, or why achieving deep integration has been such a slow process.

Because integration among developing countries typically affects only a small share of their total trade, the volume effects are likely to be small; hence the revenue effects are also likely to be small. In the case of developed-developing country integration, where trade diversion is more likely, the revenue effects will be greater, highlighting the need for policy measures to offset any adverse effects on income distribution.

We briefly consider whether *services* liberalization at the regional level provides better outcomes than liberalization at the world level, and whether RTAs could affect the poverty focus of trade in services. Stephenson (2002) defines four different categories of services:

(i)   infrastructure-type services: financial, telecommunications, energy and transport
(ii) business-type services: distribution, professional services, other business services, tourism, construction and engineering services, and environmental services
(iii) social services: educational and health services
(iv) other services: recreational, cultural.

In order to attract the most efficient service provider in the capital-intensive category (i), it would make sense to liberalize beyond the region. Global service providers are likely to have better access to capital than service providers whose market is a Southern region (the global provider may, of course, be from a developing country). For the less capital-intensive category (ii), tourism is a relatively liberalized sector (although the GATS often includes qualified commitments, such as subject to national approval); construction and engineering services and professional services, on the other hand, depend on qualifications and national standards, so that RTAs may play a useful role in facilitating recognition across borders (within the region first). The third category is sensitive to national concerns and it could be easier to liberalize these sectors among countries with similar levels of development, language, culture, etc. RTAs could act as a catalyst.

---

[2]   Small does not imply necessarily poor. For instance, Singapore is very rich compared with other ASEAN members. That is why we refer to small in economic size.

The fourth category is mixed. Hence, for some sectors RTAs could be an appropriate starting level. However, it is premature to analyze differences in services liberalization fully now, since many regional protocols have not been ratified by all parties and those that have, have been in force for only a short period.

4.3 Does regional integration change the poverty focus of FDI?

Various factors determine whether RI changes the poverty focus of FDI. Table 4.2 uses the FDI and development framework set out in Chapter 1 to examine whether global MNEs could be expected to have an impact on development and hence poverty distinctive from that of regional MNEs. It shows that regional MNEs (in a typical developing-country region) have both advantages and disadvantages over global MNEs. While there is by now quite a lot of evidence on differences between foreign and local firms (see Section 2.2), there is not much on the effect of the source country on FDI. Some evidence for developed countries suggests that US firms pay higher wages and are more productive than other MNEs, including from the EU, that have set up in the UK (te Velde, 2002). In general, it seems that the potential benefits of global liberalization are greater than those of regional integration, but that the potential losses will also be greater. This implies that active public policies (as we discussed in Section 4.2) increase in importance with global as opposed to regional integration.

It is usually the dynamic effects that are emphasized. Blomström and Kokko (1997) argue that regional integration leads to efficiency gains and higher growth. FDI can actually act as such a catalyst through spillovers in terms of technology transfer and other linkages with local firms. There can thus be long-lasting effects on growth and productivity, in addition to the one-off effect based on a more efficient allocation of resources. Not surprisingly, many studies examining the wealth effects of regional trade arrangements find that they are large. Wealth (or GDP) effects can ultimately benefit the poor, depending on the distribution of the gains.

In practice, integration among developing countries affects only a small share of total FDI; in other words, intra-regional FDI is low as a percentage of total FDI for low-income regions such as the South Asian Association for Regional Cooperation (SAARC), ASEAN, and even for SADC. One could infer from this that regions do not have an important role to play with respect to the overall poverty focus and impact of FDI. However, this would be wrong. Crucially, while trade rules in regions aim, at best, to create trade amongst members, trade and investment rules aim to raise investment from both members and non-members.

The possible divergence amongst members of developing-country regions as a result of an uneven spread of benefits, can be further enhanced by agglomeration effects (Venables, 1999). Agglomeration effects refer to a spatial clustering of

Table 4.2   FDI and host-country development

Impact Area	Indicators	Regional vs Global Integration
Employment and Income	• Employment generation inside foreign firms • Wage levels for staff with given characteristics	• Global MNEs from the EU and US may pay higher wages than regional developing country MNEs. • Global MNES may be more productive and hence create more employment in the long run, but their superior productivity may also crowd-out more domestic employment
Physical capital Market access	• Fixed capital formation • Financial transfers • Share of inputs imported • Share of output exported	• Global MNEs will have better access to finance than regional MNEs • Global MNEs may export more than regional MNEs • Regional MNEs will source more regionally (because they may have regional networks); but this is not the case when global MNEs invest in order to source locally
Structure of factor and product markets	• Concentration in product and factor markets • Profit margins	• Profits of regional MNEs are more likely to stay within region, while global MNEs may repatriate profits to their headquarters. But the effect for the host country may still be the same.
Technology, skills and management techniques	• Skill level of employees • Training budgets • Output per employee • R&D budgets • Types of technologies used	• Global MNEs will have more access to skills, technology and management techniques, compared with regional MNEs
Fiscal revenues	• Fiscal payments • Grants to foreign firms	• Many fiscal grants have been wasted to attract global MNEs; there may be regional competition but this is often for global MNEs such as Intel and General Motors
Political, social and cultural issues		• Regional MNEs are more likely to be culturally and politically acceptable

Source: Authors' own classification.

economic activities, and are another way through which investment affects poverty. Agglomeration can occur within a country (for example, cities) or across countries. Clusters of economic activities can lead to efficiency gains, for instance because a pool of specialized support services is feasible due to economies of scale (see, for example, Porter, 1998). If relocation effects occur within a region, this may lead to efficiency gains which may reinforce further relocation effects. This would lead to further divergence or convergence, which could affect the distribution of gains from, and ultimately the motives for, regional integration processes. On the other hand, as argued in Ethier (1998), smaller (and possibly poorer, though this is obviously not the case in regions such as ASEAN) countries may actually have incentives to form a region in order to attract investment away from other members, particularly extra-regional FDI. This may be the case when regional tariff preferences allow foreign investors to set up beachhead locations in a small (or poor) country to serve the entire regional market.

Agglomeration effects occur through local and foreign investment. It would therefore be important to ask how (intra- and extra-) FDI would affect regional integration processes, in addition to other factors (parallel national reforms, country size, political and security issues, etc.). Competition for FDI may lead to the introduction of more efficient and better organized regional policy and institutions, but there is also a possibility that such competition may undermine regional integration efforts. Similarly, if not all countries can benefit from an increased amount of FDI or do not have the capabilities to benefit from it, this may also undermine RI efforts. FDI may affect the establishment of regional institutions relevant to FDI. For example, competition for FDI between member states is thought to be one of the reasons why MERCOSUR is beginning to have talks on investment incentive issues (Chudnovsky and Lopez, 2003).

4.4 Does regional integration change the poverty focus of migration?

The first notable issue is that intra-regional migration is low in developed and developing country regions, as a percentage of total population (see Table 4.3). Obviously this can differ in other regions, for example, in the Southern African Development Community where South Africa is experiencing significant immigration. On the other hand, the intra-regional share of immigration is a quarter for MERCOSUR and a half for ANDEAN. This is higher than the intra-regional shares of FDI and trade, and may indicate that migration is likely to take place amongst neighbours. For the EU, the intra-regional share of immigration appears to be lower than that of trade and FDI. Also, the Filipino contract workers seem to prefer the Middle East to their own region ASEAN (8 per cent). This can also be said for Indonesian labour flows. Overall the numbers are of limited significance, certainly compared with the importance of FDI as a percentage of total investment or trade as a percentage of GDP.

Table 4.3   Intra-regional migration

	Intra-regional migration as % of population	Total migration as % of population	Intra-regional as ratio of total immigration
Immigration			
Argentina	1.28	4.92	0.26
Brazil	0.05	0.52	0.10
Uruguay	1.31	2.92	0.45
Paraguay	3.81	4.51	0.84
MERCOSUR	0.37	1.42	0.26
Bolivia	0.11	0.93	0.12
Colombia	0.17	0.32	0.53
Ecuador	0.44	0.76	0.58
Peru	0.04	0.2	0.17
Venezuela	3.21	5.66	0.57
ANDEAN	0.78	1.47	0.53
CARICOM (early 90s)	1		
EU (2000)	0.80	Ranges from 2.2% in Spain to 4% in UK and Netherlands to 5.6% in France and 8.9% in Germany and 37% in Luxembourg	< 0.20 for most EU member states (except 0.33 in Spain)
Emigration			
Philippines contract workers			0.08 (to ASEAN)

Sources: Fuchs and Straubhaar (2003); World Bank (2003); Thomas-Hope (2002); *World Development Indicators*; Wickramasekera (2002).

Secondly, both the main source of remittances and most of the skills gained are more likely to be associated with South–North migration rather than with South–South. We can thus offer the preliminary conclusion that RTAs have a limited impact on poverty through migration (compared with, say, trade or investment), although we should emphasize that further research is required. Also, this does not deal with temporary movement of people, which can also be important in delivering services, and has in essence become a trade issue under the GATS.

4.5 Regional integration and poverty: non-trade and non-FDI routes

Various processes usually coincide with regional integration in various degrees depending on the region. Besides direct effects such as improved market access for trade in goods, investment, and more recently trade in services, there can be increased functional cooperation in regional infrastructure, security and protection of democracy, increases in market size and income levels, convergence and divergence amongst members of RTAs, cooperation in terms of movement of natural persons and regional investment funds and social programmes.

4.5.1 Regional social programmes and investment funds

Some regions (for example, ANDEAN, EU) specifically include regional investment banks or structural funds, often to finance development of the least developed parts (countries, provinces) of the region. For example, within the EU, Ireland received some 6 per cent of GDP in structural funds in the 1990s to finance infrastructure projects. Most recently, the Free Trade Area of the Americas has attempted to include a regional fund to support the adjustment effects for small and vulnerable states in the region.

4.5.2 Trade – investment – migration linkages

While this chapter considers the effects of RI on trade, investment and migration, there could also be effects on the connections between these, which may ultimately affect poverty. Various studies discuss links between FDI and trade (for example, Barrell and te Velde, 2002), which can be substitutes or complements, between trade and migration (Schiff, 1997), and between FDI and migration (there is likely to be an association, given the fact that there is significant capital flight and a considerable brain drain from several developing countries). However, it is not clear how RI processes affect these interactions. Such interactions may also be important when examining the effects of RI on poverty via the effects on trade, FDI and migration.

4.5.3 Stepping-stone or stumbling blocks

There are a number of explanations for the increase in popularity of RTAs. One view is based on frustrations with the lack of speed of multilateral liberalization, such as in the GATT and the WTO. For example, Krugman (1993) argues that RTAs are easier to negotiate and implement than multilateral agreements as they typically involve fewer negotiating parties endeavouring to reach agreement on a narrower range of issues (though this may now no longer be the case). Bhagwati (1993) advances a related argument in putting the new regionalism down to US interests in a greater regional focus on trade negotiations through NAFTA and more recently the FTAA. The same issues can be raised with the current Doha Round of WTO negotiations.

An alternative explanation is the 'domino theory' which exploits the fact that RTAs may result in trade and investment diversion. The greater the number of nations included, the greater the pressures on non-parties. Thus, a single initial agreement, if it is important enough, can stimulate expansion of that agreement and/or proliferation of others.

Researchers disagree on whether RTAs are stepping stones or stumbling blocks to further liberalization. Would a RTA which was easier to negotiate imply a slower level of multilateral integration (which would theoretically be more efficient) or would such a RTA decrease the interest in, and ability to negotiate, further multilateral integration? For instance, negotiating RTAs would attract scarce institutional resources away from other applications, possibly from effectively negotiating at the multilateral level. On the other hand, negotiating experience gained at regional level might be relevant for negotiations at multilateral level.

There are others reasons why RTAs might be stumbling blocks (or stepping stones). First, regions can lead to trade creation. Secondly, regional agreements could be less secure than other types of integration (see Page, 2000). This can have consequences for policy responses and benefits to the poor. If the benefits to the poor depend on the long-term effects of trade, such long-term effects may be less forthcoming within unstable regional agreements. Hence, if poor people would like to capture benefits from regions, the immediate effects become more important, and will alter the choice of policy as identified in Section 2.1 on trade and poverty. If there are negative effects from trade diversion, then the benefits will be reduced.

4.5.4 Voices of the poor in RTAs

In Sections 4.2 and 4.3 we posed the questions as to whether regional integration could alter the poverty focus of trade and FDI. In part, this may depend on the economic conditions of the members of a RTA compared with non-members. It may also depend on whether certain interest groups are able to negotiate certain outcomes. For instance, would vulnerable groups within countries be better represented in a region than at multilateral levels? There does not seem to be much direct evidence for this, but it is nevertheless a question worth asking, because better representation at the negotiating table may lead to more desirable outcomes (namely, a more desirable poverty focus).

4.6 Towards a framework for analyzing regional integration and poverty

The aim of this chapter was to set out linkages between regional integration and poverty. This section outlines the routes from RI to poverty on the basis of a simple mapping of four sets of links describing how poverty in a country is affected by the processes of regional integration.

The first set of links between RI and poverty is through *trade*. Chart 4.1 covers a number of building blocks. Regional Trade Agreements include certain provisions that may affect the volume, price and 'poverty focus' of trade. This may, in turn, affect different characteristics of poverty intermediated through complementary conditions, including public policies. For a country which is a member of a particular RTA, we should be asking a number of questions in order to unravel the effects of RTAs on poverty through trade (the same could be done for regions of which the country is not a member in order to detect possible trade diversion effects).

- **Regional Trade Agreement** (of which the country under examination is/is not a member):

  - what are the goods trade provisions (tariffs, rules of origin, NTB)?
  - what are the services provisions?
  - what are the investment provisions?
  - other provisions?

- **Trade (volume, price and focus):**

  - How have provisions in the RTA affected the volume and price of intra- and extra-regional exports and imports (and the trade balance) of goods and services?
  - How has the RTA affected the poverty focus of trade?
    - Does regional liberalization lower import and domestic prices of products (goods and services) consumed directly by the poor or used in production processes that benefit the poor indirectly?
    - Has the RTA resulted in increased output in every country or have certain countries gained more than others?
    - Does the RTA lead to trade creation or trade diversion, and what are the effects of this on fiscal receipts?

- **Complementary conditions:**

  - Does the RTA include provisions that are different from other international policies and agreements such as the WTO?
  - Does the country have the capabilities to withstand competition with imports or exports in sectors with comparative advantage in the region?
  - Are public policies (labour, infrastructure, trade facilitation, education) geared towards enhancing import competition and export capabilities?
  - Does the government redistribute income or assets, through taxes, support for incomes, and provision of public goods, temporarily through safety nets or permanently to compensate (relative) losers from RTAs?

- **Poverty – how does trade affect:**

  - incomes and employment of the poor
  - capital assets (equipment, land)
  - other assets: health characteristics, education levels, access to financial capital, empowerment and exclusion?

Chart 4.1   Regional integration and poverty via trade

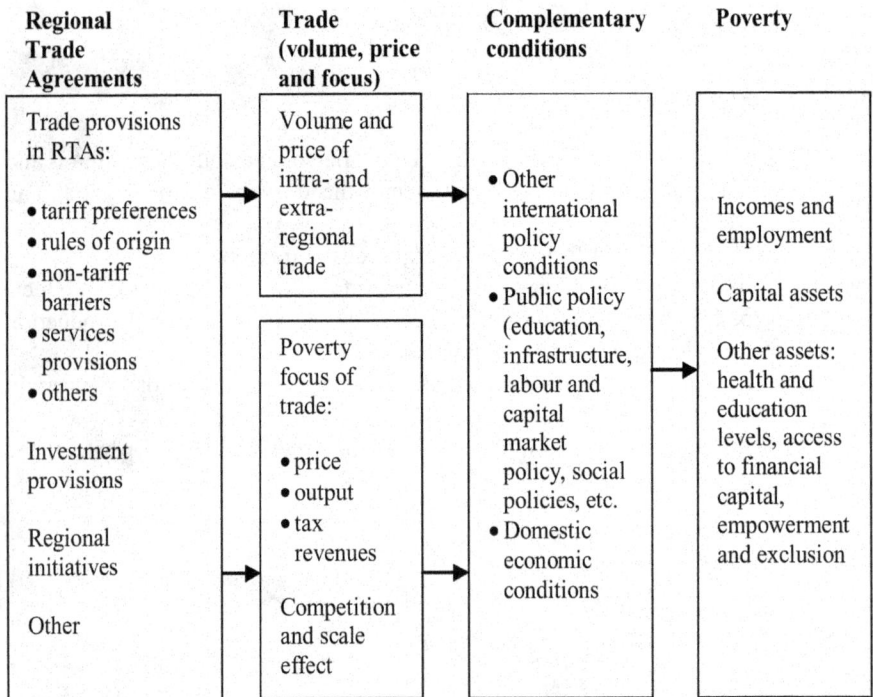

Regional Trade Agreements	Trade (volume, price and focus)	Complementary conditions	Poverty
Trade provisions in RTAs: • tariff preferences • rules of origin • non-tariff barriers • services provisions • others Investment provisions Regional initiatives Other	Volume and price of intra- and extra-regional trade Poverty focus of trade: • price • output • tax revenues Competition and scale effect	• Other international policy conditions • Public policy (education, infrastructure, labour and capital market policy, social policies, etc. • Domestic economic conditions	Incomes and employment Capital assets Other assets: health and education levels, access to financial capital, empowerment and exclusion

The second set of links between RI and poverty is through *foreign direct investment*. Chart 4.2 covers a number of building blocks. RTAs include certain provisions that may affect the volume and 'poverty focus' of investment. These may, in turn, affect different characteristics of poverty intermediated through complementary conditions, including public policies. For a member of a particular RTA we should be asking a number of questions in order to unravel the effects of RTAs on poverty through investment.

- **Regional Trade Agreement** (of which the country is member):

  - what are the goods trade provisions (tariffs, rules of origin, NTB)?
  - what are the services provisions?
  - what are the investment provisions?
  - other provisions?

- **Foreign Direct Investment (volume and focus):**

  - How have provisions in the RTAs affected the volume of intra- and extra-regional investment?
  - How has the RTA affected the poverty focus of investment, in other words, what are the differences between global MNEs, regional MNEs and domestic firms with respect to:
    - wages, jobs
    - capital
    - trade
    - structure of markets
    - tax revenues
    - technology, skills?

- **Complementary conditions:**

  - Does the RTA include provisions that are different from other international policies and agreements such as the WTO (for example, GATS, TRIMs) or bilateral investment treaties?
  - Does the domestic private sector have the capabilities to withstand competition with foreign firms in order to capture productivity spillovers?
  - Are public policies (labour, infrastructure, trade and investment facilitation, education, MNE-local firms linkage stimulation) geared towards capturing the productivity spillovers?
  - Does the government redistribute income or assets, through taxes, support for incomes, and provision of public goods, temporarily through safety nets or permanently?

- **Poverty – how does investment affect:**

  - incomes and employment of the poor
  - capital assets (equipment, land)
  - other assets: health characteristics, education levels, access to financial capital, empowerment and exclusion?

Chart 4.2   Regional integration and poverty via investment

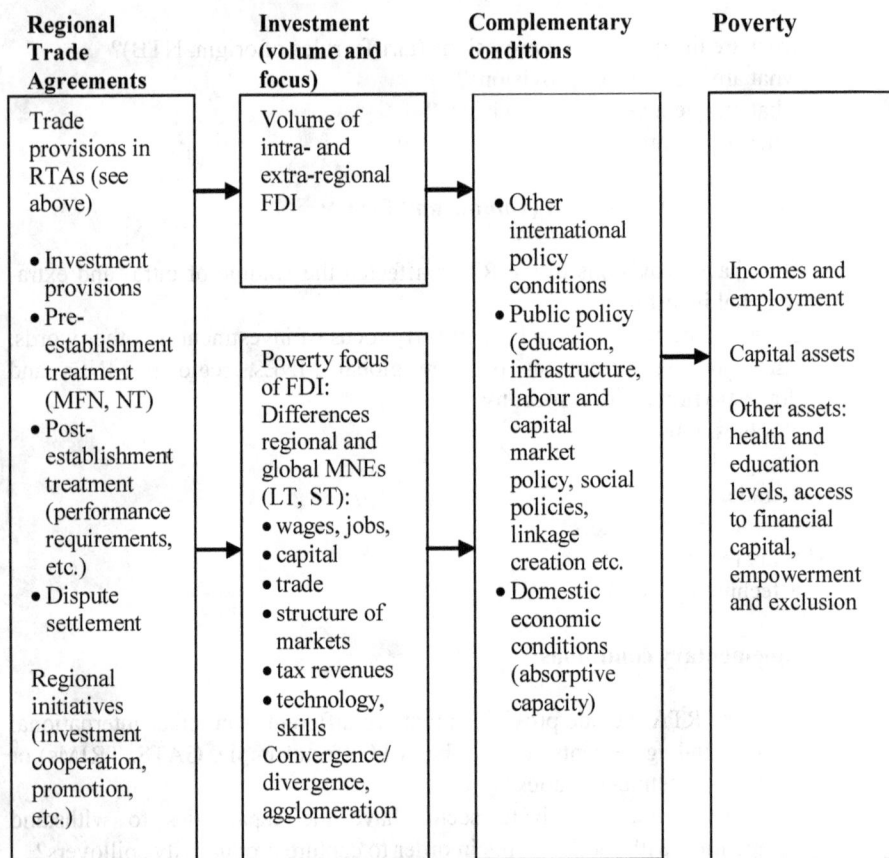

Regional Trade Agreements	Investment (volume and focus)	Complementary conditions	Poverty
Trade provisions in RTAs (see above) • Investment provisions • Pre-establishment treatment (MFN, NT) • Post-establishment treatment (performance requirements, etc.) • Dispute settlement Regional initiatives (investment cooperation, promotion, etc.)	Volume of intra- and extra-regional FDI Poverty focus of FDI: Differences regional and global MNEs (LT, ST): • wages, jobs, • capital • trade • structure of markets • tax revenues • technology, skills Convergence/ divergence, agglomeration	• Other international policy conditions • Public policy (education, infrastructure, labour and capital market policy, social policies, linkage creation etc. • Domestic economic conditions (absorptive capacity)	Incomes and employment Capital assets Other assets: health and education levels, access to financial capital, empowerment and exclusion

The third set of links between RI and poverty is through *migration*. Chart 4.3 covers a number of building blocks. RTAs include certain provisions that may affect the volume and 'poverty focus' of migration. This may, in turn, affect different characteristics of poverty intermediated through complementary conditions, including public policies that facilitate the use of remittances. For a member of a particular RTA we should be asking a number of questions in order to unravel the effects of RTAs on poverty through migration.

Chart 4.3   Regional integration and poverty via migration

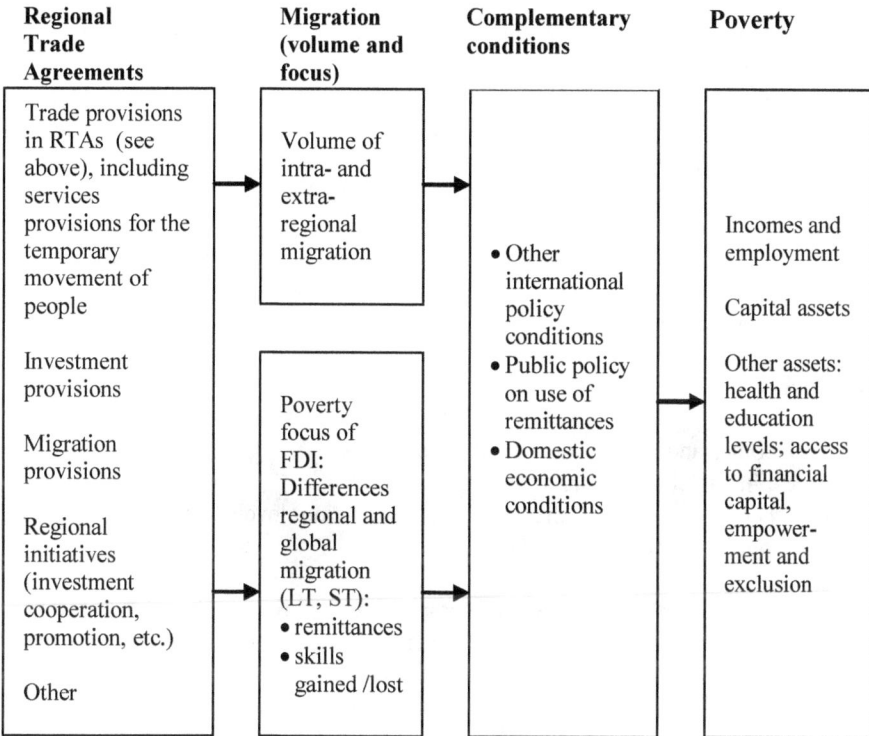

Regional Trade Agreements	Migration (volume and focus)	Complementary conditions	Poverty
Trade provisions in RTAs (see above), including services provisions for the temporary movement of people	Volume of intra- and extra-regional migration	• Other international policy conditions • Public policy on use of remittances • Domestic economic conditions	Incomes and employment Capital assets Other assets: health and education levels; access to financial capital, empower-ment and exclusion
Investment provisions Migration provisions Regional initiatives (investment cooperation, promotion, etc.) Other	Poverty focus of FDI: Differences regional and global migration (LT, ST): • remittances • skills gained /lost		

- **Regional Trade Agreement** (of which the country is/is not a member):

  - what are the goods trade provisions (tariffs, rules of origin, NTB)?
  - what are the services provisions (including related to temporary movement of natural persons)?
  - what are the investment provisions?
  - other provisions?

- **Migration:**

  - How have provisions in the RTAs affected the volume of intra- and extra-regional migration?
  - How has the RTA affected the poverty focus of migration, in other words, what is the difference between global and regional MNEs' migration with respect to:
    - skills gained/lost
    - remittances?

- **Complementary conditions:**

  - Does the RTA include provisions that are different from other international policies and agreements such as the WTO (for example, GATS) or bilateral treaties?
  - Do the domestic private and public sectors have the capabilities to withstand the temporary loss of skills and can they absorb the skills gained in return migrants?
  - Are public policies geared towards channelling remittances towards the poor?
  - Does the government redistribute income or assets, through taxes, support for incomes, and provision of public goods, temporarily through safety nets or permanently?

- **Poverty – how does migration affect:**

  - incomes and employment of the poor
  - capital assets (equipment, land)
  - other assets: health characteristics, education levels, access to financial capital, empowerment and exclusion?

The fourth set of links can be termed 'other' links and relate to non-trade and non-FDI issues in RTAs that may affect poverty or trade and FDI issues that affect regional integration processes. These issues include:

- Is the RTA associated with long-run or dynamic effects through competition and scale effects?
- Is the RTA associated with convergence or divergence of income levels and how has this affected the regional integration processes?
- Does the RTA include regional social programmes and investment funds?
- Are there any significant links between the RTA and poverty through migration?
- What are the links among trade effects – investment effects – migration effects of RTAs?
- Can the RTA be seen as a stepping stone or stumbling block towards further (multilateral) integration?
- Have negotiations on the RTA included the effective representation of poor people?

Chart 4.4   Regional integration and poverty: non-trade and non-investment routes

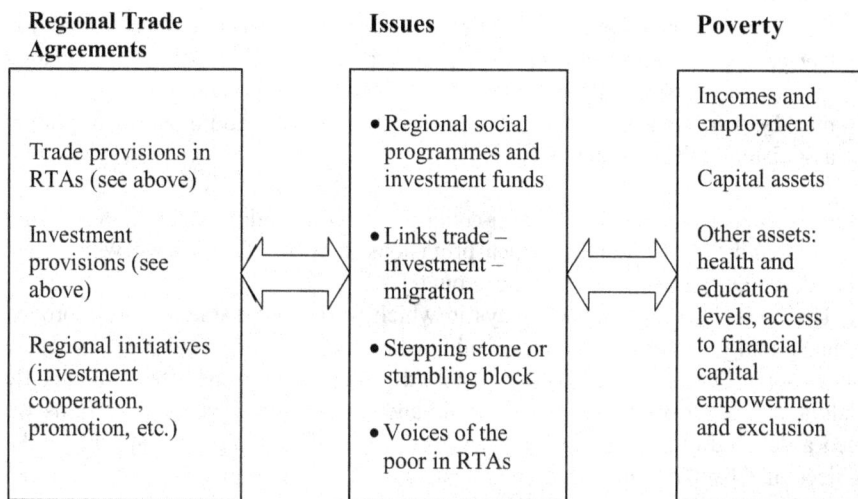

Regional Trade Agreements	Issues	Poverty
Trade provisions in RTAs (see above) Investment provisions (see above) Regional initiatives (investment cooperation, promotion, etc.)	• Regional social programmes and investment funds • Links trade – investment – migration • Stepping stone or stumbling block • Voices of the poor in RTAs	Incomes and employment Capital assets Other assets: health and education levels, access to financial capital empowerment and exclusion

4.7 Conclusion and further research

This chapter has indicated for a number of potential links what the expected (and sometimes actual) effects of regional integration are on poverty. Awareness of such linkages should make it possible to gain a better understanding of how regional integration affects poverty. For instance, some general empirical findings in the literature include:

- RTAs boost intra-regional trade through tariff reduction; very strict rules of origin may dampen intra-regional trade or the take-up of tariff references.
- Effects can interact: RoO are more relevant if preferential tariff rates are substantially lower than extra-regional tariffs.
- RTAs are likely to lead to increased extra-regional FDI; various RTAs have led to net investment creation. Both trade and investment provisions in RTAs can affect investment, but the precise effects will depend on a range of factors.
- Increased trade and investment are likely to lead to faster economic growth and poverty reduction, particularly when economic conditions and appropriate public policies are in place. Investment has a tendency to raise income inequalities, if not counteracted by public policies.
- The intra-regional share of trade and investment is lower for developing regions than for developed regions; regional integration in the latter therefore covers a larger share of trade and investment. While trade provisions are important for increasing intra-regional trade and hence the intra-regional share (without

aiming to divert trade), trade and investment provisions in regions are also likely to raise extra-regional FDI, and hence the effect on the intra-regional share of investment is ambiguous.

• The intra-regional share of migration is low as a percentage of total population (for example, compared with the importance of FDI as a percentage of total investment, or trade as percentage of GDP), and while South–South agreements may help to spur migration, this does not deal with South–North migration associated with remittances.

Much evidence is based on multi-country or multi-region studies, deals with averages and fails to identify which provisions in which RTAs have what effect (on trade, FDI, poverty etc.) in which country.

This overview suggests two ways in which we can contribute to an improved understanding of the effects of regional integration on poverty (but there are many other ways). The first is to conduct a more detailed study on the effects of specific trade and investment provisions on trade and investment in general. For this we need a detailed overview of investment provisions in key regions, and this is the subject of Chapter 5 in Part 2. This can be used to examine the links between investment-related provisions and FDI.

Secondly, we shall aim to test the mapping structure set out in Part 1 of this book and as summarized above, on the basis of two case studies. There are various countries that would be relevant for this. Part 3 discusses the experience of two countries. Bolivia, part of LAIA and ANDEAN (and FTAA due to start in 2005), associate member of MERCOSUR and featuring in the EU and US GSP systems, coupled with having one of worst poverty records in Latin America, has been chosen for the first case study to examine the effects of RTAs. The second case study is Tanzania to provide an African example. Tanzania is a member of the CBI, EAC (old and new) and SADC and is also part of others such as GSP systems and the Cotonou Agreement, but withdrew from COMESA. While the methodology of the case studies on regional integration has been fixed (for example, via trade and FDI), the methods varied. The Bolivia case study is able to use quite a detailed database linking trade and FDI in regional settings with incomes and employment. The Tanzania case study, on the other hand, has used in-depth interviews to obtain much relevant information.

References

Barrell, R. and te Velde, D.W. 'European Integration and Manufactures Import Demand', *German Economic Review* 3 (2002): 263–93.
Bhagwati, J., 'Regionalism and Multilateralism: An Overview,' in J. de Melo and A. Panagariya (eds), *New Dimensions in Regional Integration* (Cambridge: Cambridge University Press for the World Bank, 1993).

Blomström, M. and Kokko, A. *Regional Integration and Foreign Direct Investment,* NBER Working Paper 6019 (Cambridge, MA: National Bureau of Economic Research, 1997).

Chudnovsky, D. and Lopez, A., 'Policy Competition for Foreign Direct Investment' in D. Tussie, (ed.), *Trade Negotiations in Latin America* (Basingstoke: Palgrave Macmillan, 2003)

Coe, D.T., Helpman, E. and Hoffmeister, A.W. 'North–South R&D Spillovers', *Economic Journal* 107 (1997): 134–49.

Coe, D.T. and Helpman, E. 'International R&D Spillovers,' *European Economic Review* 39(5) (1995): 859–87.

Ethier, W.J., 'Regionalism in a Multilateral World', *Journal of Political Economy*, 106, (1998):1214–45.

Fuchs, D. and Straubhaar, T., *Economic Integration in the Caribbean: The Development towards a Common Labour Market,* International Migration Papers 61 (Geneva: ILO, 2003) http://www.ilo.org

Grossman, G.M. and Helpman, E., *Innovation and Growth in the Global Economy*, (Cambridge, MA: MIT Press, 1991).

Krugman, P.R., 'Regionalism versus Multilateralism: Analytical Notes' in J. de Melo and A. Panagariya (eds), *New Dimensions in Regional Integration* (Cambridge: Cambridge University Press for the World Bank, 1993).

McCulloch, N., Winters, L.A. and Cirera, X. *Trade Liberalization and Poverty; A Handbook* (London: Centre for Economic Policy Research, 2001).

McKay, A., 'Methodological Issues in Assessing the Impact of Economic Reform on Poverty', in M. McGillivray and O. Morrissey (eds), *Evaluating Economic Liberalization* (Basingstoke: Macmillan, 1999).

McKay, A., Winters, L.A. and Kedir, A.M. 'A Review of Empirical Evidence on Trade, Trade Policy and Poverty' (Report to DFID prepared as a background document for the Second Development White Paper, 2000).

Neary, J.P., *Foreign Direct Investment and the Single Market*, Draft paper CEPR and University College Dublin (Dublin: University College, Dublin, 2001).

Page, S. (2000), *Regionalism among Developing Countries* (London: Macmillan in association with ODI, 2000).

Porter, M. (1998), 'Clusters and the New Economics of Competition,' *Harvard Business Review*, 76 (1998): 77–90.

Schiff, M. *South–North Migration and Trade: Survey and Policy Implications,* World Bank Working Paper 1696 (Washington, DC: World Bank, 1997).

Schiff, M. and Wang, Y., *Regional Integration and Technology Diffusion. The Case of the North American Free Trade Agreement*, World Bank Policy Research Working Paper 3132 (Washington, DC: World Bank, 2003).

Stephenson, S.M. 'Can Regional Liberalization of Services Go Further than Multilateral Liberalization under the GATS?' *World Trade Review*, 1 (July 2002).

Thomas-Hope, E. 'Trends and Patterns of Migration to and from Caribbean Countries' (2002) downloaded from www.iom.org

Velde, D.W. te, 'Foreign-ownership and Wages in British Establishments', *Economic and Social Review,* 33 (2002):101–8.

Venables, A.J. *Regional Integration Agreements; A Force for Convergence or Divergence,* World Bank Policy Research Paper (Washington, DC: World Bank, 1999).

Viner J. *The Customs Union Issue.* (New York: Carnegie Endowment for International Peace, 1950).

Wickramasekera, P. *Asian Labour Migration, Issues and Challenges in an Era of Globalization,* International Migration Papers 57 (Geneva: ILO, 2002).

World Bank, *Global Economic Prospects 2004* (Washington, DC: World Bank, 2003).

PART 2

Describing and Monitoring Regional Integration

Chapter 5

Investment-Related Provisions in Regional Trade Agreements

Dirk Willem te Velde and Miatta Fahnbulleh

5.1 Introduction

There is a renewed interest in how regional trade agreements can foster foreign direct investment in developing countries. Under World Trade Organization rules members can enter into a regional integration arrangement through which more favourable conditions are granted to their trade with other parties to the arrangement than to others, thereby departing from the guiding principle of non-discrimination. The specific conditions for this are spelled out in three sets of rules: paragraphs 4 to 10 of Article XXIV of the General Agreement on Tariffs and Trade, which provide for the formation and operation of customs unions and free trade areas covering trade in goods; the Enabling Clause which refers to preferential arrangements in trade in goods between developing country members; and Article V of the General Agreement on Trade in Services which governs the conclusion of RTAs in the area of trade in services. Other non-generalized preferential schemes, for example non-reciprocal preferential agreements involving developing and developed countries (such as the EU-ACP Partnership Agreement), require a waiver from WTO rules. The number of RTAs notified to the WTO was 265 by May 2003, and the number of RTAs in force has increased, especially since the early 1990s (see Chart 1.2).

The coverage and depth of preferential treatment differs from one RTA to another. There are, however, a large number of RTAs that go beyond tariff-cutting and provide for complex regulations on intra-regional trade in goods (standards, safeguard provisions, customs administration, etc.) and preferential treatment for intra-regional trade in services. A select group of RTAs go beyond traditional trade rules and provide rules on investment, competition, environment and labour.

Countries decide to form a RTA for various reasons. One reason might be to enhance economic development and cooperation through increased trade and investment. This can, in turn, affect poverty through various routes as we identified in Part 1. The purpose of this chapter is to examine how RTAs can affect investment, in particular listing investment-related provisions that (aim to) promote intra- and extra-regional FDI. The structure is as follows. Section 5.2 describes investment-related provisions by key region, while Section 5.3 does this by key provision. Section 5.4 provides a summary of new evidence on the effects of RTAs on FDI. Section 5.5 concludes.

5.2 An overview of investment-related provisions in key regions

This section discusses what provisions have been implemented in the context of RTAs. While all RTAs have implemented or are planning to implement at least some rules that can affect investment, we shall focus on those regions that (i) are relatively large in terms of market size or number of members and (ii) have gone some way in implementing investment provisions. For these regions, we shall discuss investment provisions and trade provisions by main region. A detailed description can be found in Appendix 5.2.

5.2.1 What are the key regions?

Appendix 5.1 provides a list of developing country regions notified to the WTO before May 2003, with a list of members, including when the region was established or when members joined. We have narrowed down all regions notified under Article XXIV of the GATT to developing country regions (African, Asian and Latin American), or joint developing and developed country regions. For instance, the many RTAs that the European Union has negotiated with Central and Eastern European countries are not included, but those with North African countries are. The resulting list is still quite extensive.

Note too that regions are overlapping; in other words, a country can be in more than one region, leading some to argue that the web of regional groupings is becoming a spaghetti bowl. For the two countries we shall follow more closely in Chapters 6 and 7, Bolivia is part of Latin American Integration Association and the Andean Community (and the Free Trade Area of the Americas in the future) and also features in the GSP systems of the EU and the US, while Tanzania is a member of the East African Community and the South African Development Community and is part of others such as the GSP systems and the Cotonou Agreement.

Our narrowed-down list leaves us with the following regions: ASEAN (AFTA, or ASEAN Free Trade Area), NAFTA, MERCOSUR, CARICOM, ANDEAN, COMESA and SADC. We do not include APEC because its investment provisions are explicitly non-binding, or the Cotonou Agreement because it is not an RTA (its investment provisions are also essentially voluntary) but gained a waiver at the WTO and is discussed in further detail in te Velde and Bilal (2003). We have also not included the Free Trade Area of the Americas as this was due to finish at the beginning of 2005 but has been postponed. The resulting list contains mainly South–South regions, though NAFTA is an example of a North–South region.

5.2.2 Description by region

For each region we discuss investment rules, trade rules and other significant initiatives. We discuss investment rules in more detail, whereas we deal with trade rules more briefly because information on this subject is available in a number of secondary sources. We have not addressed information on technical barriers to trade or sanitary and phytosanitary regulations or anti-dumping, though this would be possible in a more detailed analysis for which we would need to collect more technical information. The discussion on trade rules will therefore simply report on MFN tariffs, tariffs applicable regionally and the nature of rules of origin.

NAFTA

The North American Free Trade Agreement (NAFTA), negotiated by the United States, Canada and Mexico, came into force in 1994. It represented the first North–South regional integration agreement of its kind in the Western hemisphere. NAFTA has taken significant strides in the area of regional economic cooperation. In particular, it encompasses one of the most comprehensive frameworks of regional investment provisions.

These are set out in Chapter 11 of the Agreement. NAFTA assumes a broader definition of investment than is usually applied to investment provisions. These rules are applicable to the investors and investment of a NAFTA member state, but some also extend to non-NAFTA investors with investments in one NAFTA country who decide to expand their operations into other NAFTA countries. Such expansion is predicated, however, on the condition that the investors have 'substantial business activities in the territory of the Party' where they were originally established. Although NAFTA's investment provisions are applicable to all sectors in principle, each member country has identified key sectors that are exempted from the agreement. Mexico excludes its petroleum sector and all state-owned sectors. Canada excludes cultural industries, health and social services and aboriginal affairs. The United States excludes health and social services, in addition to all maritime activities being highly restrictive.

Chapter 11 grants national treatment for the establishment (market access), acquisition, expansion, management, conduct, operation and sale or other disposition of investments; this is complemented and strengthened by the provision of Most Favoured Nation (MFN) treatment. In addition, it prohibits restrictions on ownership rules and the use of performance requirements on all investments by its members. This covers a broader range of performance requirements which go beyond those prohibited by the WTO Trade-related Investment Measures (TRIMs) Agreement and include trade balancing, technology transfer and 'exclusive supplier' requirements. Finally, Chapter 11 guarantees investors free transfer of funds across borders and protection from expropriation and nationalization.

NAFTA also established a comprehensive disputes settlement mechanism for both intergovernmental and investor-state disputes, the latter representing one of the first regional agreements to encompass a distinct mechanism for the arbitration of state-investor disputes. Mechanisms for both types of dispute have been used a number of times. It also provides access to international arbitration bodies through the International Centre for the Settlement of Disputes (ICSID) and the UN Commission on International Trade Law (UNCITRAL).

The first decade saw 9 investor-state cases brought against Canada, 9 against the US and 10 against Mexico. Of these Canada lost two cases and paid out Canadian $27 million and Mexico also lost two, paying out $18.2 million; the US has lost no cases so far. Some cases have been settled out of court, dismissed or are still pending. Measures challenged include environmental protection, industrial policy, softwood lumber, and property development among others and relate mostly to treaty articles on national and MFN treatment.

There have also been important developments in the trade regime in the region. Most merchandise was liberalized between 1994 and 1998. Intra-regional trade faces average applied tariffs of between zero and 2 per cent. In contrast, applied MFN tariff rates averaged 16.5 per cent (2001) for Mexico, 5.5 per cent (2000) for the US and 7.7 per cent (1998) for Canada. Rules of origin exist and are based on a value content criterion that stipulates a 50–60 per cent regional value content.

MERCOSUR

The Southern Common Market (MERCOSUR) was established in 1991 by the Treaty of Asuncion, and comprises Argentina, Brazil, Uruguay and Paraguay. Since its inception, MERCOSUR has achieved important developments in both regional trade and investment cooperation.

The investment provisions created for its members were established under the Colonia Protocol for the Promotion and Protection of Investment in 1994. This grants national treatment for the establishment, acquisition, expansion, management, operation and disposition of investment to MERCOSUR members, complemented and strengthened by the provision of MFN treatment. The Colonia Protocol also guarantees MERCOSUR investors free transfer of funds across borders and protection against expropriation and nationalization. Although the protocol prohibits the use of performance requirements, Argentina and Brazil have reserved the right to maintain performance requirements in the automobile sector. A number of sectors were temporarily exempted from the wider agreements, including border real estate, energy sectors, mineral extraction and exploitation sectors and telecommunications.

A less extensive range of provisions were established for non-MERCOSUR investors under the Buenos Aires Protocol in 1994. In principle, this grants MFN treatment to non-members. However, the application of MFN treatment is left to the discretion of each member country. In addition to this, it guarantees investors free transfer of funds across borders.

The Brasilia Protocol for the Settlement of Disputes in 1991 established the initial framework which was then expanded by the Ouro Preto Protocol in 1994. This provides a dispute settlement mechanism for both intergovernmental disputes and investor-state disputes, in addition to access to a number of international arbitration bodies.

MERCOSUR has taken important steps in enhancing regional trade integration. The implementation of the Common External Tariff in 1995 has facilitated the gradual harmonization of the trade regime in the region and full implementation is expected by 2006. Applied average MFN rates in 2001 were 12.7 per cent for Argentina, 14.6 per cent for Brazil and 13.8 per cent for Uruguay, and averaged 13.2 per cent for Paraguay in 2000. With respect to intra-regional trade, a gradual phasing out of intra-regional tariffs has taken place since 1991; as early as 1995, 85 per cent of intra-regional trade was duty-free. Currently most intra-regional trade is duty-free with the exception of capital goods, informatics and telecommunications products. Rules of origin exist and are based on a value content criterion that stipulates a 60 per cent domestic/regional value content.

CARICOM

The Caribbean Community and Common Market was established in 1973. The original members were Antigua and Barbuda, Barbados, Belize, Dominica, Grenada, Guyana, Jamaica, Montserrat, St Kitts and St Nevis, St Lucia, St Vincent and the Grenadines and Trinidad and Tobago. The Bahamas joined in 1983 but opted not to become a member of the common market. Suriname became the fourteenth member in 1995, followed by Haiti in 2002.

Since its inception, CARICOM has made greater progress in the area of trade cooperation than in investment cooperation. The Eighth Heads of Government Meeting in 1987, however, signalled one of the most comprehensive attempts to promote greater economic integration in the region. Significantly, plans were made to replace the Common Market with the CARICOM Single Market and Economy (CSME), preparations for the establishment of which included the negotiation of nine Protocols which effectively amended the original Treaty of Chaguaramas. Of these, the Protocols relating to investment and the free movement of people across borders have been most relevant for facilitating investment cooperation.

Few investment provisions were included in the 1973 Treaty of Chaguaramas. The 1980s and '90s, however, witnessed the introduction of more investment provisions. Some initial provisions were set out in the Principles and Guidelines on Foreign Investment approved by the CARICOM Heads of State and Government Conference in 1982. These were later developed and consolidated by Protocol II in 1997; however, some members have yet to enact this protocol.

Although Protocol II does not include national treatment provisions *per se*, it does establish that members shall not introduce any new restrictions relating to the right of establishment of nationals of other member states, except as otherwise provided for in the agreement. It allows each country to give preferential treatment to the investments of its own nationals, and stipulates that regional agreements on foreign investment should accord preferential treatment to investors in the following order: nationals of the host country, nationals of other CARICOM member countries, nationals of the source country and finally other countries. In terms of performance requirements, the Principles and Guidelines on Foreign Investment permitted their use. Although no further provisions were defined in Protocol II on the subject, CARICOM does conform to the WTO's Trade-related Investment Measures (TRIMs). Protocol II establishes provisions for the free transfer of funds across borders and protection from expropriation and nationalization. It also creates a dispute settlement mechanism for intergovernmental disputes, and under certain circumstances investment-state arbitration. In addition, it provides access to international arbitration through the ICSID.

CARICOM has achieved important development in its regional trade regime, however. A common external tariff, ranging from 20 to 35 per cent, has been in place since 1991, and is being implemented through four stages of tariff reductions. There is currently a wide variation in the level of implementation obtained by different members. Intra-regional trade is duty-free, the few exceptions including some agricultural produce and highly revenue-sensitive sectors such as alcoholic beverages, tobacco and oil products.

Andean Community

The origins of the Andean Community date from 1969, and the signing of the Andean Pact (Cartagena Agreement). The original members included Bolivia, Chile, Colombia, Ecuador, and Peru. Venezuela joined in 1973 and Chile left the Pact in 1976. The Andean Group was established in 1988. Its members are Bolivia, Colombia, Ecuador, Peru and Venezuela. Peru suspended its membership in 1992 but resumed it in 1997. The Andean Group became the Andean Community (ANDEAN) in 1997 following the adoption of the Protocol of Trujillo. Over the past decade and a half, ANDEAN has achieved a greater level of regional trade cooperation than investment cooperation, although the reverse seemed to apply back in the 1970s.

Investment has been on the agenda from the start. The first regional approach to investment dates back to 1970 and established a system of common treatment of foreign investment. Decision 24 of the Andean Commission (Commission of the Cartagena Agreement, 'Common Regime of Treatment of Foreign Capital and of Trademarks, Patents, Licenses and Royalties') aimed to create international legal obligations with respect to investment. This decision instituted several new restrictions on investment, including a disinvestment scheme for foreign investors to become semi-nationally-owned companies after a certain period of time, a limitation on the repatriation of profits, a reservation of certain sectors for domestic enterprises, an investment screening mechanism setting high standards of entry for foreign investors, and the establishment of a sub-regional office on industrial property and transfer of technology. The decision was silent on matters of expropriation. Chile withdrew from the Cartagena Agreement partly because of the controversial and tight restrictions on investment. Other member states also began to distance themselves from the regional treaty (which was mandatory), and by 1987 Decision 220 allowed each member state greater autonomy in setting investment policy as well as granting greater freedom to investors (for example, lengthening the time period for companies to become semi-public). Decisions 24 and 220 were replaced by Decision 291 in 1991.

The main investment provisions currently applicable to investment were defined under Decisions 291 and 292 in 1991. The former is applicable to both members and non-members. Its provisions are subject, however, to national stipulation on the subject, which effectively abandons any common policy on investment. ANDEAN grants national treatment to investors, but Decision 291 stipulates that national treatment can be regulated according to the laws of each member country. It also guarantees the free transfer of funds (and profits) across borders and protection against expropriation and nationalization. With respect to performance requirements, it establishes provisions only for technological contracts and technical assistance. Finally, it provides a disputes settlement mechanism for intergovernmental disputes through the Andean Court of Justice and access to an international arbitration body through the ICSID.

Decision 292 allows for the formation of Andean multinational enterprises. The establishment of such enterprises is predicated, however, on the condition that capital contributions by national investors of two or more member countries must make up more than 60 per cent of the capital of the enterprise. Among the privileges granted to such enterprises are national treatment with respect to government procurements, export incentives and taxation, the right to participate in economic sectors reserved for national companies and the right to open branches in any member country, and free transfer of funds related to investment. Other institutions that seek to facilitate investment include the Andean Development Corporation which raises funds to provide for a range of financial services and the Andean Business Advisory Council.

ANDEAN has made huge advances in liberalizing the trade regime in the region. The Andean Free Trade Area was formed in February 1993, when Bolivia, Colombia, Ecuador, and Venezuela completed the elimination of their customs tariffs and opened up their markets to each other. Intra-regional trade is currently duty-free, with all of the products in its tariff universe deregulated. Peru became a member in 1997, and it has been gradually deregulating its trade with its Andean partners; thus far, it has completed more than 90 per cent of this undertaking. The Andean Customs Union has been in operation since 1995, when the Common External Tariff approved by Colombia, Ecuador and Venezuela at the basic levels of 5, 10, 15 and 20 per cent came into effect. The Customs Union is incomplete, however. Bolivia enjoys preferential treatment and applies levels of only 5 and 10 per cent, whilst Peru did not sign the agreement. Average applied MFN rates were 9.1 per cent for Bolivia, 12.2 per cent for Colombia and 12.4 per cent for Venezuela in 2001. They averaged 11.2 per cent for Ecuador in 2000 and 13.4 per cent for Peru in 1998. Rules of origin exist and are based on a value content criterion that stipulates a 50 per cent import content.

COMESA

The Common Market for Eastern and Southern Africa (COMESA) was established in 1994 to replace the Preferential Trade Area for Eastern and Southern Africa which had been in existence since 1981. It members include Angola, Burundi, the Comoros Islands, the Democratic Republic of Congo, Djibouti, Egypt, Eritrea, Ethiopia, Kenya, Madagascar, Malawi, Mauritius, Namibia, Rwanda, the Seychelles (which may leave SADC), Sudan, Swaziland, Uganda, Zambia and Zimbabwe.

COMESA currently grants few investment provisions. Its founding treaty provides fair and equitable treatment to COMESA investors. It also guarantees the free transfer of funds across borders and protection from expropriation and nationalization. In addition, it provides a settlement dispute mechanism for intergovernmental disputes and access to an international arbitration body through the ICSID. Although the treaty encompasses only the most basic of investment provisions, recent plans to develop a more comprehensive regional investment framework through a Common Investment Area are indicative of COMESA's desire to enhance regional economic cooperation.

COMESA has, however, made some significant achievements in terms of trade liberalization. A free trade area (FTA) was established in November 2000, and it currently has nine members: Djibouti, Egypt, Kenya, Madagascar, Malawi, Mauritius, Sudan, Zambia and Zimbabwe, which have eliminated their tariffs on COMESA originating products. Burundi, the Comoros, Eritrea, Rwanda and Uganda have obtained a rate of tariff reduction of between 80 and 90 per cent. The rest have yet to take decisive steps to enter the FTA. A Customs Union was expected to come into effect in November 2004, with a common external tariff comprising four rates: 0, 5, 15, and 30 per cent. Rules of origin exist and are based on a value content criterion that permits a 60 per cent import content and 35 per cent domestic/regional value content.

SADC

The Southern African Development Community (SADC), formerly known as the Southern African Development Coordination Conference (SADCC), was established in 1992. Its member states are Angola, Botswana, Lesotho, Malawi, Mauritius, Mozambique, Namibia, South Africa, Swaziland, Tanzania, Zambia and Zimbabwe. The membership has remained the same with the exception of South Africa, which was not a member of the SADCC.

There are currently very few investment provisions guaranteed by SADC. However, plans to establish more comprehensive provisions under the Protocol on Finance and Investment indicate an increasing awareness of the need for greater regional investment cooperation. Although the most basic of investment provisions are lacking, SADC does provide a disputes settlement mechanism for intergovernmental disputes and access to international arbitration through the ICSID.

There has only recently been some progress towards greater trade liberalization. The SADC Trade Protocol came into operation in January 2001. A number of countries have begun to implement their commitments under this agreement and grant duty-free access, on a reciprocal basis, to imports of category A products (mostly capital goods and equipment) from other members that have also adopted the Protocol. These include Malawi, Mauritius and Zambia. In contrast, those members that are also members of Southern African Customs Union, such as South Africa, Botswana and Lesotho, apply SACU's common external tariff. Rules of origin exist and are based on a value content criterion that permits 70–35 per cent import content.

ASEAN

The Association of South-East Asian Nations (ASEAN) was established in 1967, with Indonesia, Malaysia, Philippines, Singapore and Thailand as its original members. Brunei Darussalam joined later in 1984, followed by Vietnam in 1995 and Laos and Myanmar in 1997. Cambodia became the tenth member, acceding to all agreements in 1998. Since its inception, ASEAN has made significant progress in the attainment of greater regional trade and investment cooperation.

The first major attempt to enhance regional investment cooperation was the 1987 ASEAN Agreement on the Promotion and Protection of Investment, the provisions of which were improved under a 1996 amending Protocol. These achievements were further developed and consolidated with the signing of the Framework Agreement on the ASEAN Investment Area (AIA) in 1998. This endeavours to establish a regional investment area incorporating all ten members, thus representing a significant step towards greater regional investment cooperation. Other programmes that have been developed to facilitate investment in the region include the ASEAN Industrial Cooperation scheme (AICO Scheme) which seeks to promote joint manufacturing activities between ASEAN-based companies.

The Agreement on the Promotion and Protection of Investment guaranteed ASEAN investors free transfer of funds across borders and protection from expropriation and nationalization. It also established a dispute settlement mechanism for intergovernmental disputes and access to a number of international arbitration bodies, most notably ICSID and UNCITRAL. ASEAN's dispute settlement mechanism has been effective, with at least one case put forward for arbitration.

The AIA enhanced this framework with the establishment of a more comprehensive range of provisions. It grants national treatment immediately for the establishment, acquisition, expansion, management, operation, and disposition of investment to ASEAN members. Sectors exempted under either the Exclusion or the Sensitive List were to be progressively liberalized by 2010. National treatment was also to be extended to non-ASEAN investors by 2020, later foreshortened to

2010. In addition, MFN treatment was also granted to ASEAN investors. Finally, laws restricting foreign shareholders in national companies have been deregulated. A short-term measure has been implemented which suspended laws regulating equity joint ventures between foreign and local enterprises and 100 per cent foreign equity. ASEAN has also launched a series of joint outward investment events and other activities to promote investment opportunities in the region including high-level meetings for relevant ministers to discuss investment-related issues.

There have also been important developments in the trade regime in the region. Although a Common External Tariff does not exist, the signing of the ASEAN Free Trade Area (AFTA) in 1992 has witnessed significant steps towards regional trade liberalization. Intra-regional tariffs have been gradually reduced from the 1992 average of 12 per cent to less than 5 per cent. AFTA was expected to reduce tariffs to between zero and 5 per cent for all trade between member nations by 2008, and this was brought forward to 2002 for the six original founding members. The Common Effective Preferential Tariff scheme is the main trade instrument of AFTA, which covers on average 90 per cent of the tariff lines of all ASEAN member nations. The intra-regional tariff rates range from 7 per cent (Cambodia) to zero (Singapore). Rules of origin exist and are based on a value content criterion that allows a 60 per cent import content.

The experience over the past three decades or so shows that regions can be subdivided into four categories with respect to investment provisions: (i) regions that do not have investment-related provisions except for trade rules; (ii) regions that impose a common policy towards investment (ANDEAN in the early 1970s) which is more restrictive than the initial individual member policies; (iii) regions that choose to develop a common approach gradually over time, introducing provisions that stimulate regional investment cooperation and regional investment promotion and (beginning to) grant national and MFN treatment (pre- and post-establishment) to foreign firms (ASEAN); and (iv) regions that include comprehensive investment provisions from the start, including pre-establishment national treatment and effective investor-state dispute mechanisms (NAFTA).

5.3 An overview of regional provisions by investment provision

We now discuss investment-related provisions by provision for the key regions identified above. The aim is to find the variation in key provisions (as discussed under the trade and investment rules in Chapter 2) and to quantify these, thus providing a cross-section element to investment provisions in the regions. This can help to prepare an index of integration relevant for investment. We discuss investment rules, trade rules and others.

5.3.1 Scope and coverage

Even though RTAs are normally preferential agreements for their members, in some cases the provisions are wider and apply to non-members. Under certain conditions, this is the case in NAFTA and MERCOSUR and it is planned for ASEAN/AFTA (AIA). Other RTAs such as CARICOM act more discriminatorily in favour of intra-regional FDI.

5.3.2 National treatment and MFN

Some regions are now offering national treatment to regional investors pre- and post-establishment, for example, in NAFTA and recently in ASEAN. However, for others (such as COMESA) free movement of capital remains an aspiration.

5.3.3 Performance requirements, transfer of funds and expropriation

Some regions are quite strict on performance requirements and will not allow any (NAFTA), while others maintain the possibility by containing a list of preferences and requirements applied to existing investment (CARICOM), though not to new investment.

5.3.4 Dispute settlement mechanisms

While most regions have some intergovernmental dispute settlement mechanisms, few have effective investor-state dispute mechanisms. NAFTA is the best example of such a mechanism, while ASEAN has also had at least one dispute – allegedly between a Singaporean investor and Myanmar – referred to arbitration under the ASEAN Investment Agreement. But less is known about the effectiveness of the investor-state provision in MERCOSUR or the intergovernmental provisions in SADC and COMESA.

Several studies have highlighted rules of origin as affecting locational decisions (Estevadeordal and Suominen, 2003). The RoO differ amongst regions, and Table 5.1 contains a summary on the basis of existing surveys of them in selected RTAs. While it is very difficult to calculate overall restrictiveness since much of it is sector-, chapter-, heading- or product-specific, it is possible to obtain some simple ordering of RoOs in RTAs by following Chart 5.1 in Estevadeordal and Suominen (2003) which documents the mean restrictiveness. Note that certain sectors have stricter rules of origin than others: for instance, the textiles and clothing sector faces higher than average restrictiveness in NAFTA, SADC and the Pan-Euro system.

5.3.5 Rules of origin

Table 5.1   Summary of WTO survey of rules of origin; selected regions

A General criteria of the rules of origin

RTAs	Criterion			Tolerance rule	
	CTH	Percentage	Technical test	Limitation (% of value)	Exceptions
NAFTA	√	√	√	7%	Textiles: 7% Agricultural, few industrial prod.
ASEAN		√	√	No	
CARICOM	√				
COMESA	√	√		No	
MERCOSUR	√	√		No	
SADC	√	√	√	10%	Textiles and others
ANDEAN		√			

B Rules of origin based on percentage criterion

RTAs	General criterion and Limitations			Basis for calculation			
	Import content	Domestic content	Value of parts	c.i.f.	f.o.b.	Ex-works	Cost prod.
NAFTA		√ 60–50%			√ 60%		√ 50%
ASEAN	√ 60%				√		
CARICOM	n.av.						
COMESA	√ 60%	√ 35%		√			
MERCOSUR	√ 40%	√ 60%			√		
ANDEAN	√ 50%				√		
SADC	√ 70–35%					√	

C Exceptions to the general criteria

| RTAs | Criterion for exceptions | | | |
	CTH	Percentage	Technical Test	Sector-specific
NAFTA		√		Yes (auto)
ASEAN			√	Yes (textiles)
CARICOM	-			
COMESA		√ (DC, 25%)		
MERCOSUR		√ (DC, 33–60% for certain automotive)	√	Yes (dairy, chemicals, steel, auto)

D Drawback provisions

| RTAs | Allow for drawback | No-drawback | | Drawback not mentioned |
		Rule	Derogation	
NAFTA		√	2 y. (Canada, US), 7 y. (Mex.)	
ASEAN	√			
CARICOM	√			
COMESA	√			
MERCOSUR	√	√		

Sources: WTO (2002), Estevadeordal and Suominen (2003).

We can also devise a simple measure using the percentage criterion for maximum import value or domestic content (section B of the table). On the latter measure, NAFTA and MERCOSUR have stricter RoO than the other regions.

5.3.6 Tariff structures

An important element for extra-regional investors is how intra-regional tariffs compare with MFN tariffs, because this determines the 'market size effect' of an RTA. It depends on the regional preferences and the level of initial tariffs. In some cases regional preferences are set at a fixed percentage of MFN tariffs, or at a certain level below the MFN (which may have to be revised if and when the MFN is revised), while in other regions there is a schedule for the phasing out of intra-regional tariffs altogether.

As Table 2.2 revealed, there are quite big variations in preferences granted as a percentage of total import prices. For the regions shown they are low for SAARC because it grants very low regional preferences, low for AFTA because it already has low tariffs, but high for the Latin American regions, partly because their intra-regional tariffs are very low, of course with exceptions for some products.

5.3.7 Others

No two regions are the same. The regions under discussion have designed various schemes to foster regional enterprises (ANDEAN), investment cooperation and promotion (ASEAN), and movement of people (CARICOM). These are likely to affect mainly intra-regional FDI.

5.3.8 Conclusions

The above Sections 5.2 and 5.3 show that there is a wide variation in regional provisions across regions (this is summarized in Table 5.2). On the basis of the above information, it is possible to design a basic integration index with respect to investment-related provisions (trade rules and investment rules) which varies across regions. This is shown at the bottom of the table. It basically reflects whether trade rules or investment rules in regions can be expected to increase FDI. Because regions have implemented different provisions, the expected effects on FDI will be different, indicated by a different index. For example, granting pre-establishment national treatment is one of the reasons why the investment rule index scores high for NAFTA. On the other hand, there seems to be only limited progress in the implementation of the SADC trade protocol, so that is why the trade rule index scores low for SADC. It is possible to design different indices weighting individual rules differently. Note too that this integration index is cross-sectional and it is possible to design integration indices that vary over time – for example, to reflect changes in investment provisions in ASEAN or ANDEAN. The main conclusion is that, apart from changing over time, regions can also be very different depending on which provisions have been implemented. This has clear implications for the expected effects of regions on extra-regional FDI.

Table 5.2 Summary of investment-related provisions in selected RTAs

	NAFTA	MERCOSUR	CARICOM	ANDEAN	ASEAN	SADC	COMESA
INVESTMENT RULES							
Year investment provisions came into force at regional level	1994	1994	1982 & 1997	1991	1987 & 1998	Few provisions	1994
1 Scope and coverage							
a. Applicable to non-parties (when or when not)	Yes	Yes	No	Yes	AIA National Treatment		No
b. Positive or negative list approach	Negative	Colonia – Negative Buenos Aires– positive	Positive	Positive	1987 – positive AIA-negative		Positive
c. Main exceptions (safeguards, sectors, etc.)							
2 National Treatment							
a. Pre-establishment (all sectors?)	Yes	Yes	No	Not specified	Yes	No	No
b. Are there restrictions on ownership rules? (e.g. min equity share)	Yes	No	No	No	Yes	No	No

Table 5.2 (continued)

	NAFTA	MERCOSUR	CARICOM	ANDEAN	ASEAN	SADC	COMESA
c. Operations by MNEs in the country	Yes	Yes	No	Not specified	Yes	No	No
3 Most Favoured Nation and fair and equitable treatment							
a. granted to parties	Yes	Yes	No	No	Yes	No	Yes – fair & equitable
b. non-parties	Yes	Yes	No	No	No	No	No
4 Performance requirements							
a. Are they banned for new and existing investment?	Yes	Yes	No	Yes	No	No	No
b. Do they go beyond TRIMs?	Yes	Yes		No			
5 Transfers of funds							
a. .Are transfers of funds across borders allowed?	Yes	Yes	Yes	Yes	Yes	No	Yes
6 Do provisions with respect to expropriation exist (nationalization, etc.)?	Yes	Yes	Yes	Yes	Yes	No	Yes

Table 5.2 (continued)

	NAFTA	MERCOSUR	CARICOM	ANDEAN	ASEAN	SADC	COMESA
7 Settlement of Disputes							
a. State-to-state	Yes	Yes	Yes	Yes	Yes	Yes	Yes
b. Investor-state	Yes	Yes	Yes under certain conditions.	No	Yes	No	No
c. Access to international dispute settlement (ICSID, UNCITRAL)	Yes	Yes	Yes	Yes	Yes	Yes	Yes
TRADE RULES							
8 Rules of Origin							
a. Do rules or origin exist?	Yes	Yes	Yes	Yes	Yes	Yes	Yes
b. Value Content Criterion: Domestic/Regional Value Content (RVC)	RVC 50–60%	MC40% RVC60%	N/A	MC: 50%	MC: 60%	MC: 70–35%	MC:60% RVC:35%
c. Are there roll-up arrangements?	Yes	Yes	-			Yes	Yes
d. Are drawbacks allowed?	No	Yes	-		Yes		Not after 10 years
e. Mean/median value of restrictiveness	4	3			4	4	3

Table 5.2 (continued)

	NAFTA	MERCOSUR	CARICOM	ANDEAN	ASEAN	SADC	COMESA
9 Tariff structures							
a. Does a Common External Tariff exist?	No MFN varies from 5.5–16.5%	Yes since 1995	Yes since 1991	Yes since 1993	No	No	No. Plans for CET
b. Level of intra-regional tariffs and plans	0–2%	Duty-free	Duty-free	Duty-free	0–7%	Mixture of duty-free and SACU CET	Different levels of tariff elimination
c. Exceptions	Yes	Yes	Yes Free movement of people				
10 Other relevant provisions (regional enterprise schemes, regional investment funds, etc.)				Andean Multinational Enterprises. Andean Development Cooperation. Andean Business Advisory Council.	ASEAN Industrial Cooperation Regional Investment Promotion Events. ASEAN Investment Portals.		
Investment relevant integration index (1=	3	2	2	2	2/3	1	1

Table 5.2 (continued)

	NAFTA	MERCOSUR	CARICOM	ANDEAN	ASEAN	SADC	COMESA
no; 2=middle;3=integrated) INV							
Investment relevant integration index (1= no; 2=middle;3=integrated) TRADE	2	3	3	2	1	1	1

Sources: Tables in Appendix 5.1. Note that cells represent a likely outcome, but will in reality depend on specific circumstances.

5.4 New evidence on the effects of regional integration on FDI

The effects of investment-related provisions in regions can be treated more formally. Extending the review by Dunning (1997b), there are basically two ways in which this can be done. First, we can take a standard FDI model with standard explanatory variables such as costs, market size, risk, etc. and include an additional variable measuring the degree of implementation of the investment provisions. In this way we can isolate a separate RTA (provision) effect

$$FDI_{ijt} = f(FDI_{ijt-1}, HOME_{ijt}, HOST_{ijt}, OTHER_{ijt}, RTA_{kjt})$$

where FDI is the real stock of FDI, i is the home country, j is the host country, t time. *HOST* country factors can include, amongst others, market size, relative labour costs, human capital, indicators for natural resource availability and privatization efforts and risk measures. *HOME* country factors from country i are provided in country j. *OTHER* includes such variables as distance or shared language. *RTA* denotes measures of (the sum of) investment-related provisions k in an RTA applicable in host country j at time t. Rules that are expected to raise FDI (extra-, and/or intra-regional FDI) would show in the regression with a significant and positive regression coefficient.

A second way to assess the effects of regional investment-related provisions on FDI is by considering the impact of provisions on individual determinants of FDI (host market size, regional market size, efficiency or costs, risk, etc.) in addition to an effect independent of the other determinants. For instance, the following simple equation tries to account for this

$$FDI_{ijt} = f(FDI_{ijt-1}, Y_{jt}, RY_{jt}, RELCOST_{jt}, RISK_{jt}, OTHER_{ijt}, RTA_{kjt})$$

where *RELCOST* is a measure of relative investment costs such as relative unit labour costs, *RISK* is a measure of risk factors, Y is the market size of the host economy, and *RY* is the 'regional market size' that countries of a region create by lower intra-regional tariffs for the members of the region. Investment-related provisions in RTAs can potentially affect (sign of provision above the variable) most of these explanatory variables, see Table 5.3.

Dunning (1997b) argues that the main effects of RTAs work through the explanatory variables and are dynamic. We can control for the regional market size effect, by including it as an explanatory variable in the regression. However, this is not so straightforward for the other effects on explanatory variables, so the variable RTA in the above equations will pick up such effects.

Table 5.3   Investment-related provisions and explanatory variables of FDI

Investment provision	Relationship with determinant of FDI	*Relationship explanatory variable and FDI*
Tariffs	$Y = f(\overline{T}, OTHER)$, as lower tariffs, T, (regionally or MFN) foster growth	More growth, more FDI
Tariffs, Rules of Origin	$RY = f(\sum_{members=1} \overset{+}{Tpref_i Y_i}, \overset{+}{RoO})$ as larger regional preferences through lower intra-regional tariffs provide for a 'larger' or more accessible regional market; similarly, the stricter the rules of origin the more important is the regional market	A larger regional market, may lead to more (extra-regional) FDI
Tariffs	$RELCOST = f(\overset{+}{T}, OTHER)$, as lower tariffs (regionally or MFN) foster competition and more efficiency and thus lower costs relative to outside the region	More efficiency leads to more FDI in the longer term
Investment provisions	$RISK = f(\overset{-}{RTA inv}, OTHER)$, as more investment provisions safeguarding the interest of investors vis-à-vis governments would mean lower (political) risks	Lower risk fosters more FDI when the economic fundamentals are right
All RTA provisions	*RTA* measures all other aspects, e.g. a signalling or locking-in effect	

Te Velde and Bezemer (2005) estimated a model explaining the real stock of UK and US FDI in developing countries which identified the effects on FDI of specific regional investment-related provisions in the seven key regions identified in Table 5.2, controlling for key factors behind investment decisions, such as education, infrastructure and market size. The provisions in regions with substantial provisions were measured not just across regions but also over time, as is shown in Table 5.4. A higher value of the index is associated with more FDI (from outside the region). Implementation will vary by country, but for trade provisions, such as tariff preferences, for example, we have used averages for the region.

It was found (Table 5.5) for seven RTAs that (i) membership of a region leads to further FDI inflows from outside (stock of UK and US FDI), but the type of regional provisions matters, in other words, whether or not regions include certain trade and investment provisions (column 1); and (ii) the position of countries within a region matters, in other words, that smaller countries and countries located further away from the largest country in the region benefit less from being part of a region than larger countries and those closer to the core of the region (column 2). The final column of Table 5.5 shows that total inward FDI is higher in regions with provisions pointing to investment creation effects (column 3).

Table 5.4 Regional integration index for key regions

	Investment provisions			Trade provisions		
RTA (date of establishment)	1970s	1980s	1990s	1970s	1980s	1990s
NAFTA (1994)	0	0	3 (1994)	0	0	2 (1994)
MERCOSUR (1991)	0	0	2 (1994)	0	0	3 (1991)
CARICOM (1973)	0	1 (1982)	2 (1997)	1 (1973)	2	3 (1997)
ANDEAN (1969)	-1 (1970)	1 (1987)	2 (1991)	1	1	2 (1993)
ASEAN (1967)	0	1 (1987)	2 (1996) 3 (1998)	1	1	1
SADC (1992)	0	0	1 (1992)	0	0	1 (1992)
COMESA (1994)	0	0	1 (1994)	0	0	1 (1994)

Note: Years between parentheses indicate when certain provisions were announced.
Source: Authors' own analysis.

Investment Index:

= 0 if not member of group
= 1 if some investment provisions in region (as in COMESA, SADC),
= 2 if advanced investment provisions in region (e.g. improved investor protection in ASEAN)
= 3 if complete investment provisions in region (e.g. Chapter XI of NAFTA)
= -1 if more restrictive provisions (restrictions on foreign investors in ANDEAN in '70s)

Trade Index:

= 0 if not member of group
= 1 if some trade provisions (e.g. tariff preferences),
= 2 if low MFN, (close to) zero intra-regional tariffs
= 3 if high MFN, (close to) zero intra-regional tariffs

Table 5.5   Regional integration and FDI in developing countries

	UK and US FDI (log of real stock) (1981-2000)		Total FDI (flows) (1981-2000)
GDP in host country (log)	0.68[a]	0.67[a]	0.79[a]
GDP growth			0.035[a]
Education (average primary, secondary and tertiary)	0.004[a]	0.004[a]	0.006[a]
Inflation	0.00	0.00	-0.00
Phone lines per 1000 inhabitants	0.003[a]	0.003[a]	0.0007[b]
Roads (% paved)	0.17[a]	0.11[b]	0.01
Regional investment provisions (index Table 5.4) – for key regions only	0.41[a]	0.17[b]	0.38[b]
Regional investment provisions * ratio of host country to largest GDP in the region		0.80[a]	
No. of observations	1521	1521	2230
No. of countries	68 for UK 97 for US	68 for UK 97 for US	
R-squared	0.44	0.45	0.61

Notes: Constant, US fixed effect and time dummies omitted from tables; (a) (b) denotes 5% (10%) significance level.

5.5 Conclusion

This chapter has discussed the expected effects of investment-related provisions in RTAs and has assessed the way in which they have been implemented in a number of key regions. Important in all RTAs are trade rules. Trade liberalization is likely to foster extra-regional FDI, particularly in those sectors with high MFN tariffs (for example, car components in MERCOSUR) and tight rules of origin. But it is more ambiguous with regard to intra-regional FDI, as there is a trade-off between the importance of transport costs, firm-level specific and plant-level fixed costs. Investment rules, when offered in a package with other location-specific factors including basic fundamentals, should provide a more welcoming investment climate. However, in reality there will be many specific factors that play a role when determining the effects of RTAs on FDI:

- the extent of regional tariff preferences (and other trade barriers)
- the restrictiveness of rules of origin
- the differences from actual regional investment rules

- the initial situation, including the structure of investment and the existing liberalization
- plant-level and firm-level fixed costs
- existing economic factors.

We have shown that regions differ in two fundamental respects:

- *over time* when one region can change or add investment-related provisions
- *across regions* when investment-related provisions differ at one single point in time.

A comparison of regions also showed that investment-related provisions in key regions differ significantly, including differences in:

- the extent of regional tariff preferences
- the restrictiveness of rules of origin
- the investment rules, including national treatment for pre- and post-establishment and the presence of effective dispute settlement mechanisms
- the regional coordination on investment
- the type of membership: North–North, South–South, North–South, South–South–North.

A summary of the effects of RTAs on FDI shows that regional integration raises investment (from outside the region), but the benefits are likely to be distributed unequally across the region.

References

Association of South East Asian Nations Secretariat (ASEAN), *Compendium of Investment Policies & Measures in ASEAN Countries* (ASEAN Secretariat, 1998a)

ASEAN, *Handbook of Investment Agreements in ASEAN* (ASEAN Secretariat, 1998b)

Blomström, M. and Kokko, A., *Regional Integration and Foreign Direct Investment*, NBER Working Paper 6019 (Cambridge, MA: National Bureau of Economic Research, 1997).

Brainard, S.L., 'An Empirical Assessment of the proximity-Concentration Trade-Off Between Multinational Sales and Trade', *American Economic Review*, 87, (4), (1997): 520–44.

Carr, D.L., Markusen, J.R. and Maskus, K., 'Estimating the Knowledge-Capital Model of the Multinational Enterprise', *American Economic Review*, 91, (2001): 693–708.

Chudnovsky, D. and Lopez, A., 'La inversion extranjera directa en el Mercosur: un análisis comparativo', in D. Chudnovsky (ed.), *El Boom de Inversión Directa en el Mercosur* (Madrid: Siglo XXI Editoria Iberoamericana, 2001): 1–50.

Chudnovsky, D. and Lopez, A., 'Policy Competition for Foreign Direct Investment' in D. Tussie (ed.), *Trade Negotiations in Latin America* (Basingstoke: Macmillan, 2003)

Dahl, J., *Incentives for FDI: The Case of SADC in the 1990s*, NEPRU Working Paper, 81(2002).

Dunning, J. 'The European Internal Market Programme and Inbound Foreign Direct Investment', *Journal of Common Market Studies*, 35, (1997a): 1–30.

Dunning, J. (1997b), 'The European Internal Market Programme and Inbound Foreign Direct Investment', *Journal of Common Market Studies*, 35, (1997b): 189-223.

Estevadeordal, A. and Suominen, K., 'Rules of Origin: A World Map', Draft IADB Paper (2003).

Gestrin, M. and Rugman, A., 'The North American Free Trade Agreement and Foreign Direct Investment', *Transnational Corporations*, 3 (1994).

Globerman, S. and Walker, M. (eds), *Assessing NAFTA: A Trinational Analysis*, (Vancouver: The Fraser Institute, 1993).

Görg, H. and Greenaway, D., *Is There a Potential for Increases in FDI for Central and Eastern European Countries Following EU Accession*, GEP Research Paper 2002//31 (Nottingham: University of Nottingham, 2002).

Graham, E. and Wilkie, C., 'Regional Economic Agreements and Multinational Firms: The Investment Provisions of the NAFTA', in T. Brewer (ed.), *Trade and Investment Policy* (2 Volumes) in Mark Casson (series ed.), *The Globalization of the World Economy* (London: Edward Elgar, 1999).

Greenaway, D. and Milner, C., *Regionalism and Gravity*, GEP Research paper 2002/20 (Nottingham: University of Nottingham, 2002).

Helpman, E., 'A Simple Theory of Trade with Multinational Corporations', *Journal of Political Economy*, 92 (1984): 451–71.

Heydon, K., 'RTA Market Access and Regulatory Provisions. Regulatory Provisions in Regional Trade Agreements: 'Singapore Issues', a paper for the World Trade Organization Seminar on Regionalism and the World Trade Organization (2002).

Hufbauer, G. and Schott, J., *NAFTA: An Assessment* (Washington, DC: Institute for International Economics, 1993).

IPS Sri Lanka, 'Foreign Direct Investment and Economic Integration in the SAARC region', a paper presented at SANEI (August 2000).

Kurtz, J., *A General Investment Agreement in the World Trade Organization? Lessons from Chapter 11of NAFTA and the OECD Multilateral Agreement on Investment*, Jean Monnet Working Paper 6/02 (2002).

Levy, Y.E., Stein, E. and Daude C., 'Regional Integration and the Location of FDI', IADB Draft (2002),

Markusen, J.R., *Trade versus investment liberalization*, NBER Working Paper 6231 (Cambridge, MA: National Bureau of Economic Research, 1997).

Markusen, J.R., 'The Boundaries of Multinational Enterprises and the Theory of International Trade', *Journal of Economic Perspectives*, 9 (1995): 169–89,

Markusen, J.R., 'Multinationals, Multi-plant Economies, and the Gains from Trade', *Journal of International Economics*, 16 (1984): 205–26

Markusen, J.R. and Venables, A.T., 'The Role of Multinational Firms in the Wage-Gap Debate', *Review of International Economics*, 5 (4) (1997): 435–51.

Monge-Naranjo, A., 'The impact of NAFTA on Foreign Direct Investment flows in Mexico and the Excluded countries' (Draft paper, Northwestern University: 2002).

Muradzikwa, S., *Foreign Investment in SADC* (Cape Town: Development and Policy Unit, University of Cape Town, 2002).

Neary, J.P., 'Foreign Direct Investment and the Single Market', Draft paper CEPR and University College Dublin (Dublin: University College, Dublin, 2001).

Oman, C., *Policy Competition for Foreign Direct Investment: A Study of Competition among Governments to Attract FDI* (Paris: OECD Development Centre, 2000).

Organization of American States Trade Unit, *An Analytical Compendium of Western Hemisphere Trade Agreements* (1996).

Page, S., *Regionalism Among Developing Countries* (London: Overseas Development Institute, 2000).

Pain, N., 'Continental Drift: European Integration and the Location of UK Foreign Direct Investment', *The Manchester School Supplement,* LXV (1997): 94–117.

Roberts, M., *Multilateral and Regional Investment Rules: What Comes Next?* (Organization of American States Trade Unit, 2001).

Rugman, A. and Brain, C., 'Intra-regional Trade and Foreign Direct Investment in North America' (Draft paper, Indiana University, 2002).

Rugman, A. and Gestrin, M., 'The Investment Provisions of the NAFTA' in Globerman and Walker, 1993.

UNCTAD, *International Investment Agreements: Issues Paper Series* (Geneva: UNCTAD).

UNCTAD, *International Investment Instruments: A Compendium,* 1–10 (Geneva: UNCTAD).

UNCTAD, *World Investment Report,* annual report (Geneva: UNCTAD, various issues).

Velde, D.W. te., 'Policies towards Foreign Direct Investment', in G. Wignaraja, (ed.), *Competitiveness Strategy and Industrial Performance: A Manual for Policy Analysis* (London: Routledge, 2003).

Velde, D.W. te., and Bezemer, T., 'Regional Integration and Foreign Direct Investment in Developing Countries', *Transnational Corporations Journal*, UNCTAD (2004).

Velde, D.W. te and Bilal, S., 'Foreign Direct Investment and Home Country Measures in the Lomé Conventions and Cotonou Agreement', Report for UNCTAD (Geneva: UNCTAD, 2003).

Waldkirch, A., 'The "New Regionalism" and Foreign Direct Investment: The Case of Mexico, *Journal of International Trade & Economic Development*, 12 (2003): 151–84

Wilkie, C., 'The Origins of NAFTA Investment Provisions: Economic & Policy Considerations', paper presented at the Centre for Trade Policy and Law conference on NAFTA Chapter 11 (Ottawa: Carleton University, 18 January 2002).

World Trade Organization, *Regional Trade Agreements Notified to the GATT/WTO and in Force* (Geneva: WTO, 2003).

World Trade Organization, *Trade Policy Reviews* (various).

World Trade Organization, *Mapping of Regional Trade Agreements* (Committee on Regional Trade Agreements, 11 October 2000).

World Trade Organization, 'Rules of Origin', WT/REG/W/45 (2003).

Primary Sources: Agreements, Treaties and Protocols

NAFTA:
North Atlantic Free Trade Agreement (1992)

MERCOSUR:
Colonia Protocol for the Promotion and Protection of Mercosur Investment (1994)
Buenos Aires Protocol (1994)

CARICOM:
Treaty of Chaguaramas (1973)
Agreement for the Establishment of a Regime for Caricom Enterprises (1987)
Protocol Amending the Treaty Establishing the Caribbean Community (Protocol II: Establishment, Services, Capital) (1997)
Revised Treaty of Chaguaramas Establishing the Caribbean Community Including the CARICOM Single market and Economy (2001)

Andean Community:
Decision 291 of the Commission of the Cartagena Agreement: Common Code for the Treatment of Foreign Capital and on Trademarks, Patents, Licenses and Royalties (1991)
Decision 292 of the Commission of the Cartagena Agreement: Uniform Code on the Andean Multinational Enterprises (1991)

ASEAN:
ASEAN Agreement for the Protection and Promotion of Investment (1987)
Revised Basic Agreement on ASEAN Industrial Joint Ventures (1987)
Framework Agreement on the ASEAN Investment Area (1998)
Protocol to Amend the Framework Agreement on the ASEAN Investment Area (2001)

SADC:
Treaty establishing Southern African Development Community (1992)

COMESA:
The COMESA Treaty (1994)

Web Sources

ASEAN Secretariat. www.aseansec.org
ANDEAN. www.comunidadandina.org
CARICOM Secretariat. www.caricom.org
COMESA. www.comesa.org.
Free Trade Area of the Americas. www.ftaa-alca.org
Foreign Trade Information Systems. www.sice.org
Mercosur Red Academica Uruguaya. www.rau.edu.uy/mercosur
Organization of American States. www.oas.org
OECD. www.oecd.org
SADC. www.sadc.int
UNCTAD. www.unctad.org
World Trade Organization. www.wto.org

Appendices

Appendix 5.1 Membership of regional trade agreements involving developing countries

Asia Pacific Economic Cooperation Forum 1989
Australia, Brunei Darussalam, Canada, Chile (entered November 1994), China (entered November 1991), Hong Kong (entered November 1991), Indonesia, Japan, Korea, Malaysia, Mexico (entered November 1993), New Zealand, Papua New Guinea (entered November 1993), Peru (entered November 1998), Philippines, Russia (entered November 1998), Singapore, Chinese Taipei (entered November 1991), Thailand, United States, Vietnam (entered November 1998).

Association of South East Asian Nations 8 August 1967
Brunei Darussalam (entered 8 January 1984), Cambodia (entered 30 April 1999), Indonesia, Malaysia, Myanmar (entered 23 July 1997), Laos (entered 23 July 1997), Philippines, Singapore, Thailand, Vietnam (entered 28 July 1995).

Bangkok Agreement 17 June 1976
Bangladesh, China (formally became a member in 2000), India, Republic of Korea, Laos, Sri Lanka.

Economic Cooperation Organization 1985
Afghanistan (entered 1992), Azerbaijan (entered 1992), Iran, Kazakhstan (entered 1992), Kyrgyz Republic (entered 1992), Pakistan, Tajikistan (entered 1992), Turkey, Turkmenistan (entered 1992), Uzbekistan (entered 1992).

Indian Ocean Rim Association for Regional Cooperation 1997 (March)
Australia, Bangladesh, India, Indonesia, Iran, Kenya, Madagascar, Malaysia, Mauritius, Mozambique, Oman, Seychelles, Singapore, South Africa, Sri Lanka, Tanzania, Thailand, United Arab Emirates, Yemen.

South Asian Association for Regional Cooperation 8 December 1985
Bangladesh, Bhutan, India, Maldives, Nepal, Pakistan, Sri Lanka.

ACS Association of Caribbean States 24 July 1994
Antigua and Barbuda, Bahamas, Barbados, Belize, Colombia, Costa Rica, Cuba, Dominica, Dominican Republic, El Salvador, Granada, Guatemala, Guyana, Haiti, Honduras, Jamaica, Mexico, Nicaragua, Panama, St Kitts and Nevis, St Lucia, St Vincent and the Grenadines, Surinam, Trinidad and Tobago, Venezuela.

CACM Central American Common Market 12 October 1961
Costa Rica, El Salvador, Guatemala, Honduras, Nicaragua.

CAN Andean Community 25 May 1988
Bolivia, Colombia, Ecuador, Peru, Venezuela.

CARICOM Caribbean Community and Common Market 1 August 1973
Antigua and Barbuda, Bahamas (entered 4 July 1983 – not a member of the common market), Barbados, Belize, Dominica, Granada, Guyana, Haiti (entered July 2002), Jamaica, Montserrat, St Kitts and St Nevis, St Lucia, St Vincent and the Grenadines, Surinam, Trinidad and Tobago.

G3 Group of Three 1995
Colombia, Mexico, Venezuela.

LAIA Latin American Integration Association 18 March 1981
Argentina, Bolivia, Brazil, Chile, Colombia, Cuba (entered 6 November 1998), Ecuador, Mexico, Paraguay, Peru, Uruguay, Venezuela.

MERCOSUR Southern Common Market 29 November 1991
Argentina, Brazil, Paraguay, Uruguay.

NAFTA North American Free Trade Agreement 1 January 1994
Canada, Mexico, United States.

OECS Organization of Eastern Caribbean States 18 June 1981
Antigua and Barbuda, Dominica, Grenada, Montserrat, St Kitts and Nevis, St Lucia, St Vincent and the Grenadines.

SICA Central American Integration System 1993 (February)
Belize, Costa Rica, El Salvador, Guatemala, Honduras, Nicaragua, Panama.

AMU Arab Maghreb Union 17 February 1989
Algeria, Libya, Mauritania, Morocco, Tunisia.

CBI Cross Border Initiative 1993 (August)
Burundi, Comoros, Kenya, Madagascar, Malawi, Mauritius, Namibia, Rwanda, Seychelles, Swaziland, Tanzania, Uganda, Zambia, Zimbabwe.

CEMAC Economic and Monetary Community of Central Africa 24 June 1999
Cameroon, Central African Republic, Chad, Congo, Equatorial Guinea, Gabon.

CEPGL Economic Community of the Great Lakes Countries 20 September 1976
Burundi, Democratic Republic of Congo, Rwanda.

COMESA Common Market for Eastern and Southern Africa 8 December 1994
Angola, Burundi, Comoros, Democratic Republic of Congo, Djibouti, Egypt, Eritrea, Ethiopia, Kenya, Madagascar, Malawi, Mauritius, Namibia, Rwanda, Seychelles, Sudan, Swaziland, Uganda, Zambia, Zimbabwe.

EAC East African Community 7 July 2000
Kenya, Tanzania, Uganda.

ECCAS Economic Community of Central African States 18 October 1983
Angola (entered 1999), Burundi, Cameroon, Central African Republic, Chad, Democratic Republic of Congo, Republic of Congo, Equatorial Guinea, São Tomé and Principe.

ECOWAS Economic Community of West African States 28 May 1975
Benin, Burkina-Faso, Cape Verde, Côte d'Ivoire, Gambia, Ghana, Guinea, Guinea-Bissau, Liberia, Mali, Mauritania, Niger, Nigeria, Senegal, Sierra Leone, Togo.

MRU Mano River Union 3 October 1973
Guinea (entered 25 October 1980), Liberia, Sierra Leone.

SACU Southern African Customs Union 3 March 1970
Botswana, Lesotho, Namibia, South Africa, Swaziland.

SADC Southern African Development Community17 August 1992
Angola, Botswana, Democratic Republic of Congo, Lesotho, Malawi, Mauritius, Mozambique, Seychelles (may leave SADC), South Africa, Swaziland, Tanzania, Zambia, Zimbabwe.

TRIPARTITE Tripartite Agreement 1 April 1968
Egypt, India, Yugoslavia.

UEMOA West African Economic and Monetary Union 1 August 1994
Benin, Burkina Faso, Côte d'Ivoire, Guinea Bissau (entered 2 May 1997), Mali, Niger, Senegal, Togo.

Other agreements involving developing countries
EC–Chile 2003
EU–South Africa Free Trade Agreement 1 January 2000
EU–Morocco Free Trade Agreement 1 March 2000
EU–Mexico Free Trade Agreement 1 July 2000
EU–Mexico Services Agreement 1 March 2001
EU–Tunisia Free Trade Agreement 1 March 1998
EC–Egypt Free Trade Agreement 1 July 1977
EC–Algeria Free Trade Agreement 1 July 1976
EU–ACP Cotonou Agreement Signed 23 June 2000
US–Vietnam Free Trade Agreement 10 December 2000
US–Singapore Free Trade Agreement Signed 5 June 2003
US–Chile Free Trade Agreement Signed 6 June 2003

Appendix 5.2 Investment-related provisions in key regions

NAFTA

Members (late membership in parentheses)	Canada, Mexico, United States	Established 1 January 1994.
INVESTMENT RULES		
What year did investment provisions come into force (variable?)	1 January 1994	
1 Scope and coverage	Investors of a NAFTA state and investment of investors of a NAFTA state.	Article 1101.
a. Applicable to non-parties (when or when not)	Non-NAFTA investors with investments in one NAFTA country are assured the benefits of Chapter 11 if they decide to expand their operations into the other NAFTA countries as long as they have 'substantial business activities in the territory of the Party' where they were originally established. Particular disciplines re: performance requirements and environmental measures apply to all investment (inc domestic investment and investment from non-NAFTA parties).	Article 1106 (Performance requirements) Article 1114 (Environmental measures).
b. Positive or negative list approach	Negative list	
c. Main exceptions (safeguards, sectors etc.)		
Mexico	Excludes: petroleum sector; electricity; nuclear power and treatment of other radio-active materials; telecommunications and media – all state owned sectors. Health and social services. Control of air and maritime ports.	Annex III, Chapter 11.
Canada	Excludes: Cultural Industries; health and social services; aboriginal affairs; large scale water exports.	Article 2106/Annex 2106.
United States	Excludes: health and social services. All maritime activities are highly restrictive.	

NAFTA

2 National Treatment	Yes with respect to the establishment, acquisition, expansion, management, conduct, operation and sale.	Article 1102.
a. Pre-establishment (all sectors?)	Yes – covers all sectors unless exempted. Exemptions: Canada: Aboriginal affairs, some communications sectors, social services, some transportation. Mexico: Media, some communications and transport, energy and social services. US: Communications, social services, some media and transportation.	
b. Are there restrictions on ownership rules? (e.g. min equity share)	Yes - No Party may impose a requirement that a minimum level of equity in an enterprise be held by its nationals, other than nominal qualifying shares for directors etc or require an investor of another Party, by reason of its nationality, to sell or dispose of an investment in the territory of the party.	
c. Operations by MNEs in the country	Yes	
3 Most Favoured Nation and fair and equitable treatment		Article 1103/Article 1104.
a. granted to parties	Yes	
non-parties	Yes – No less favourable treatment than that granted to non-parties and that provided by international law.	Exceptions: Article 1113.
	Yes – Applies to 'third party' investors and their investments.	
4 Performance requirements	Yes – Outright prohibition on the use of certain performance requirements by NAFTA states. Exceptions: environmental standards; standards for employee training are permitted; no ban on requirements for R&D.	Article 1106 Article 1106.2 & 1114 (Environmental Standards) Article 1106.4 (Employee training/R&D).
	NB. Applies to requirements placed on any investment (inc non-NAFTA).	Article 1106.
a. Are they banned for new and existing investment?	Yes	

Appendix 5.2 (continued)

NAFTA

	NAFTA
b. Do they go beyond TRIMs?	Yes – no party may impose the following requirements: export requirements; minimum domestic content; domestic sourcing requirements; trade balancing; technology transfer; 'exclusive supplier' requirements.	
5 Transfers of funds	
a. Are transfer of funds across borders allowed	Yes – all transfers relating to an investment can be made freely without delay.	Article 1109.
6 Do provisions with respect to expropriation exist (nationalization, etc.)?	Yes – no party may directly or indirectly nationalize/expropriate an investment of an investor of another party in its territory. Except: for public purposes; on a non-discriminatory basis; in accordance with due process of law and fair and equitable treatment; on payment of compensation.	Article 1110.
7 Settlement of Disputes		Article 1115.
a. State-to-state	Yes	Chapter 20.
b. Investor-state	Yes	Article 1116 – Article 1120.
c. Access to International Dispute Settlement (ICSID, UNCITRAL)	Yes – Arbitration under World Bank ICSID/UNCITRAL. A Tribunal is established that is empowered to order interim measures to protect the rights of disputing investor.	
8 Provisions for incentives and subsidies	
TRADE RULES	
9 Rules of Origin	
a. Do rules or origin exist?	Yes	
b. Value Content Criterion:	RVC: 60– 50%	

Appendix 5.2 (continued)

NAFTA

Domestic/Regional Value Content (RVC)	
c. Are there roll-up arrangements?	Yes except automotive.
d. Are drawbacks allowed?	No after 7 years for Mexico.
e. Mean/median value of restrictiveness	4
10 Tariff structures	
a. Does a Common External Tariff exist? If so what is it and will it be? If not, indicate country dispersion.	No. Applied MFN was 16.5 in 2001 for Mexico; 5.5 in 2000 in US; *ad valorem* MFN is 7.7 in Canada in 1998.
b. Level of intra-regional tariffs and plans.	Most merchandise liberalized between 1994 and 1998; Intra-regional trade face 0–2% average applied tariffs.
c. Exceptions	High applied MFN for food, animal, footwear textile and clothing products in Mexico, Canada and US and textile and clothing in US and Canada; expected phase out of sensitive products until 2019 of motor vehicles, maize, milk and beans.
11 Other relevant provisions (regional enterprise schemes, regional investment funds, etc.)	

MERCOSUR

Members (late membership in	Argentina, Brazil, Paraguay, Uruguay

Established 29 November

Appendix 5.2 (continued)

MERCOSUR

parentheses)		1991.
INVESTMENT RULES		
What year did investment provisions come into force (variable?)	The Colonia Protocol for the Promotion and Protection of Investments in MERCOSUR was approved by Decision No. 11/93 of the Common Market Council of 17January 1994. The Buenos Aires Protocol for the Promotion and Protection of Investments in MERCOSUR from Non-Member Countries was approved by Decision No. 11/94 5 August 1994.	
1 Scope and coverage	Any natural person who is a national of, permanently resides, or is domiciled in a Contracting Party in accordance with its laws. The Protocol does not apply to investments made in the territory of one Contracting Party by natural persons who are nationals of the other Contracting Party if they, by the date the investment is made, permanently reside or are domiciled in the host country, unless it is proved that the investment was admitted from abroad. Any legal person constituted under the laws and regulations of a Contracting Party, and having its seat in the territory of said Party; and, any legal person constituted under the laws of the host country but effectively controlled, directly or indirectly, by a natural or legal person as defined above.	Article 1 (2) Colonia Protocol.
a. Applicable to non-parties (when or when not).	Yes – The Buenos Aires Protocol creates provisions for Non-parties with respect to MFN and transfer of funds.	(Article 2(C) (3) of the Buenos Aires Protocol).
b. Positive or negative list approach.	Colonia Protocol: negative. Buenos Aires Protocol: Positive.	
c. Main exceptions (safeguards, sectors etc.)	A number of transitory exceptions were agreed.	

Appendix 5.2 (continued)

MERCOSUR

Argentina	Border real estate; air transportation; shipbuilding; nuclear power generation; uranium mining; insurance and fisheries.
Brazil	Exploration and exploitation of minerals; hydroelectric power; health care, telecommunications; rural property; banking and insurance services; construction and shipping.
Paraguay	Real property in the frontier zones; communication/media; air land or maritime transportation; electricity; water and telephones; exploitation of hydrocarbons and strategic minerals; importation and refining petroleum products and postal service.
Uruguay	Electricity; hydrocarbons; petrochemicals and plastic industries; nuclear energy; strategic mineral extraction and exploitation; financial industries; rail transportation; telecommunications; radio and television and journalism.
2 National Treatment	Yes – Parties must accord to investment of investors of member parties treatment which is no less favourable than accorded to investment of its own investors or investors of third states.	Article 3 Protocol of Colonia.
a. Pre-establishment (all sectors?)	Yes	
b. Are there restrictions on ownership rules? (e.g. min equity share).	No	
c Operations by MNEs in the country	Yes	
3 Most Favoured Nation and fair and equitable treatment		
a granted to parties	Yes	Article 3 Protocol of Colonia
	Yes	Article 3 Colonia Protocol

Appendix 5.2 (continued)

MERCOSUR

non-parties	Yes – But the application of MFN treatment is left to the discretion of each MERCOSUR country: Each Member Party **may** accord to investments of investors of third States treatment no less favourable than that accorded to investments of investors of other States.	Article 2 Buenos Aires Protocol
4 Performance requirements	Yes – Brazil and Argentina have reserved the right to maintain performance requirements in the automobile sector.	Article 3 Protocol of Colonia
a. Are they banned for new and existing investment?	Yes – No party shall impose performance requirements as a condition for establishment, expansion or maintenance of investments.	
b. Do they go beyond TRIMs?	Yes	
5 Transfers of funds		
a Are transfer of funds across borders allowed.	Yes – Free transfer of investment and returns	Article 5 Protocol of Colonia; Article 2E of Protocol of Buenos Aires.
6 Do provisions with respect to expropriation exist (nationalization, etc.)?	Yes – Except on public interest grounds; on a non-discriminatory basis with respect to due process and prompt and fair compensation.	Article 4 Protocol of Colonia.
7 Settlement of Disputes		Initially established under Brasilia Protocol for the Settlement of Disputes in 1991 (in force as of 1993) were expanded by the Ouro Preto Protocol in 1994.
a. State-to-state	Yes – Disputes between states will be settled according to the terms and conditions	Colonia Protocol Article 8.

Appendix 5.2 (continued)

MERCOSUR

	set out in the protocol of Brasilia.
b. Investor-state	Yes – In the first instance amicable negotiations. If the dispute is not settled in six months, an investor may seek resolution via national legal means, international arbitration or by a system of permanent dispute settlements that will be established under the framework of the Treaty of Asuncion.	Colonia Protocol Article 9.
c. Access to International Dispute Settlement (ICSID, UNCITRAL)	Yes – Investor may choose CIADI or United Nations system for the settlement of disputes.
8 Provisions for incentives and subsidies	
TRADE RULES	
9 Rules of Origin	
a. Do rules or origin exist?	Yes
b. Value Content Criterion: Domestic/Regional Value Content (RVC) or Import Content (MC)	MC:40% RVC: 60%
c. Are there roll-up arrangements?	Yes except automotive.
d. Are drawbacks allowed?	Yes except automotive imports from Argentina and Brazil.
e. Mean/median value of restrictiveness	3 (Based on MERC– Bol/Chi).
10 Tariff structures	
a. Does a Common External	Yes since 1995; full implementation by 2006.

Appendix 5.2 (continued)

MERCOSUR

Tariff exist? If so what is and will be average? If not, give indication of country dispersion	
b. Level of intra-regional tariffs and plans	Phase out of intra-regional tariffs has proceeded since 1991 (85% of intra-regional trade became duty free in 1995). Intra-regional trade is duty free.
c. Main exceptions	General: Capital goods, informatics and telecommunications products. Argentina: Automobiles, sugar and footwear have high CET or MFN (up to 30%).
11 Other relevant provisions (regional enterprise schemes, regional investment funds, etc.)	

CARICOM

Members (late membership in parentheses)	Antigua & Barbuda, Bahamas (entered 4 July 1983 – not a member of the common market), Barbados, Belize, Dominica, Granada, Guyana, Haiti (entered July 2002), Jamaica, Montserrat, St. Kitts and St Nevis, St Lucia, St Vincent and the Grenadines, Surinam (1995), Trinidad and Tobago.	Established 1 August 1973. The Single Market and Economy was launched 1 January 1991.
INVESTMENT RULES	

Appendix 5.2 (continued)

CARICOM

What year did investment provisions come into force (variable?)	Treaty of Chaguaramas establishing the Caribbean Community and the Caribbean Common Market, 4 July, 1973. Protocol II which concerns the right of establishment, provisions for services and the movement of capital was signed in 1997. Not all members have enacted Protocol II. Some provisions were laid out in the Principles and Guidelines on Foreign Investment approved by the Caricom Heads of States of Government Conference 1982.
1 Scope and coverage	
a. Applicable to non-parties (when or when not)	No
b. Positive or negative list approach	positive
c. Main exceptions (safeguards, sectors etc.)	In general foreign investment shall not be allowed in a sector/activity where there is need to; protect small entrepreneurs; insulate areas of the economy where investment is already adequate and where the effect of new overseas investment would be to drive out present investment; avoid threats to national security; create economic opportunities for nationals and nationally-controlled enterprises which need protection from more efficient foreign enterprises until, in the long run, they can develop the necessary entrepreneurial managerial and technological; capabilities to adequately service the sector/activity; curtail increased investment in service

Appendix 5.2 (continued)

CARICOM

activities, thus giving preference to the goods-producing sector.

2 National Treatment	No – recognizes preferential treatment with regards to investments of its nationals. However it does establish that members shall not introduce in their territories any new restrictions relating to the right of establishment of nationals of other member states except as otherwise provided in the agreement.	Treaty of Chaguaramas, Caribbean Common Market Annex Article 35 .1; Protocol II
a. Pre-establishment (all sectors?)		
b. Are there restrictions on ownership rules? (e.g. min equity share)	No	
c. Operations by MNEs in the country		
3 Most Favoured Nation and fair and equitable treatment	No: Cooperation agreements on foreign investments shall tend to accord preferential treatment to the following groups of entities, ranked as follows: 1) nationals of the host Caricom country, 2) nationals of other Caricom member countries, 3) Nationals of the sources countries – both developed and developing, 4) Other Countries	Head of Government Conference
a. granted to parties		
non-parties		

Appendix 5.2 (continued)

CARICOM

4 Performance requirements	No – All foreign investments shall be required to meet performance criteria on a case by case basis as determined by Caricom host governments. Five criteria that will be required to be met; removal or reduction of restrictions under licensing agreements on production for both national and extra -regional markets; employment priority to be given first to nations of the host country, second to Caricom nationals and nationals of source country; and policies instituted to ensure that nations of the host country receive the necessary training and achieve the required experience to equip them top assume senior management positions; the use, where appropriate of local and regional; raw materials, other mineral inputs and services; the provision of externally generated financial resources to meet a reasonable proportion of long term and working capital needs of foreign enterprises; where there are joint venture enterprises, 'fade out, arrangements over time to enable ultimate local or regional control. However Caricom does conform to WTO TRIMs.	Heads of Government Conference 1982.
a. Are they banned for new and existing investment?	No	
b. Do they go beyond TRIMs?		
5 Transfers of funds		
a. Are transfers of funds across borders allowed?	Yes	Revised Treaty of Chaguaramas establishing the Caribbean community including the Caribbean Single Market and Economy, Article 40.
6 Do provisions with respect to	Yes	

Appendix 5.2 (continued)

CARICOM

expropriation exist (nationalization, etc.)?		Chapter 9, Revised Treaty.
7 Settlement of Disputes		
a. State-to-state	Yes	
b. Investor-state	Yes	Article 222, Revised Treaty.
c. Access to International Dispute Settlement (ICSID, UNCITRAL).	Under certain circumstances – persons of a contracting party, with the special leave of the court, may be allowed to appear as parties in proceedings. Yes – most members have acceded to ICSID.	
8 Provisions for incentives and subsidies	No	
9 Rules of Origin		
a. Do rules of origin exist	Yes	
b. Value Content Criterion: Domestic/Regional Value Content (RVC).	N/A	
c. Are there roll-up arrangements?	Not mentioned	
d. Are drawbacks allowed?	possibly	
e. Mean/median value of		

Appendix 5.2 (continued)

CARICOM

restrictiveness.

10 Tariff structures

a. Does a Common External Tariff exist? If so what is it and will it be? If not, give indication of country dispersion.

Yes since 1991. CET rates range from 20–35%. 4 stage schedule of CET tariff reductions, starting in 1993. The final Phase 4 of full implementation, with a tariff ceiling of 20% for non-exempt industrial goods and 40% for non-exempt agricultural goods was to be reached by 1998.

b. Level of intra-regional tariffs and plans.

Intra-regional trade is duty free

c. Exceptions

Agricultural; highly revenue sensitive sectors, mainly alcoholic beverages, tobacco, oil products, jewellery, electrical appliances and motor vehicles.; some electrical appliances.

11 Other relevant provisions (regional enterprise schemes, regional investment funds, etc.)

Free movement of people

Article 45/46, Revised Treaty

ANDEAN

Members (late membership in parentheses)

Bolivia, Colombia, Ecuador, Peru, Venezuela

Established 25 May 1988. Andean Group became the Andean Community in 1997 with the adoption of the Trujillo protocol

INVESTMENT RULES

Appendix 5.2 (continued)

ANDEAN

What year did investment provisions come into force (variable?)	Decision 291 established the obligations regarding foreign investment. Made in March 1991. Decision 292 deals with Andean Multinational Enterprises. Its provisions generally yield to national stipulation on the subject.	
1 Scope and coverage		
a . Applicable to non-parties (when or when not)	yes	
b. Positive or negative list approach	positive	
c. Main exceptions (safeguards, sectors etc.)	Reserved sectors according to national law	
2 National Treatment	Yes but.... foreign investors shall have the same rights and obligations as those to which national investors are subject, except as provided for in the national legislation of each Member Country. Decision 292 grants national treatment to Andean MNCs. National treatment with respect to government procurements, export incentives and taxation, the right to participate in economic sectors reserved for national companies and the right to open branches in any member country, and free transfer of funds related	Decision 291 Article 2.

Appendix 5.2 (continued)

ANDEAN

	to investment.	
a. Pre-establishment (all sectors?)	Not specified	
b. Are there restrictions on ownership rules? (e.g. min equity share).	No	
c. Operations by MNEs in the country.	Not specified	
3 Most Favoured Nation and fair and equitable treatment		
a granted to parties non-parties	No	
4 Performance requirements	Yes but only establishes particular provisions for the performance of contracts for the license of technology, technical assistance, technical services, and other technological contracts under the national laws of each Member.	Decision 291 Article 14.
a. Are they banned for new and existing investment?		
b. Do they go beyond TRIMs?		
5 Transfers of funds		
a. Are transfers of funds across borders allowed?	Yes	Decision 291 Article 4 & 5.
6 Do provisions with respect to	Yes	

Appendix 5.2 (continued)

ANDEAN

expropriation exist (nationalization, etc.)?

7 Settlement of Disputes

a. State-to-state. — Yes through the Andean Court of Justice

b. Investor-state. — No

c. Access to International Dispute Settlement (ICSID, UNCITRAL) — Yes – ICSID

8 Provisions for incentives and subsidies

9 Rules of Origin

a. Do rules or origin exist? — Yes

b. Value Content Criterion: Domestic/Regional Value Content (RVC) or Import Content (MC). — MC: 50%

c. Are there roll-up arrangements?

d. Are drawbacks allowed?

e. Mean/median value of restrictiveness.

10 Tariff structures

Appendix 5.2 (continued)

ANDEAN

a. Does a Common External Tariff exist? If so what is it and will it be? If not, give indication of country dispersion.	Yes since 1993. The resulting Customs Union is incomplete – the CET (with rates of 0, 5, 10, 15 and 20 per cent) is applied only to Colombia, Ecuador and Venezuela. Bolivia has been exempted from implementing it and maintains its flat national tariff.
b. Level of intra-regional tariffs and plans.	Intra-regional trade is duty free
c. Exceptions.	
11 Other relevant provisions (regional enterprise schemes, regional investment funds, etc.)	Decision 292 provides for the formation of Andean Multinational Enterprises. Andean Development Corporation. Andean Business Advisory Council.

ASEAN

Members (late membership between parentheses)	Brunei Darussalam entered 8/1/1984), Cambodia (entered 30/4/1999), Indonesia, Malaysia, Myanmar (entered 23/7/1997), Laos (entered 23/7/1997), Philippines, Singapore, Thailand, Vietnam (entered 28/7/1995).	Established **8 August 1967**. ASEAN Free Trade Area was set up in 1992.
INVESTMENT RULES		
What year did investment	Agreement for the Protection and Promotion of Investment, 1987. The	

Appendix 5.2 (continued)

ASEAN

provisions come into force (variable?)	Framework agreement on the ASEAN Investment Area (AIA) was signed on 7 October 1998.	
1 Scope and coverage	This Agreement shall apply only to investments brought into, derived from or directly connected with investments brought into the territory of any Contracting Party by nationals or companies of any other Contracting Party and which are specifically approved in writing and registered by the host country and upon such conditions as it deems fit for the purposes of this Agreement.	AIA
a. Applicable to non-parties (when or when not)	Yes – with respect to national treatment in AIA.	
b. Positive or negative list approach	1987 Agreement: positive. AIA: negative (Temporary Exclusion List & Sensitive List).	
c. Main exceptions (safeguards, sectors etc.)	Temporary Exclusion List and Sensitive List.	
2 National Treatment	Yes – To ASEAN members immediately and to non-ASEAN investors by 2020. National treatment to the admission, establishment, acquisition, expansion, management, operation, and disposition of investment.	Article 7 AIA
a. Pre-establishment (all sectors?)	Yes – subject to temporary exclusion list and sensitive list. As of 1 January 2003, the Temporary Exclusion Lists (TEL) for the manufacturing sector of Brunei Darussalam, Indonesia, Myanmar, Philippines, and Thailand have been phased out thereby broadening the scope of economic activities where ASEAN investors are given national treatment. Malaysia and Singapore have no temporary exclusion list.	

Appendix 5.2 (continued)

ASEAN

b Are there restrictions on ownership rules? (e.g. min equity share)	Yes – as a short term measure: a suspension of laws regulating equity joint venture between foreign and local enterprises and 100% foreign equity is allowed. Laws restricting foreign shareholders in national companies are also deregulated. However, since the 100% foreign equity and other special privileges granted in the short-term measures are not set as permanent measures, they are subject to change and may alter in the future or be extended depending on later circumstances. Currently, Brunei Darussalam, Indonesia, Laos, Malaysia allows 100% foreign equity ownership in certain sectors.	
c. Operations by MNEs in the country	Yes	
3 Most Favoured Nation and fair and equitable treatment		
a. granted to parties non-parties	Yes	
	No – however it does not exclude non-ASEAN investors who have formed a company in a member country, and they may be entitled to 'ASEAN investor' status.	Article 8 & 9
4 Performance requirements a. Are they banned for new and existing investment? b. Do they go beyond TRIMs?	No	
5 Transfers of funds a. Are transfers of funds across borders allowed?	Yes	Article 7, 1987

Appendix 5.2 (continued)

ASEAN

6 Do provisions with respect to expropriation exist (nationalization, etc.)?	Investments of nationals or companies of any Contracting Party shall not be subject to expropriation nationalization or any measure equivalent thereto (in the article referred to as 'expropriation'), except for public use, or public purpose, or in the public interest, and under due process of law, on a non-discriminatory basis and upon payment of adequate compensation.	Article 6, 1987
7 Settlement of Disputes		
a State-to-state	Yes – Any dispute between and among, the Contracting Parties concerning the interpretation or application of this Agreement shall, as far as possible, be settled amicably between the parties to the dispute. Such settlement shall be reported to the ASEAN Economic Ministers (AEM). If such a dispute cannot thus be settled it shall be submitted to the AEM for resolution.	Article 9, 1987
b. Investor-state	Yes	Article 10, 1987
c. Access to International Dispute Settlement (ICSID, UNCITRAL)	The dispute may be brought before the International Centre for Settlement of Investment Disputes (IGSID), the United Nations Commission on International Trade Law (UNCITRAL), the Regional Centre for Arbitration at Kuala Lumpur or any other regional centre for arbitration in ASEAN, whichever body the parties to the dispute mutually agree to appoint for the purposes of Conducting the arbitration.	
8 Provisions for incentives and subsidies	No	

Appendix 5.2 (continued)

ASEAN

9 Rules of Origin

a. Do rules or origin exist?	Yes
b. Value Content Criterion: Domestic/Regional Value Content (RVC) or Import Content (MC)	MC: 60%
c. Are there roll-up arrangements?	Not mentioned
d. Are drawbacks allowed?	Yes
e. Mean/median value of restrictiveness	4

10 Tariff structures

a. Does a Common External Tariff exist? If so what is it and will it be? If not, give indication of country dispersion	No. Afta was expected to reduce tariffs to between 0–5% for all trade between member nations by 2008. Common Effective Preferential Tariff scheme covers on average 90% of the tariff lines of all ASEAN members nations.
b. Level of intra-regional tariffs and plans (2003)	Brunei Darussalam: 0.92 Cambodia: 7.96 Indonesia: 3.70 Laos: 5.66 Malaysia: 3.19
	Myanmar: 2.05 Philippines: 3.79 Singapore: 0 Thailand: 4.63 Vietnam: 2.02

COMESA

Members (late membership	Angola, Burundi, Comoros, Democratic Republic of Congo, Djibouti, Egypt, Eritrea,	Established 8

Appendix 5.2 (continued)

COMESA

between parentheses)	Ethiopia, Kenya, Madagascar, Malawi, Mauritius, Namibia (left in 2003), Rwanda, Seychelles (may leave SADC), Sudan, Swaziland, Uganda, Zambia, Zimbabwe
INVESTMENT RULES	
What year did investment provisions come into force (variable?)	Comesa Treaty 1994
1 Scope and coverage	
a. Applicable to non-parties (when or when not).	No
b. Positive or negative list approach.	positive
c. Main exceptions (safeguards, sectors etc.)	
2 National Treatment	No
a. Pre-establishment (all sectors?)	
b. Are there restrictions on ownership rules? (e.g. min equity share)	
c. Operations by MNEs in the country	
3 Most Favoured Nation and fair and equitable treatment	fair and equitable treatment to private investors

December 1994

Article 159.1

Appendix 5.2 (continued)

COMESA

a. granted to parties non-parties		
4 Performance requirements		
a. Are they banned for new and existing investment?	No	
b. Do they go beyond TRIMs?		
5 Transfers of funds		
a. Are transfers of funds across borders allowed?	Yes	Article 159.5
6 Do provisions with respect to expropriation exist (nationalization, etc.)?	Yes – subject to the accepted principle of public interest, refrain from nationalizing or expropriating private investment and in the event private investment is nationalized or expropriated, pay adequate compensation.	Article 159.3
7 Settlement of Disputes	Yes – Court of Justice for arbitration between member states and legal and natural persons.	
a. State-to-state	Yes	
b Investor-state	No	
c Access to International Dispute Settlement (ICSID, UNCITRAL)	Yes – most members have acceded to ICSID	
8 Provisions for incentives and subsidies		
TRADE RULES		
9 Rules of Origin		
a. Do rules or origin exist	Yes	

Appendix 5.2 (continued)

COMESA

b. Value Content Criterion: Domestic/Regional Value Content (RVC) or Import Content (MC)	MC: 60% RVC35%
c. Are there roll-up arrangements?	Yes
d. Are drawbacks allowed?	Not after 10 years
e. Mean/median value of restrictiveness	3

10 Tariff structures

a. Does a Common External Tariff exist? If so what is it and will it be? If not, give indication of country dispersion	No. Its free-trade area (FTA) was set up on 1 November 2000; nine of its member countries were able to respect this deadline, whereas Burundi has been given a waiver to allow it to apply a 60 % reduction of its MFN tariffs on exports from COMESA. The customs union should come into effect on 1 November 2004, with a common external tariff (CET) comprising four rates: 0, 5, 15, and 30 %. The tariff reduction schedule was as follows: 60% by 1993; 70% by 1994; 80% by 1996; 90% by 1998 and 100% by 2000.
b. Level of intra-regional tariffs and plans	Nine member States – Djibouti, Egypt, Kenya, Madagascar, Malawi, Mauritius, Sudan, Zambia and Zimbabwe have eliminated their tariffs on COMESA originating products, in accordance with the tariff reduction schedule which was adopted in 1992 for the gradual removal of tariffs to intra-COMESA trade.

Appendix 5.2 (continued)

COMESA

	Angola: rate of tariff reduction is 0. Burundi: Under the reform process launched in January 2003, Burundi has introduced a new preferential tariff for COMESA member countries, providing for a standard reduction of 80 per cent of all MFN rates in force since 1 January 2003. As from January 2004, all products from COMESA countries are due to be granted duty-free entry into Burundi. Comoros: 80% tariff reduction; DR Congo: zero; Eritrea: 80% tariff reduction; Ethiopia: 10%; Rwanda: 90% tariff reduction; Uganda: 80% tariff reduction; Swaziland – CET for SACU. Has undertaken to seek the concurrence of SACU to join the FTA in 2004; Namibia – apply CET SACU; Seychelles.
c. Exceptions	Some sub-sectors of agriculture
11 Other relevant provisions (regional enterprise schemes, regional investment funds, etc.)	

SADC

Members (late membership between parentheses)	Angola, Botswana, Democratic Republic of Congo, Lesotho, Malawi, Mauritius, Mozambique, Seychelles, South Africa, Swaziland, Tanzania, Zambia, Zimbabwe.
	Southern African Development Coordination Conference was established in 1 March 1970. It was replaced by SADC on 17 July 1992
INVESTMENT RULES	

Appendix 5.2 (continued)

SADC

What year did investment provisions come into force (variable?)	Few investment provisions. Though plans to establish more comprehensive investment provisions under the Protocol on finance and investment.
1 Scope and coverage	
a. Applicable to non-parties (when or when not)	
b. Positive or negative list approach	
c. Main exceptions (safeguards, sectors etc.)	
2 National Treatment	No
a. Pre-establishment (all sectors?)	
b. Are there restrictions on ownership rules? (e.g. min equity share)	
c. Operations by MNEs in the country	
3 Most Favoured Nation and fair and equitable treatment	No
a. granted to parties	

Appendix 5.2 (continued)

SADC

	non-parties
4 Performance requirements	
a. Are they banned for new and existing investment?	No
b. Do they go beyond TRIMs?	
5 Transfers of funds	
a. Are transfer of funds across borders allowed	No
6 Do provisions with respect to expropriation exist (nationalization, etc.)?	No
7 Settlement of Disputes	Tribunal to settle disputes between state and community, between natural and legal persons and community. Article 17–19, protocol on Tribunal and the rules of procedure thereof.
a. State-to-state	Yes
b. Investor-state	No
c. Access to International Dispute Settlement (ICSID, UNCITRAL)	Yes
8 Provisions for incentives and subsidies	No
TRADE RULES	
9 Rules of Origin	
a. Do rules of origin exist?	Yes
b. Value Content Criterion:	MC: 70–35%

Appendix 5.2 (continued)

SADC

Domestic/Regional Value Content (RVC) or Import Content (MC)	
c. Are there roll-up arrangements?	Yes
d. Are drawbacks allowed?	Not mentioned
e. Mean/median value of restrictiveness	4

10 Tariff structures

a. Does a Common External Tariff exist? If so what is it and will it be? If not, give indication of country dispersion	No. Botswana applies the CET for SACU area, Lesotho applies the CET for SACU.
b. Level of intra-regional tariffs and plans	Malawi: Under the SADC Trade Protocol, which commenced operation from January 2001, Malawi has begun to implement its commitments, and grants duty-free access, on a reciprocal basis, to imports of category A products (mostly capital goods and equipment) from other members that have also adopted the Protocol.
c. Exceptions	Mauritius: Under the SADC Trade Protocol, Mauritius grants duty-free access, on a reciprocal basis, to imports of category A products (mostly capital goods

Appendix 5.2 (continued)

SADC

and equipment) from the other members that have already deposited their implementation instruments.

Namibia: applies CET for SACU.

Swaziland: CET for SACU.

Zambia: From 30 April 2001, Zambia began to implement its commitments under the SADC Trade Protocol and to grant duty-free access, on a reciprocal basis, to imports of Category A products from SADC members that have also deposited their implementation instruments.

11 Other relevant provisions (regional enterprise schemes, regional investment funds, etc.)

PART 3
Case Studies of Bolivia and Tanzania

Chapter 6

Regional Integration and Poverty: The Case of Bolivia

Osvaldo Nina and Lykke E. Andersen

6.1 Introduction

The growth of regional trading blocks has been one of the major developments in international relations in recent years. Regional agreements vary widely, but all have the objective of reducing barriers to trade between member countries and are expected to contribute significantly to economic growth, development and the reduction of poverty.

In Bolivia, regional integration started progressing rapidly once macroeconomic stability was achieved in 1986. During the 1990s, the fundamental components of the trade reform programme were severe reduction in the coverage of non-tariff barriers, reduction of the average level of import tariffs, elimination of export taxes and expansion of export markets for Bolivian goods by signing trade agreements with the main trading partners. Moreover, the investment policies have sought to attract foreign investors to augment the country's asset base.

These policies to promote openness, especially the regional integration agreements, contributed to certain changes in the export and import structures, but to date there is little empirical evidence on the impact of regional integration on economic growth and poverty reduction in general. Thus, the objective of the present study is to analyze how regional integration has affected poverty in Bolivia. The analysis will concentrate on the structure of the labour market, where it is possible to analyze the effects of regional integration on employment and income, which is one of the transmission mechanisms described by te Velde, Page and Morrissey in Chapter 4 of this book.

The remainder of the chapter is organized as follows. Section 6.2 provides a description of the trade and investment provisions in the relevant regional trade agreements of Bolivia. Section 6.3 discusses how these provisions have affected the composition of trade and foreign direct investment. Section 6.4 discusses how such trade and investment have affected poverty. Section 6.5 concludes.

6.2 Regional integration in Bolivia

The regional integration processes involving Bolivia started in 1960 with the Latin American Free Trade Association (LAFTA), which had the objective of promoting the economic integration of the region and creating a common market.[1] The members, however, lacked political commitment to make progress towards a free trade zone (Uculmana, 2003). In 1969, based on this bad experience, the Andean countries created the Andean Pact with the objective of promoting development of the member countries through social and economic integration. Moreover, at the beginning of the 1980s, the members of LAFTA created the Latin American Integration Association (LAIA) with the objective of promoting bilateral and extra-regional agreements.

Between 1960 and 1990, Latin American countries, especially the Andean countries, introduced protectionism and widespread regulation based on the theory of import substitution. This heavy-handed government intervention generated high external barriers that obstructed the process of regional integration. However, during the 1990s, the integration forces returned, and the majority of Latin American countries signed or revived regional trade agreements as part of their structural reforms intended to open up their economies to trade and foreign direct investment. In 1991, for example, the Andean countries revived the Andean Pact, and the Southern Cone countries that were not participating in any other sub-regional agreements created the Common Market of the South (MERCOSUR).

Since 1992, Bolivia has signed three partial integration agreements through LAIA: with Chile (1993), MERCOSUR (1997) and Cuba (2000), and one free trade agreement with Mexico (1995). Moreover, Bolivia is a beneficiary country of preferences arising from the Andean Trade Promotion and Drug Eradication Act (2002), which is a continuation of the Andean Trade Preference Act (1991), from the United States, and the Andean Generalized System of Preferences (1990) from the European Union. Both agreements granted preferential tariffs as support for the Andean Community's war on drugs, on the principle of shared responsibility.

Of the above-mentioned agreements, those with Mexico and Cuba are insignificant in terms of volume of trade and investment. The remaining agreements and drug-related trade preferences are described in detail in the remainder of this section.

6.2.1 The Latin American Integration Association (LAIA)

LAIA is an intergovernmental organization, which continues the integration process started by LAFTA. The 1980 Montevideo Treaty provides its legal framework.[2] The main objective of the organization is the establishment of a

---

[1]   Up to 1966, the members were Argentina, Bolivia, Brazil, Colombia, Chile, Ecuador, Mexico, Paraguay, Peru, Uruguay and Venezuela.

[2]   The members of LAFTA signed this agreement on 12 August 1980.

common market, in order to stimulate the economic and social development of the region. LAIA is the largest Latin American integration group and has twelve member countries: Argentina, Bolivia, Brazil, Chile, Colombia, Cuba, Ecuador, Mexico, Paraguay, Peru, Uruguay and Venezuela.

LAIA established the basic provisions for trade between the member countries and promoted sub-regional agreements. Currently, the latter have advanced substantially further than the basic LAIA agreements, somewhat diluting the advantage of this mechanism (Uculmana, 2003). However, LAIA has good prospects of contributing to the creation of a Free Trade Area (FTA) in South America by coordinating and combining the sub-regional integration agreements.

Trade provisions

LAIA promotes the creation of an area of economic preferences in the region, aiming at a Latin American common market, by means of three mechanisms: (i) regional tariff preferences granted to products originating in the member countries; (ii) agreements of regional scope; and (iii) partial agreements, between two or more countries of the area. Regional and/or partial scope agreements may cover tariff relief and trade promotion; economic complementarity; agricultural trade; financial, fiscal, customs and health cooperation; environmental conservation; scientific and technological cooperation; tourism promotion; technical standards and many other fields.

A preference system consisting of market-opening lists, special cooperation programmes and countervailing measures on behalf of landlocked countries was granted to the Relatively Less Economically Developed Countries (Bolivia, Ecuador and Paraguay) to assist their full participation in the process of integration. Four agreements have been signed by all LAIA member countries: Market-Opening Lists on behalf of Bolivia, Ecuador and Paraguay and the Regional Tariff Preference Agreement. Market-Opening Agreements (MOAs) were signed 30 April 1983, providing Bolivia, Ecuador and Paraguay with effective preferential treatment as member countries opened their markets to a wide range of products and granting them, without reciprocity, the total elimination of customs duties and other restrictions.

Bolivia currently has around 2000 products in the market opening list. Categorized by the Harmonized Commodity Coding System (HCCS),[3] most of the main products are concentrated in: (i) textiles and textile articles (Section XI); (ii) live animals and animal products (Section I); (iii) base metals and articles of base metals (Section XV); (iv) wood and articles of wood (Section IX); and (v) vegetable products (Section II). The number of products covered has been growing significantly during the last two decades. At the beginning of the agreement, only 31 products were covered by MOAs concentrated in the base metals section.

---

[3]   See Appendix 6.1 for a description of the Harmonized Commodity Description and Coding Section.

In compliance with the provisions of Article 5 of the 1980 Montevideo Treaty, all member countries grant, on a reciprocal basis, a reduction in the rate of duties levied on imports originating in the region. The Regional Tariff Preference (RTP) differs according to the relative economic development of each country and applies to the entire tariff universe, except for a list of exempted products determined by each country. The current basic level of RTP is 20 per cent. In the case of Bolivia, the tariffs levied on its export products are lower, and tariffs on imports are higher, due to its landlocked situation.

Chart 6.1   Market opening list: Bolivia, 2002

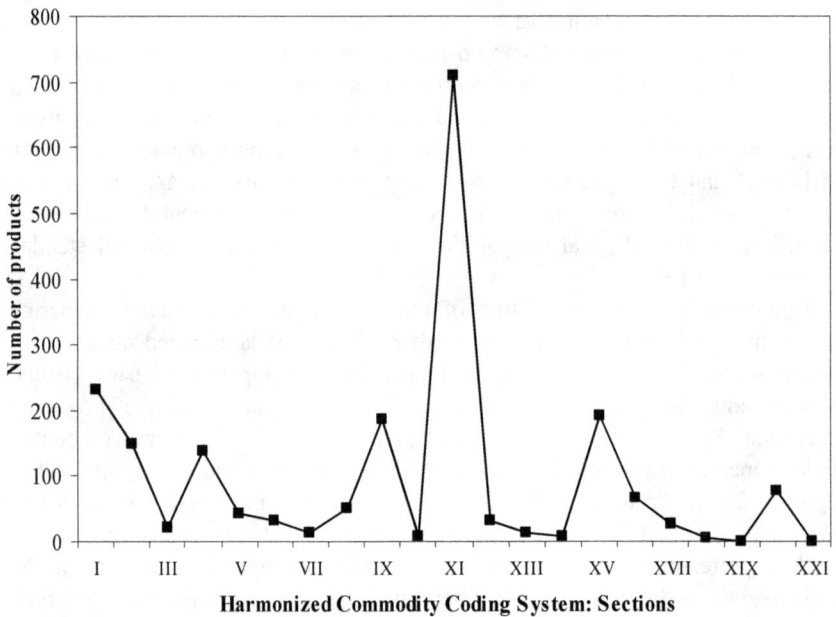

Harmonized Commodity Coding System: Sections

Source: LAIA.

In order to protect certain strategic industries, each country is allowed a list of exceptions from the tariff system of the association (NALADISA). The lists of exceptions have maximum limits: 1920 products for Relatively Less Economically Developed Countries, 960 products for Medium Economically Developed Countries and 480 products for the rest.

In order to receive the preferential treatment established in the Montevideo Treaty, goods have to qualify as 'originating', according to the general Rules of Origin of the Association. The origin of goods is categorized as follows:

1. products manufactured entirely from the native materials of any member country;
2. animal, vegetable, and mineral products extracted, harvested or collected in the territory or territorial waters and exclusive economic zones of any member country;
3. products resulting from operations or processes performed in its territory which substantially transform the materials into new and different products;
4. products manufactured with materials from non-member countries but which are processed in any member country to become new and different products as classified according to the NALADISA code system;
5. products that are assembled in any member country using native materials from member or third countries, when the value CIF port of destination or CIF maritime port of the third-country materials does not exceed 50 per cent[4] of the value FOB of the export of such merchandise.
6. These rules of origin have been applied to all sub-regional and partial agreements in Latin America, with some minor modifications, which will be noted below.

6.2.2 The Andean Community (CAN)

The Andean countries created the Andean Pact in 1969 through the Cartagena Agreement, the main objective being to increase the development of the members by means of social and economic integration. During the first couple of decades, there was little progress towards regional integration, but global developments and structural reforms renewed interest in the integration process. In 1991, the Caracas Letter implemented the Andean Free Trade Zone and renamed the agreement the Andean Community (CAN). Moreover, the members set up the Andean Integration System, to work closely in pursuit of the same objectives: to intensify Andean sub-regional integration, promote its external projection, and reinforce activities connected with the process. Currently, the members are Bolivia, Colombia, Ecuador, Peru and Venezuela.[5]

Trade Provisions
Initially, the Andean Pact implemented fundamental instruments of the integration process, such as the Liberalization Programme and the Industrial Development Programme. But, these instruments did not help to promote regional integration because the prevailing import-substitution model, which had the objective of promoting industrialization, required high external trade barriers. According to Schiff and Winters (2003), in general the countries with these characteristics were

---

[4]   60 per cent for the Relatively Less Economically Developed Countries.
[5]   Chile was a founding member but left the organization in 1976. Peru was not a member during the 1992–4 period.

very protectionist and interventionist in the sense of attempting to determine administratively which industries to undertake and where they should be located.

Following the revival of the Andean Pact, the trade provisions became substantially more liberal, creating a Free Trade Area, and eliminating tariffs and all other duties between CAN member countries. Since 1993, products have been circulating freely within the bloc, but the Common External Tariff did not enter into force due to a number of disagreements between the member countries. In March 2005, they agreed to implement a new Andean Integrated Tariff System (ARIAN), which includes a Common External Tariff, by January 2006, but they have still to agree on the level of the external tariff, and have already passed two self-imposed deadlines.

The rules of origin of LAFTA governed trade among the Andean countries until 1987, when the members approved their own provisions for determining the origin of products. Nevertheless, the rapid advances in trade integration, in particular the formation of a customs union, generated the need for updating the rules in order to establish precise criteria of origin. In 1997, Decision 416 introduced amendments to the provisions specifying the conditions products must meet in order to be goods of sub-regional origin and thereby benefit from the enlarged market. The amendments were more specific with respect to goods in whose manufacture non-native materials were used. The basic criterion used for this type of goods is that the materials of non-native origin must either have undergone processing, as reflected in the change in tariff heading, or the CIF value of the non-native materials does not exceed 50 per cent of the FOB value of the final products in the case of Colombia, Venezuela and Peru, and 60 per cent for Bolivia and Ecuador.

Between 1995 and 2001, the Andean Community approved provisions that removed unnecessary technical obstacles to trade. These provisions are the Andean System of Standardization, Accreditation, Testing, Certification, Technical Regulations and Metrology, the Andean Quality System, and the Andean Certificates of Products Marketed. The Andean System of Standardization, etc. has the objective of clearing the way for trade by removing unnecessary technical obstacles and bringing about an improvement in the quality of the goods and services produced in the Andean sub-region. The Andean Quality System covers all elements of the quality infrastructure: standardization, accreditation, testing, certification, technical regulations and metrology for all of the sub-region's products and services, except for those having to do with phytosanitary and zoosanitary matters.[6] Finally, the Andean Certificates of Products Marketed simplify conformity evaluation activities by the member countries and are aimed at establishing 'Andean standards' for the products marketed in the sub-region by harmonizing the standards applied in each member country or adopting international standards considered to be of interest to the sub-region. The

---

[6]   Phyto- and zoosanitary regulation aims at protecting plants and animals from the spread of pests and diseases.

application of these provisions is intended to shore up institutions in the member countries that are responsible for monitoring the fulfilment of the conformity evaluation provisions, technical regulations, and procedures of the World Trade Organization's Agreement on Technical Obstacles to Trade.

Investment Provisions

The Andean Community provisions with regard to investment are in two parts. The first part covers the general regime governing foreign investment and the second regulates the case of Andean multinational enterprises. However, these requirements have to be complemented by national laws and regulations, especially through bilateral arrangements or agreements that promote and protect investments signed by member countries with third countries and even among themselves.

The general regime for foreign investment contains the definitions of direct foreign investment and classifies investors and enterprises into national, mixed, and foreign. Even though the regime sets out the rights and obligations of foreign investors, it gives the individual Andean countries full freedom to regulate this field through their own national legislation.

The regulation with respect to Andean multinational enterprises ensures that these enterprises enjoy national treatment in regard to the public procurement of goods and services; the right to transfer all dividends abroad in freely convertible currency for distribution; tax matters; and the right to open up branches in other member countries. They also enjoy equality with domestic taxes; provisions to avoid double taxation of income and on the transfer of capital abroad; and facilities for the hiring of sub-regional personnel. The main condition for these facilities is that at least 60 per cent of the capital of the multinational company belongs to national investors from two or more member countries.

6.2.3 Common Market of the South (MERCOSUR)

Motivated by trade imbalances and a desire for energetic integration in South America, MERCOSUR countries signed a partial economic integration agreement with Bolivia in 1996. The main objectives were to establish the legal and institutional framework of economic and physical cooperation and integration that would facilitate the free circulation of goods and services, to create a Free Trade Area within ten years, and to establish a normative framework for promoting and protecting intra-regional investments, without limiting trade negotiations with third parties. This agreement entered into force on 2 March, 1997, when previous agreements between the countries involved became invalid.

Trade provisions

The trade relations between Bolivia and MERCOSUR members, before the agreement was signed, were according to LAIA's rules. The new agreement included a Trade Liberalization Programme consisting of immediate and progressive tariff reductions. This programme has several categories of tariff reductions, depending on the sensitivity of the products. The first group which was fully duty-free contained around 570 products for Bolivia and 800 for MERCOSUR. In the case of Bolivia, the tariff-free goods were concentrated in the following main categories: (i) foods, beverages, spirits and tobacco (Section IV); (ii) vegetable products (Section II); (iii) mineral products (Section V); and (iv) plastics and rubber (Section VII).

On the other hand, Bolivia set zero import tariffs on goods that are very important for capital investment. According to Chart 6.2, the main categories are: (i) products of the chemical or allied industries (Section VI); (ii) machinery and electrical equipment (XVI); (iii) live animals and animal products (Section I); and (iv) textiles and textile articles (Section XI).

Chart 6.2   Products with immediate tariff reductions granted by MERCOSUR and Bolivia

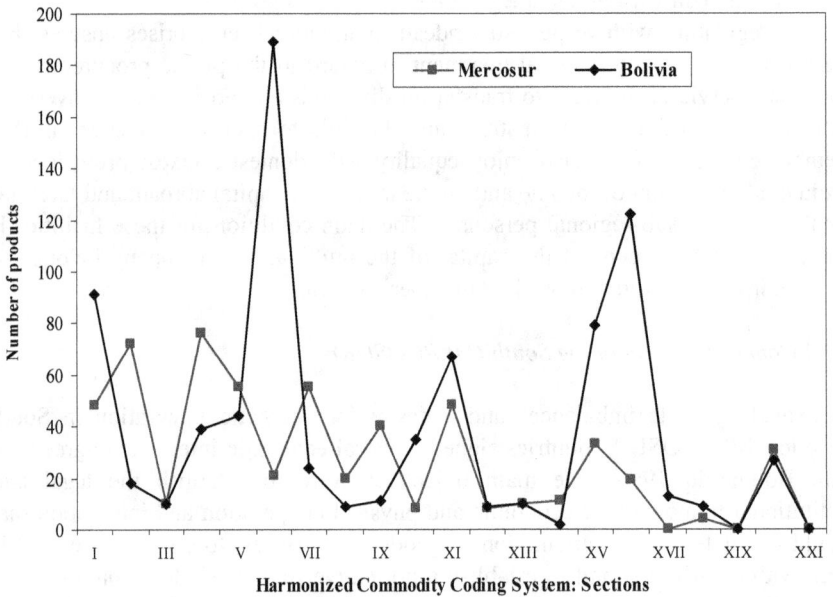

Source: Ibid.

The rules of origin of MERCOSUR have the same characteristics as those of the Andean Community and LAIA. The non-tariff barriers cover all elements of standardization, accreditation, testing, certification, technical regulations, metrology and phytosanitary and zoosanitary matters. In general, the members are governed by the rules of WTO. However, products that receive local export incentives, in the form of tariff refunds on temporarily imported inputs, are not included in the Trade Liberalization Programme.

With respect to the progressive tariff reductions, Chart 6.3 shows that Bolivia provides more benefit for MERCOSUR, especially in sections related to the agricultural sector. The progressive tariff reductions cover around 1428 goods: 74 per cent of them will have zero tariffs within 10 years of signing the agreement, and the rest within 15 to 20 years. Moreover, goods not included in the above-mentioned agreement received an immediate 30 per cent reduction in the tariff, increasing gradually to 100 per cent by 2006.

Chart 6.3   Products with progressive tariff reductions granted by MERCOSUR and Bolivia

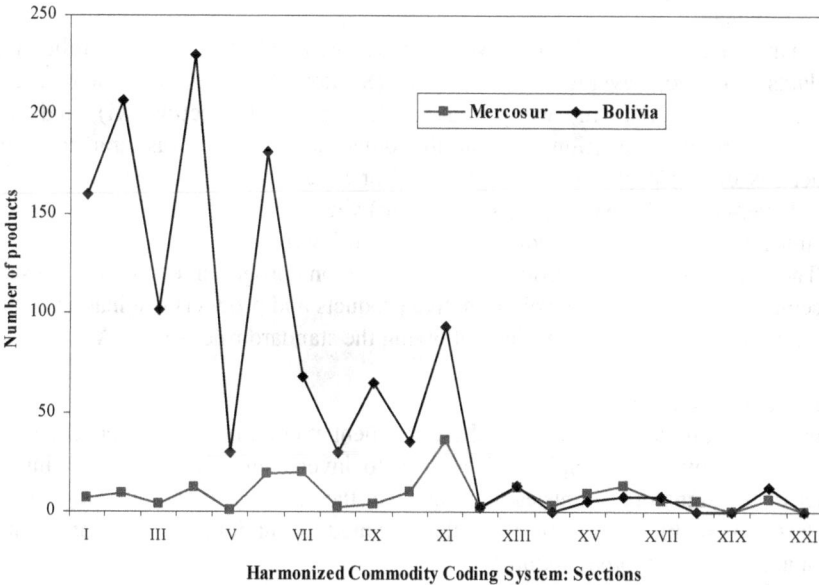

Harmonized Commodity Coding System: Sections

Source: Ibid.

Investment provisions
The agreement did not have any explicit rules on FDI or multinational enterprises. Certain articles mention that members should try to stimulate reciprocal investment, with the objective of intensifying the bilateral flows of trade and technology. These initiatives will respect national legislation.

In addition, the agreement provides the possibility of making agreements on the Promotion and Reciprocal Protection of Investments, while all bilateral agreements signed before the agreement maintain their full validity. The members have agreed to examine the possibility of signing agreements to avoid double taxation.

6.2.4 Chile

After Chile had decided to leave the Andean Pact, trade relations between Bolivia and Chile became limited. In order to increase trade and economic relations, Bolivia signed a partial integration agreement with Chile in April 1993.

Trade provisions
According to the agreement, the economic liberalization was to be carried out at three levels. The first level provides duty-free access to Chilean markets without reciprocity or volume constraints for certain Bolivian products. The second level provides duty-free access for certain products with reciprocity. Finally, at the third level, each country grants a reduction on the rate of duties according to a specific list of products.

Chart 6.4 shows that Bolivia was granted tariff reductions for the following products: (i) food, beverages, and tobacco (Section IV); (ii) textiles and textile articles (Section XI); (iii) wood and articles of wood (Section XI); and (iv) vegetable products (Section II). On the other hand, Chile was granted tariff reductions on: (i) products of the chemical or allied industries (Section VI); (ii) food, beverages and tobacco (Section IV); (iii) vegetable products (Section II); and (iv) machinery and electrical equipment (Section XVI).

The benefits derived from the liberalization programme of the present agreement will apply exclusively to native products and products originating in the territories of the member countries, following the standard rules of LAIA.

Investment provisions
In order to stimulate investment, the agreement recommends that the countries adopt the following principle with respect to investment: Capital originating in either of the signatory countries will enjoy, in the territory of the other signatory, no less favourable treatment than that granted to national capital or capital originating from any other country.

6.2.5 Andean Trade Promotion and Drug Eradication Act (ATPDEA)

The Andean Trade Preference Act (ATPA) was signed into law on 4 December 1991, providing for a 10-year period of duty-free or reduced-rate treatment of selected US imports from Bolivia, Colombia, Ecuador, and Peru. The ATPA improved the access to US markets of such exports in order to encourage economic alternatives to illicit drug activity and drug-crop production in the Andean region.

The ATPA expired on 4 December 2001, but the US Trade Act of 2002 renewed this programme under the Andean Trade Promotion and Drug Eradication Act (ATPDEA) on 15 February 2002. In addition, the United States, under the

Generalized System of Preferences (GSP), provides preferential duty-free entry to approximately 3,000 products. The purpose of this programme is to encourage economic growth in the beneficiary countries.

Chart 6.4 Products with immediate tariff reductions granted by Chile and Bolivia

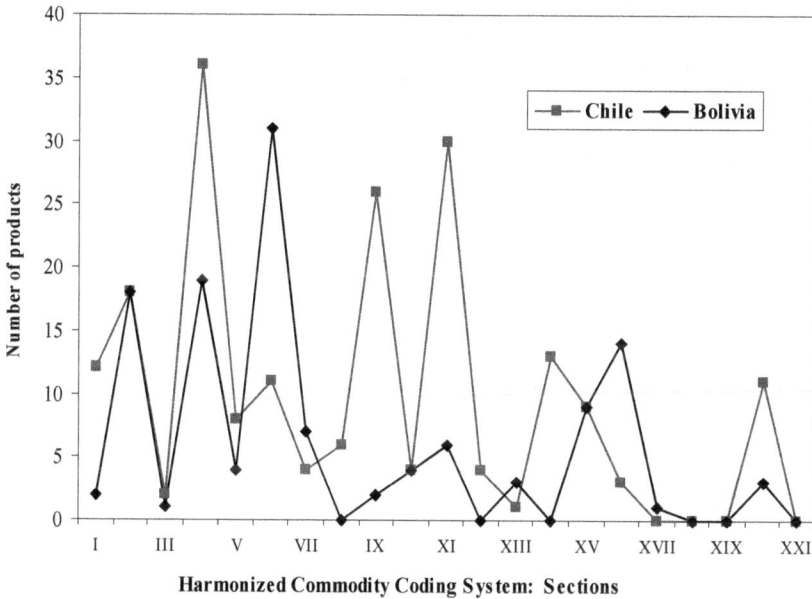

Source: Ibid.

Trade provisions
The ATPA provided duty-free access to US markets for some 5,600 products. The duty-free access of ATPDEA is similar to that of ATPA but some of the programme's parameters were modified and extended to other Andean exports, such as textile articles, to broaden the programme's effects. The ATPDEA extended new benefits to 700 additional products.

According to the Trade Act of 2002, duty-free treatment did not apply to the following products: rum and tafia; sugars, syrups, and sugar-containing products; and tuna. On the other hand, footwear; petroleum or any products derived from it; watches and their parts; and handbags, luggage, flat goods, work gloves, and leather wearing apparel may claim duty-free treatment if the President of the United States determines that such articles are not import-sensitive in the context of imports from ATPDEA beneficiary countries.

Moreover, ATPDEA provides duty-free access and access free of any quantitative restrictions or limitations to articles of apparel and certain textile articles. These products have to be: (i) manufactured or assembled from products of the United States or ATPDEA beneficiary countries; (ii) assembled in one or more ATPDEA beneficiary countries from regional fabrics or regional components; or (iii) hand-loomed, hand-made, or folklore articles. No article or material of a beneficiary country will be eligible for such treatment by virtue of having merely undergone simple combining, packaging operations, or mere dilution that does not materially alter the characteristics of the article.

In 2002, the products benefiting from ATPDEA numbered around 6545 products, around 655 more than the GSP. Chart 6.5 shows that the products are concentrated in the following categories: (i) chemical or allied industries (Section VI); (ii) base metals and articles of base metal (Section XV); (iii) machinery and electrical equipment (Section XVI); and (iv) optical, photographic, medical or surgical instruments and apparatus (Section XVIII). In contrast to the GSP programme, the ATPDEA provides duty-free access for more products from Section XVIII, Section XI (textiles and textile articles) and Section VII (wood and wood articles).

Chart 6.5   Products with duty-free access to US markets

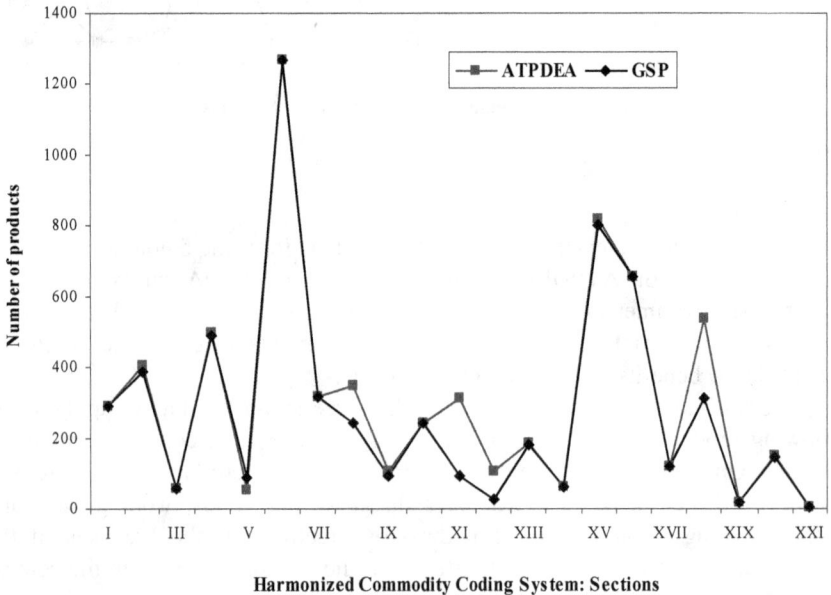

Harmonized Commodity Coding System: Sections

Source: Ibid.

In contrast to standard regional trade agreements, the ATPDEA requires that each country must meet all the following ATPDEA criteria in order to be a beneficiary:

1. The beneficiary country should demonstrate a commitment to undertake its obligations under the WTO and participate in negotiations toward the completion of the FTAA or another free trade agreement.
2. The country should provide protection of intellectual property rights consistent with or greater than the protection afforded under the Agreement on Trade-Related Aspects of Intellectual Property Rights included in the Uruguay Round Agreements Act.
3. The country should provide internationally recognized worker rights and implement commitments to eliminate the worst forms of child labour.
4. The country should meet the counter-narcotics certification criteria set out in the Foreign Assistance Act of 1961 for eligibility for US assistance.
5. The country should have taken steps to become a party to and to implement the Inter-American Convention against Corruption. Moreover, it should apply transparent, non-discriminatory, and competitive procedures in government procurement equivalent to those contained in the Agreement on Government Procurement of the Uruguay Round Agreements Act.
6. The country should support the efforts of the United States to combat terrorism.

Currently, Bolivia satisfies all these conditions.

6.2.6 Andean Generalized System of Preferences (Andean GSP)

The European Union granted tariff preferences to Andean countries by the creation of the Andean Generalized System of Preferences (Andean GSP), as support for the Andean Community's war on drugs, on the principle of shared responsibility. The scheme has been in effect since 13 December 1990.

In 2001, the EU Council approved regulations for the application of a generalized tariff preferences plan for the period 2002–4. This scheme was extended to 2005 in December 2003. In principle, countries that grow so fast that they become a high-income country (according to World Bank definitions) would graduate from the programme, in the sense that they would no longer qualify for this special treatment. However, the new regulation contains a provision that excludes, in a non-discriminatory way, all beneficiary countries accounting for less than 1 per cent of GSP imports from graduation. Because of this, no Andean Community countries will see their products graduate any more. The possible renewal of the Andean preferential system for the decade 2006–14 is also being considered; this will depend upon a general evaluation of the results over the three-year period 2002–5.

The Andean GSP has enjoyed special and privileged treatment as compared with the general GSP in the EU. Not only did it permit the preferential entry of a broad range of Andean products with a zero tariff, but it also guaranteed that these preferences could not be suspended according to general GSP provisions.

Trade provisions

To benefit from the Andean GSP on imports into the EU, three conditions must be fulfilled: (i) the goods must originate in a beneficiary country in accordance with the rules of origin; (ii) they must be transported directly from the beneficiary country to the EU; and (iii) valid proof of origin must be submitted.

Tariffs differ between non-sensitive and sensitive products. The Most Favoured Nation (MFN) duties rate on products listed as non-sensitive are entirely suspended, except for some agricultural components (Sections I to V of the HCCS). For sensitive products, the MFN *ad valorem* duties are reduced by 3.5 per cent. For textile and textile articles (Section XI), the reduction is 20 per cent and for the specific duties 30 per cent. Moreover, there are special incentive arrangements for any country that meets the norms for the protection of labour rights and the environment. In both cases, all MFN duties are reduced by a further 5 per cent.

The Andean Community has special and privileged treatment compared with the general GSP. According to the arrangements to combat drug production and trafficking, MFN *ad valorem* duties are entirely suspended on all products of Sections I to XXI of the HCCS, except arms and ammunition. According to Chart 6.6, which shows the number, group and sections of products included in the special arrangements to combat drug production and trafficking, there are many products that benefit from zero duty and they are the products that are in the sensitive products category. For instance, all textiles and textile articles (Section XI) benefit from this special arrangement.

Similar to the other trade initiatives to encourage access to new markets, the benefits derived from the Andean GSP apply exclusively to goods that originate in a beneficiary country in accordance with the following rules of origin: (i) they must be wholly obtained in that country, or (ii) sufficiently processed there. The list of products basically uses three methods, or combinations of methods, to lay down the amount of processing that can be considered as 'sufficient' in each case: (i) the change of heading criterion,[7] (ii) the value or *ad valorem* criterion, where the value of the non-originating materials used may not exceed a given percentage of the post-processing price of the product; and (iii) the specific process criterion, with certain operations or stages in a manufacturing process having to be carried out on any non-originating materials used.

---

[7]   This means that a product is considered to be sufficiently processed when the product obtained is classified in a 4-digit heading of the Harmonized Commodity Coding System, which is different from those in which all the non-originating materials used in its manufacture are classified.

Chart 6.6   **Products with preference tariff to European Union**

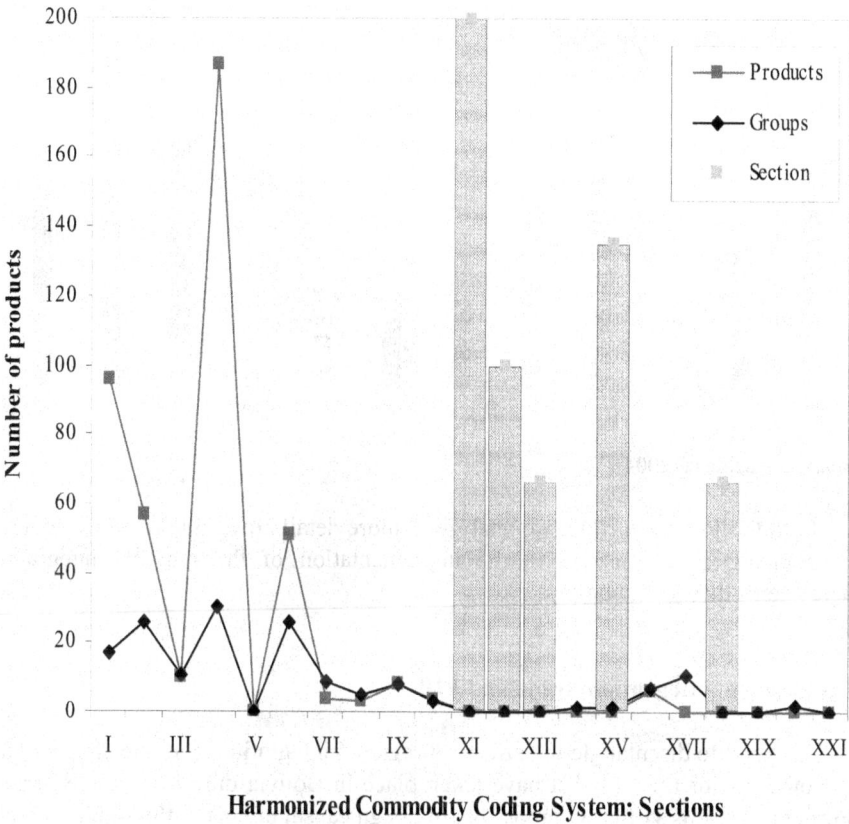

Harmonized Commodity Coding System: Sections

Source: Ibid.

6.2.7 Conclusions

The review of trade agreements and drug-related trade preferences, in general, demonstrates that a significant number of Bolivian goods have been granted preferential access to export markets, especially to US and CAN markets. Chart 6.7 indicates that Bolivia has been able to take advantage of these provisions, since the share of export value with preferential tariffs increased from just 9 per cent in 1991 to 54 per cent by 2003. This trend towards more trade under preferential agreements applies to all countries in Latin America, underscoring the progress towards regional integration of goods markets.

Chart 6.7   Percentage of export value with preferential agreement

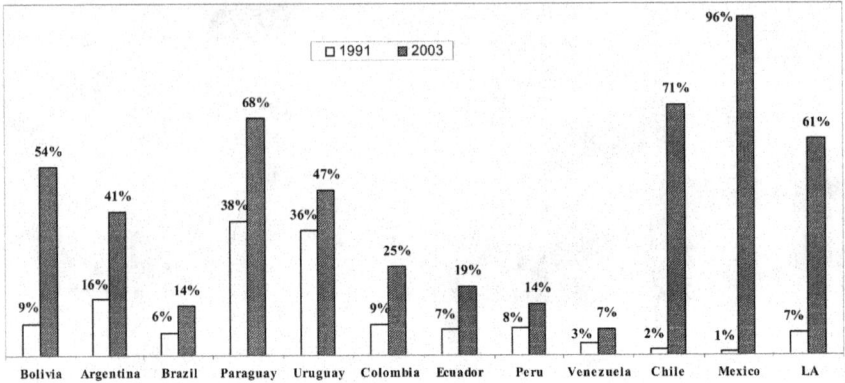

Source: Machinea (2004).

In the following section, we analyze in more detail how trade and FDI patterns have changed in response to the implementation of the regional integration agreements discussed above.

6.3 Regional integration, trade and FDI

It is difficult to disentangle the effects of regional integration from the effects of all the other major reforms that have taken place in Bolivia during the same period. Furthermore, it is virtually impossible to assign causal effects to the signing of any specific agreement or to the formulation of any specific provisions in these agreements. In this section we review the changes in trade and FDI patterns that have followed the signing of the different integration agreements. We then estimate a gravity model of trade, which can be used to formally test the impacts of these agreements.

6.3.1 Trade

Trade policy during the last two decades can be divided into three periods. The first period, 1986–90, had the main objective of reversing the negative consequences of protectionism and its anti-export bias. The policies were characterized by four basic elements: (i) reduction in the average level of tariffs;

(ii) simplification of the tariff structure; (iii) incentive mechanisms for exports; and (iv) a single[8] and realistic exchange rate.

During this period, tariffs decreased significantly, from an average of 30 per cent to a single rate of 10 per cent on all goods except capital goods for which the tariff is only 5 per cent (Peñaranda, 1993). These changes were based on the rules of the GATT, of which Bolivia has been a member since 1990. In the case of exports, the government created the National Institute of Exports to facilitate an efficient legal framework and to reduce the bureaucracy associated with exporting. Chart 6.8 suggests that these policies may have helped to reverse the negative trends in exports and GDP experienced during the early 1980s.

Chart 6.8   Official exports and imports, 1980–2002

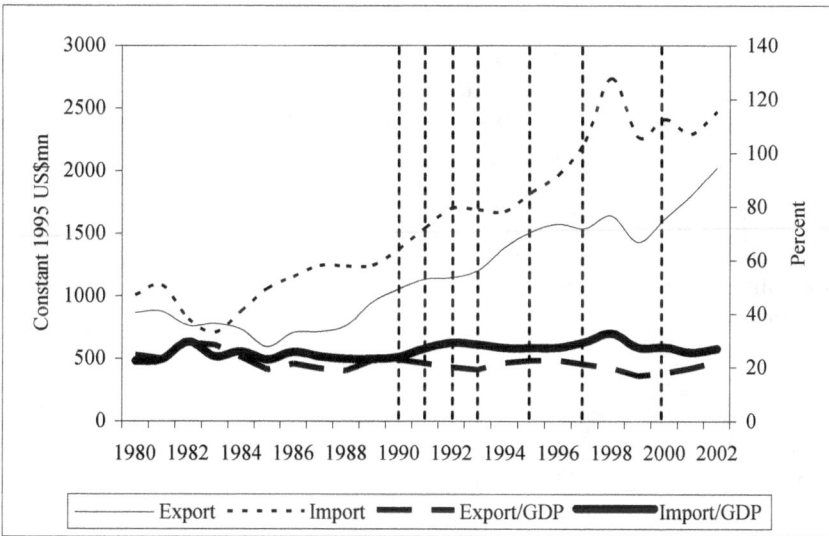

Note: Regional Agreements: Andean Community (1991-revived); Chile (1993); Mexico (1995); MERCOSUR (1997); and Cuba (2000). Preferential Trade: Andean GSP (1990); ATPA (1992); and ATPDEA (2002).
Source: National Statistical Institute (INE).

During the second period, 1991–7, trade policies concentrated on expanding the export markets for Bolivian goods by signing trade agreements with the main trading partners. Bolivia signed agreements with Chile, Mexico and MERCOSUR and became a member of the WTO in 1995. Chart 6.8 shows that both imports and

---

[8]   Meaning that the official exchange rate is identical to the black market exchange rate.

exports grew strongly during the period of increased integration. For example, they both increased significantly immediately after signing the agreement with MERCOSUR in 1997.

A major accomplishment during this period was the approval of the Export Tax Law in 1993, which compiled and consolidated a range of previous rules regarding exports. The law stipulates: free exports and imports without any licence or permission, and government guarantees for international export financing. Moreover, the government created six free trade zones (FTZs). Currently, FTZs exist in the three main cities and three cities on the borders with Brazil and Peru. They have not yet proved attractive to investors, however, because of the lack of roads and other basic infrastructure.

Trade grew steadily until 1998, when it started to decrease because of external shocks and the coming into operation of the Customs Law in 1999. The latter had the objective of decreasing illegal imports and increasing the collection of import tariffs.

The third period, 1998–2002, was characterized by economic recession, and the government implemented several temporary measures to try to revive the economy. Among these were tariff reductions on capital goods from 10 per cent to 5 per cent and tax exemptions for exporters.

Although trade has increased substantially in terms of value since the introduction of the New Economic Policy, as a share of GDP it has remained roughly constant (see Chart 6.8). Thus, regional integration has apparently not made Bolivia a more open economy, but, as we shall see below, it did affect which goods are exported and to which countries they are exported.

The impact of regional integration on trade

The trade agreements apparently contributed to changes in the relative importance of each trading bloc. Chart 6.9 shows that trade with CAN and MERCOSUR has increased substantially at the expense of trade with the US and the European Union. For example, one year before the signing of the CAN agreement, only 6 per cent of Bolivian trade was with this bloc. Five years later, this percentage had increased to 14 per cent, and by 2002 had reached 18 per cent. In contrast, trade with the European Union accounted for 23 per cent of all Bolivian trade one year before the drug-related preferential trade concession was put into operation, and five years later it had dropped to 19 per cent, and by 2002 to only 8 per cent.

In particular, the MERCOSUR agreement appears to have had a very substantial trade diversion effect. Within five years, 20 per cent of all trade had been diverted from the EU and the US to MERCOSUR.

Chart 6.9   Share of trade (imports+exports) from partners one year before and five years after implementation of RIA

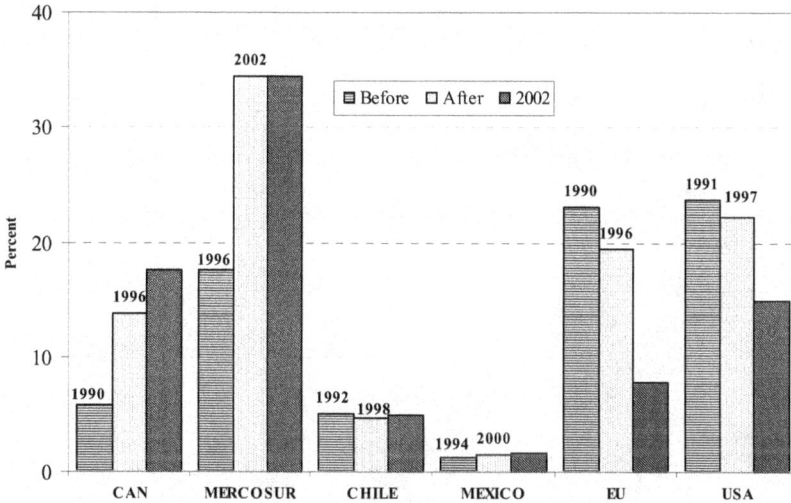

Source: Ibid.

Chart 6.10 shows that the trade diversion effect is particularly large for exports, whereas imports were slightly more rigid. Nevertheless, imports from the EU fell from 17 per cent in 1990 to 8 per cent in 2002, while imports from MERCOSUR doubled from 20 to 41 per cent between 1996 and 2002.

The trade diversion hypothesis can be formally tested in a classical gravity model of the type first applied by Tinbergen (1962) and Pöyhönen (1963). The model stipulates that the amount of trade between two countries, T_{ij}, depends on the level of income, Y_i, in each country, and the distance, D_{ij}, between them. The model also allows for some other factors, X_{ij}, which are usually dummies indicating whether the two countries share a common border or a common language. Thus, the gravity model of trade can be written as follows:

$$\ln(T_{ij}) = \alpha + \beta_1\ln(Y_i{}^*) + \beta_2\ln(Y_j) + \beta_3 D_{ij} + \beta_4 X_{ij} + \varepsilon_{ij}.$$

The model is estimated for Bolivia and its 66 trading partners using annual data from 1990 to 2002. To test whether the agreements reviewed in Section 6.2 have had a significant impact on the volume of trade, we include six trade agreement dummies in the model. The CAN dummy, for example, takes on the value 1 for the years when the agreement was in place for the countries involved, and 0 for all other countries and years. If the estimated coefficient is positive, it indicates that the agreement had a positive effect on trade, even while controlling for other factors, such as distance and income levels.

Chart 6.10   Share of exports and imports from partners one year before and five years after implementation of RIA

Exports

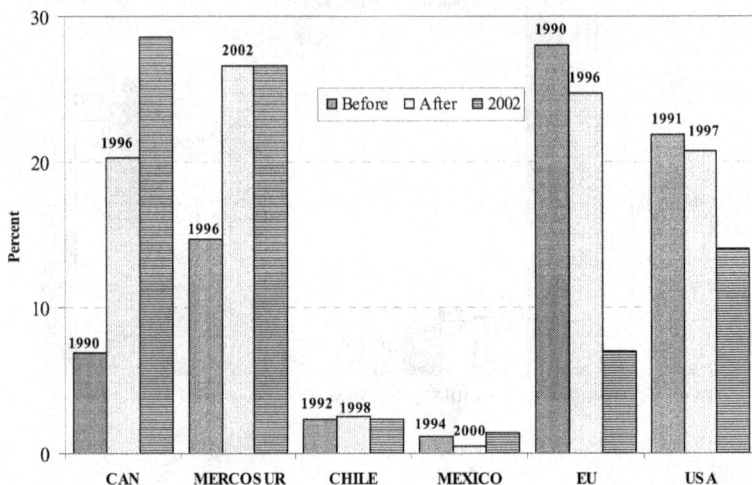

Imports

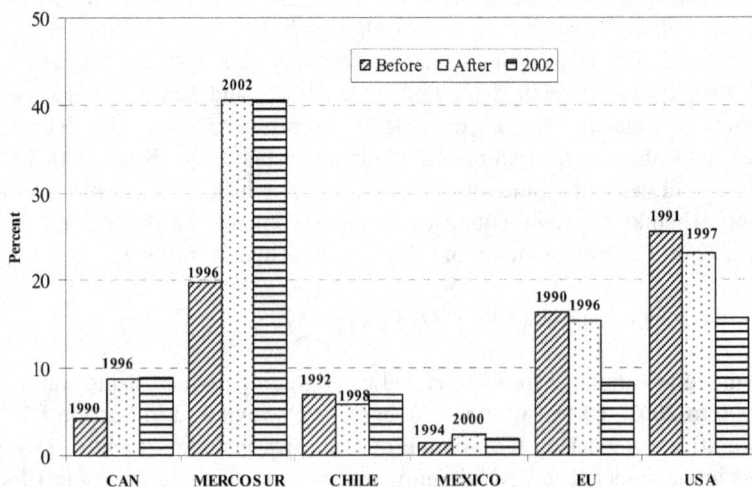

Source: Ibid.

Table 6.1 shows the regression results. Trade is defined as imports plus exports measured in fixed 1995 US dollars. Distance is measured as the distance between countries' capitals measured in kilometres.[9] The panel was intended to have 858 observations, but a few observations on imports were missing, implying a total number of 853 observations. As expected, the coefficient on both the Bolivian and the trading partner's GDP comes out positive, while distance has a highly significant negative effect on trade. A common border between the two countries tends to increase trade. There appears to be a negative trend in Bolivian trade during the 1990–2002 period, although the estimated coefficient is only significant at the 10 per cent level.

Table 6.1   Estimated gravity model of trade, Bolivia, 1990–2002

Dependent variable: ln(imports+exports+1)
Method: Pooled Least Squares
Sample: 1990 2002
Total panel (unbalanced) observations 853
White heteroskedasticity-consistent standard errors and covariance

Variable	Coefficient	Std. Error	t-Statistic	Prob.
Constant	-49.24422	22.55099	-2.183684	0.0293
ln(GDP) (95$)	1.365768	0.035496	38.47618	0.0000
ln(GDPBOL) (95$)	4.974959	2.621218	1.897957	0.0580
CAN	2.543368	0.187035	13.59837	0.0000
MERCOSUR	1.290531	0.415018	3.109575	0.0019
MEXICO	0.598812	0.167401	3.577106	0.0004
CHILE	0.186356	0.225067	0.828000	0.4079
ATPA	-0.685342	0.227003	-3.019080	0.0026
EU	0.075713	0.151131	0.500979	0.6165
Trend	-0.170553	0.094085	-1.812763	0.0702
Distance (km)	-0.000196	1.55E-05	-12.63101	0.0000
Common border	1.690658	0.234863	7.198493	0.0000
R-squared	0.733066			

Source: Authors' estimation.

According to the regression results, the CAN agreement had a highly significant positive effect on trade between Bolivia and other members of the Andean Community. The coefficient is not only significant, but also very large. A

---

[9]   The results are robust for substituting distance in kilometres with the log of distance in kilometres, except that the dummy 'Common border' becomes insignificant.

coefficient of 2.5 implies approximately a twelve-fold increase of trade (measured in real terms) after the signing of the agreement compared with before the agreement.

The MERCOSUR agreement also had a statistically significant and positive impact on trade according to the estimated model. The coefficient of 1.29 suggests that trade between Bolivia and MERCOSUR countries more than tripled after signing the agreement. The partial integration agreement with Mexico signed in 1995 also had a statistically significant and positive effect on trade between Bolivia and Mexico. The coefficient of 0.60 suggests that trade between the two countries increased by 82 per cent due to the signing of the agreement.

In contrast, the Andean Trade Preference Act (ATPA) granted by the United States appears to have had a negative effect on trade between Bolivia and the US. A coefficient of -0.69 suggests that trade fell by 50 per cent after the agreement was signed in 1991. It is unlikely that the signing of the ATPA *caused* this drop in trade. Indeed, the estimated model cannot prove causality, but can only indicate what happened to trade before and after signing the various agreements compared with what would be expected, given the GDP levels and geographical locations of each country. We do not know what would have happened to Bolivian–US trade if no ATPA had been signed, but the regression results, as well as Charts 6.9 and 6.10 above, suggest that the ATPA (followed by the ATPDEA) has not been successful in increasing trade between the two countries.

The Andean Generalized System of Preferences granted by the European Union did not have a positive effect on trade either. The estimated coefficient is positive, but not statistically significant. The same holds for the partial integration agreement signed with Chile in 1993.

The estimated gravity model of trade is consistent with the hypothesis of diversion of trade away from US and EU markets towards CAN and MERCOSUR markets. Although it is impossible to prove that this trade diversion was caused by the regional integration agreements, both empirical evidence and theory are at least consistent with this hypothesis. In the remainder of this chapter, we shall tentatively attribute all the changes that have been observed in trade patterns to the regional integration processes, thus getting an upper bound on the impact of regional integration on poverty.

Since we are interested in the impact of trade on poverty, it is also important to analyze the changes in the composition of trade. Chart 6.11 shows that, between 1992 and 2002, Bolivian exports became significantly more diversified. In 1992, exports were highly concentrated in Section V products (mineral products), whereas by 2002, this category had lost importance, while section III products (animal and vegetable fat), Section IV products (food, beverages, and tobacco), and Section XV products (base metals and products thereof) had all become significant. A large part of the current Section III exports consists of soybean exports to other Andean countries under very favourable conditions due to trade provisions in the CAN. Bolivian soybean producers cannot compete with the much more efficient Brazilian producers, and the only reason Bolivia has a significant amount of soy bean exports is the preferential access to Andean markets provided by the CAN agreement. Similarly, Section IV exports also go mainly to CAN or MERCOSUR markets and benefit from favourable trade provisions.

Chart 6.11   Structure of exports and imports: 1992 and 2002 (Constant 1995 US$m.)

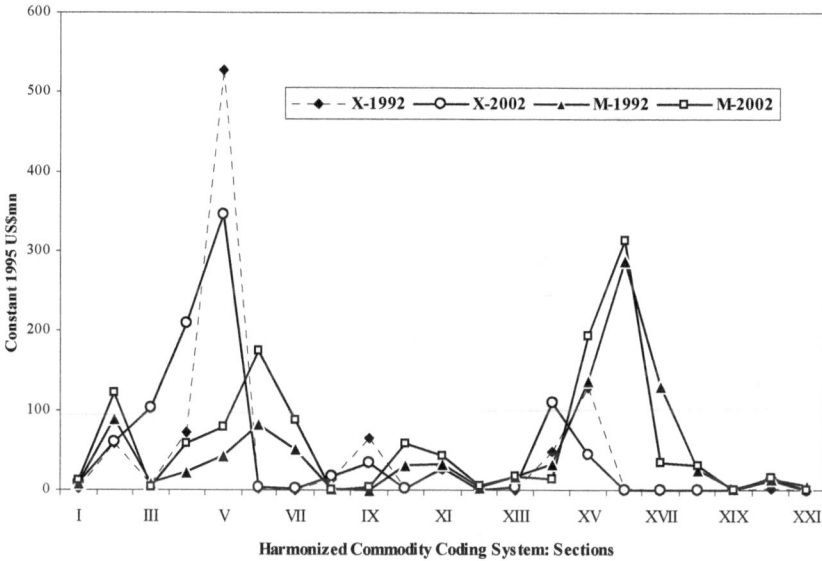

Source: National Statistical Institute (INE).

In contrast, in the case of textiles and textile articles (Section XI), the tariff reduction was gradual and zero tariff rates were reached only at the end of the period of analysis. Exports in this category had clearly not started to take off by 2002.

Chart 6.12 confirms that before signing the series of integration agreements, Bolivian exports were dominated by primary goods, mainly destined for the European Union, while MERCOSUR was relatively unimportant. By 2002, primary goods are still the most important export category, but the destination is now almost exclusively MERCOSUR. Food, beverages and tobacco have also become very important, and the destination is CAN.

In terms of poverty, we would expect labour-intensive export products (food, beverages and tobacco, all labour-intensive industries) to have the most beneficial effects. Thus, it is likely that exports to CAN and the US will reduce poverty more than exports to other blocs. This hypothesis will be formally tested in Section 6.4 below.

Chart 6.12   Structure of exports by trade blocs and goods: 1992 and 2002
            1992

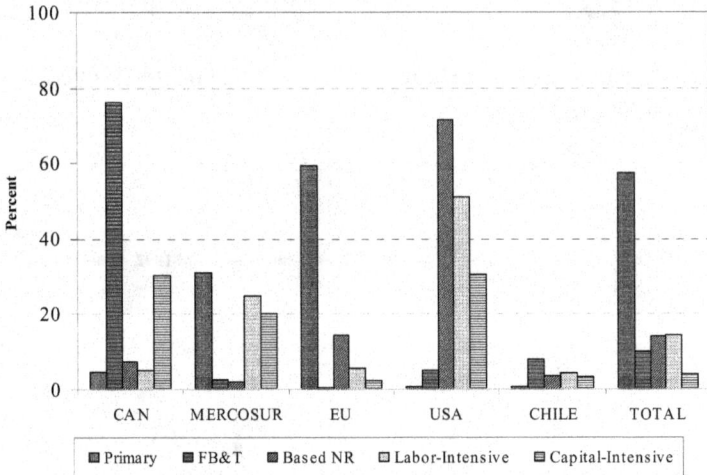

2002

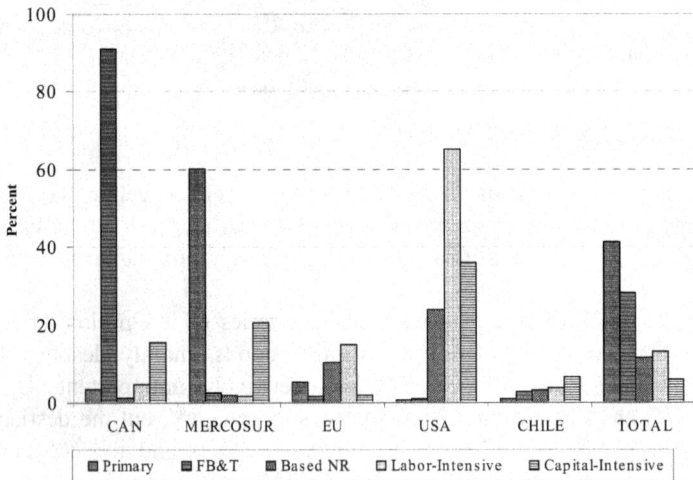

Primary: ISIC 011, 012, 013, 014, 015, 020, 050, 101, 102, 103, 111, 112, 1210, 121, 132, 141, 142. Food, beverages and Tobacco: ISIC 151, 152, 153, 154, 155, 160. Natural Resources Based: ISIC 210, 241, 243, 251, 252, 271, 272, 273. Labour-Intensive: ISIC 171, 172, 173, 181, 182, 191, 192, 201, 202, 361, 369.

Source: UN Commodity Trade Statistics Database.

Chart 6.13 Structure of imports by trade blocs and goods: 1992 and 2002

1992

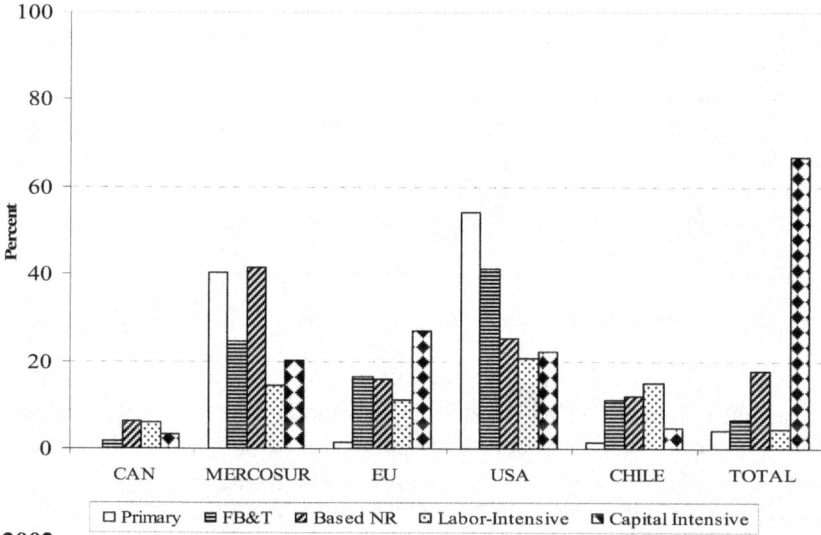

2002

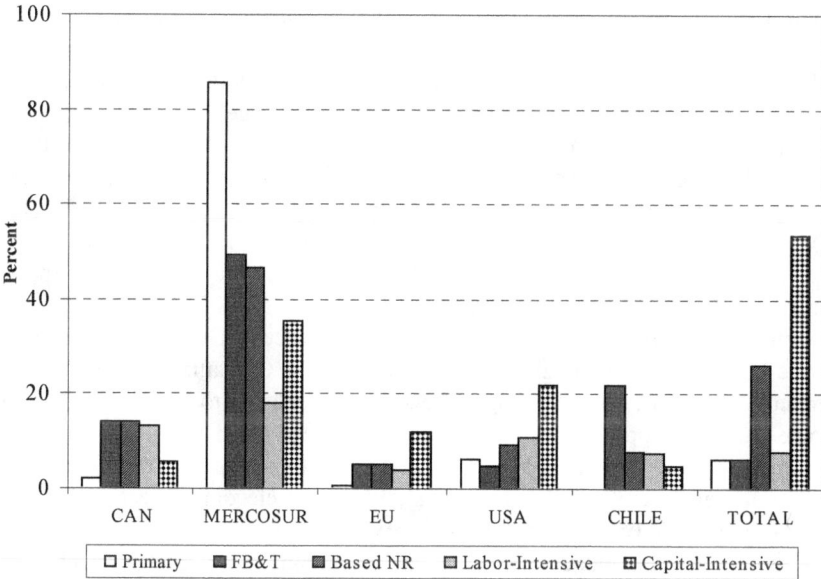

Notes: *Ibid.*
Source: *Ibid.*

Trade integration not only promotes exports, however. Increased exports go hand in hand with increased imports, as we saw in Chart 6.8. Chart 6.13 shows that Bolivia's main imports are capital goods. In 1992, these made up 68 per cent of all imports, and came mostly from the EU and the US. By 2002, the import share of capital goods had decreased to 58 per cent and, more importantly, these imports came primarily from MERCOSUR.

Capital goods are essential for Bolivian industry and do not compete with local production, as Bolivia has virtually no capital goods industry. In contrast, natural resource-based products compete directly with Bolivian production, and the increase observed between 1992 and 2002 may thus have a detrimental effect on poverty. This is the downside of increased integration, and the problem is particularly large with MERCOSUR.

6.3.2 Foreign Direct Investment

Since macroeconomic stability was achieved in 1986, investment policies have avidly sought to attract foreign investors in order to augment the country's asset base. During the first period, 1986–90, the political instability and the uncertainty regarding the success of the stabilization programme, together with an inappropriate policy framework to promote investment, can in part explain the slow growth of FDI (see Chart 6.14).

Clear rules for foreign investment were set out in the early 1990s, mainly through the Investment Law (1990) and the Privatization Law (1992). The Investment Law guarantees that foreign investors will receive national treatment, will have access to free currency conversion, will enjoy unrestricted transfers of funds, and will have the right to international arbitration. These laws, together with a complete line of investment guarantees to foreign investors by the IBRD's Multilateral Investment Guarantee Agency (MIGA), established favourable rules regarding market entry and foreign ownership. During this period, Bolivia also signed bilateral investment agreements with Argentina, Belgium/Luxembourg, China, France, Germany, Italy, Mexico, the Netherlands, Peru, Romania, Spain, Switzerland, the United Kingdom and the United States (see Appendix 6.2).

During the second half of the 1990s, when the Second Generation Structural Reforms improved the economic policy framework, the Capitalization Law (1994) generated a large infusion of foreign direct investment due to the opening up of strategic state monopolies to private investors (see Chart 6.14). Under the capitalization process, the six principal state-owned enterprises, YPFB (oil and gas), ENDE (electricity), ENFE (railways), ENTEL (telecommunications), LAB (aviation) and EMV (mining and smelting), were put up for sale by international tender and the winning bidders gained management control and a 50 per cent stake in the enterprise, while the government retained the remaining 50 per cent share.

Chart 6.14   FDI and privatization index

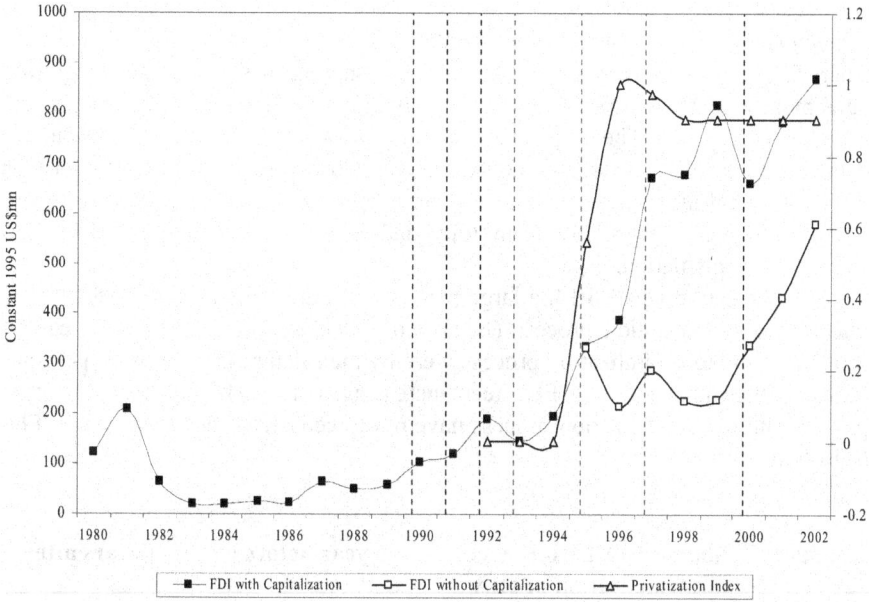

Source: National Statistical Institute (INE).

This programme nevertheless maintained five temporary monopolies, now under private control, in the hydrocarbons, transportation, telecommunications, and electricity sectors. The last of these monopoly contracts expired at the end of 2002, when the telecommunications sector was opened up to free competition.

The government set up the Sector Regulatory System (SIRESE) to offset the potential market power of the natural monopolies. SIRESE is an autonomous regulatory body, which regulates many aspects of business in the telecommunications, electricity, transport, hydrocarbons and water sectors. Prices of most public utilities are reviewed and approved by SIRESE. Market forces largely set prices, but, where necessary, a regulated price is established through relatively transparent procedures and formulas. The exception to this is potable water and garbage collection, where municipalities set the local rates.

In general, the government, over time, has been entering into a series of bilateral and multilateral agreements and covenants to promote, protect and guarantee investment. Foreign ownership is allowed virtually throughout the economy, with no requirements to register foreign direct investment separately. The legal framework restricts investments by foreigners in operations along the border areas, unless the investment or project is declared to be of national interest. Foreign investment is neither screened nor treated in a discriminatory manner. There are no registration requirements for foreign direct investors in Bolivia or any special incentives for domestic or foreign investment. Finally, there are no restrictions on any kind of remittances or currency transfers.

The impact of regional integration on FDI
Chart 6.15 shows an increase in FDI after the signing of the regional integration agreement with MERCOSUR, but hardly any effect in the cases of the agreements with CAN and Chile. The drug-related concessions with the EU and the US did not directly address FDI issues, and the large increase observed in the case of the EU is due to bilateral investment agreements (see Appendix 6.2), which have promoted large investments, especially from Italy and Spain in telecommunications and financial intermediation.

As indicated in Chart 6.14, a large part of FDI during the period 1995–2002 is due to the capitalization process (Nina and te Velde, 2003). While the capital inflows from the capitalization process were by their nature time-limited, the chart indicates that other kinds of FDI keep increasing. It is likely that the integration process and the capitalization process have reinforced each other in attracting FDI to Bolivia.

Chart 6.15   Share of FDI from partners one year before and five years after implementation of RIA

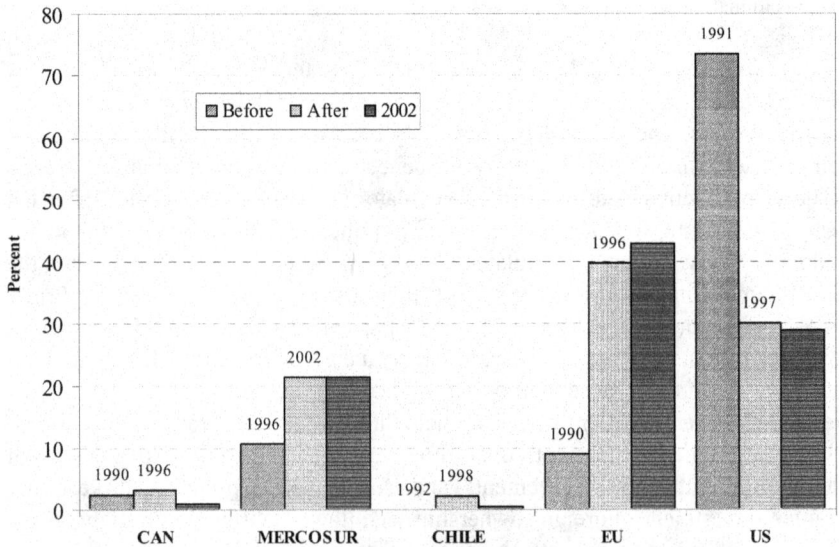

Source: Ibid.

Chart 6.16 shows the distribution of cumulative FDI during 1996–2002, by economic activity and trade bloc. The hydrocarbon (oil and gas) sector attracted 40 per cent of all FDI, with Brazil, Argentina, the US and Spain being the main investors. Utilities and transportation attracted 30 per cent of FDI, with Chile and Italy being the main actors through their investment in railways and telecommunications, respectively. The CAN bloc accounts for most of the investment in the services sector, due to the large Peruvian investments in financial intermediation. The distribution of investment across source countries is not related to regional investment provisions, as Bolivia is non-discriminatory with respect to the source of FDI.

Investment in the manufacturing and primary goods sectors accounted for only 12 per cent of total FDI during the period. Since these two sectors are much more labour-intensive than the other three groups, they would probably have had a more beneficial impact on poverty reduction in Bolivia. This issue will be investigated further in the following section.

Chart 6.16 Structure of FDI by economic blocs and economic activities – accumulated stock, 1996–2002

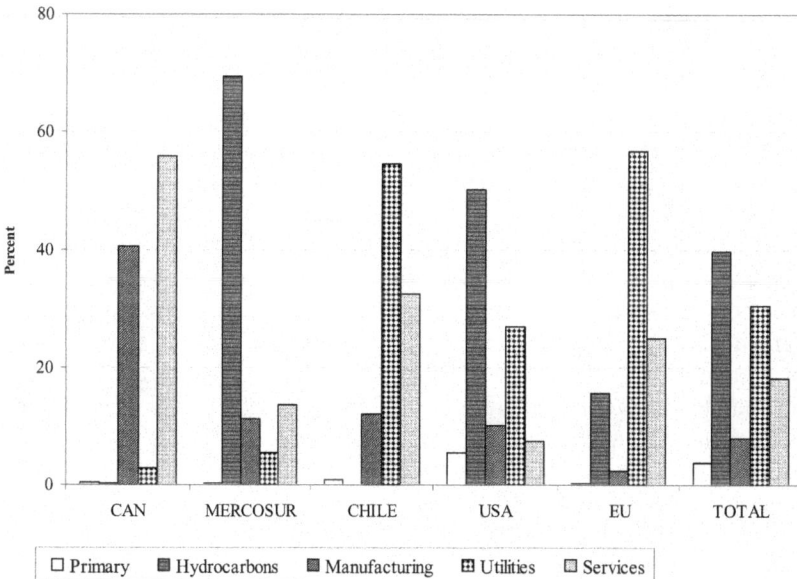

Source: Ibid.

6.3.3 Conclusions

While both distant (US, EU) and nearby (MERCOSUR, CAN) trading partners have provided free access for thousands of Bolivian products, the effect on trade has been most favourable for nearby markets. Indeed, it appears that regional integration processes have caused a diversion of trade away from US and EU markets towards MERCOSUR and CAN markets.

In addition, exports became considerably more diversified, possibly due to the different structure of demand in neighbouring countries compared with EU and US markets. Whether these changes have a positive or negative impact on poverty, is the central question in the section that follows.

6.4 Regional integration and poverty

The framework in Chapters 2–4 examines the effects of regional integration on poverty and discusses the routes from RI to poverty on the basis of a simple mapping of a set of links describing how poverty in a country is affected by RI processes. The first set of links between RI and poverty is through trade. Regional Trade Agreements (RTAs) include certain provisions that may affect the volume, price and 'poverty focus' of trade. The second set of links is through foreign direct investment. RTAs included certain provisions that may affect the volume, and 'poverty focus' of investment. The third set of links can be termed 'other' links and relate to non-trade and non-FDI issues in RTAs that may affect poverty. Finally, these links, in general, may in turn affect different characteristics of poverty intermediated through complementary conditions, including public policies.

These sets of links will depend on the structure of the labour and goods markets. In the labour markets, for example, it is possible to analyze the RTA effects on employment and income when the RTA has resulted in a change in the relative importance of each sector. On the other hand, the RTA can bring down import and domestic prices of products (goods and services) consumed directly by the poor or used in production processes that benefit the poor indirectly. Thus, it is also important to analyze the poverty effect of changes in the prices of goods and services induced by FDI.

6.4.1 Poverty

According to a recent study by Spatz (2004), Bolivia experienced a reduction in the incidence of poverty between 1989 and 1999. However, during the late 1990s, the poverty trend reversed and poverty in Bolivia started to increase again (see Chart 6.17). Moreover, the study shows that urban poverty is closely linked to macroeconomic performance, whereas rural poverty follows its own logic (linked more to weather conditions and the coca economy). The study concludes that the rural areas in Bolivia are quite detached from both improvements and deteriorations in the overall economic environment. Thus, it is reasonable to assume that the RI effect on poverty can mainly be observed in the urban areas.

Chart 6.17   Monetary poverty by region: 1989–2002

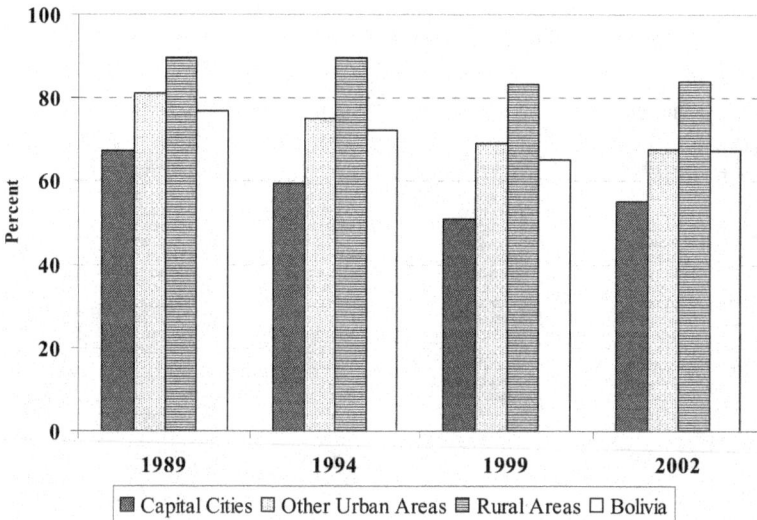

Note: [1] Poverty headcount.
Source: Spatz (2004).

According to Table 6.2, urban poverty fell rapidly during the economic boom in 1992–7, and much more slowly during the economic downturn in 1998–2002. There are large differences between sectors, however, and these differences can, to some extent, be explained by patterns in trade and FDI. For example, the table shows that poverty among workers in the hydrocarbons sector fell from 51 per cent in 1992 to zero in 2002, in capital cities. The same was the case for workers in the electricity, gas, and water sectors, and to a lesser extent for workers in the financial sector. These large reductions in poverty coincide with the sectors that attracted the main part of FDI. In contrast, the agricultural sector, which did not receive any FDI, experienced a much slower reduction in poverty.

The table also shows that the sectors that experienced rapid growth in exports (especially food, beverages and tobacco) saw faster decreases in poverty rates among workers. In contrast, the wood sector, which saw exports fall, experienced an increase in poverty. The mining sector, however, does not conform to this general trend, as poverty fell rapidly together with exports. Further below, formal

Table 6.2   Monetary poverty[a] by economic activity: 1992, 1997 and 2002

Economic Activity	Capital Cities			Bolivia		Annual average growth (%): 92–02	
	1992	1997	2002	1997	2002	Exports	Imports
Agriculture	62.5	52.8	57.5	78.7	78.8	-8.6	6.9
Hydrocarbons	50.5	19.9	0.0	23.0	2.9	5.6	60.4
Mining	82.5	64.2	41.5	63.3	57.5	-7.1	3.1
Manufacturing	78.6	55.9	61.8	59.3	63.2	4.9	2.1
Chemicals, plastics and refined petroleum	57.1	26.6	20.4	26.7	22.2	23.4	8.6
Food, beverages and tobacco	82.2	52.4	53.9	57.4	55.1	12.9	2.5
Textiles, leather and wearing apparels	82.7	63.8	59.4	66.1	65.6	3.9	8.2
Other manufacturing industries	73.4	55.1	74.2	62.5	71.5	3.6	-6.1
Paper, publishing and printing	71.6	42.0	62.5	43.5	62.9	2.9	6.4
Machinery and equipment	82.6	57.1	71.0	54.1	69.5	2.0	0.5
Basic metals and non-metallic minerals	79.6	55.1	58.9	56.3	63.9	-0.5	4.4
Wood and cork	74.9	55.1	100.0	59.5	79.9	-5.9	15.2
Electricity, gas and water supply	70.1	18.5	0.0	26.1	29.4		
Construction	81.7	59.8	63.1	60.8	69.9		
Commerce	73.8	52.5	48.7	51.9	50.7		
Hotels and restaurants	79.5	59.3	54.8	58.6	54.5		
Transport, storage and communications	67.1	44.0	39.2	45.7	43.1		
Financial intermediation	42.8	17.3	33.7	23.8	35.3		
Other services	55.5	41.9	31.6	45.7	38.9		
Total	67.2	49.7	44.3	62.2	56.9		

Note: a) We use the official poverty classification of each household as determined by the INE. The assignment to sectors is based on the work sector of the person in each household with the highest wage income. Poverty is thus 'blamed' on the main income earner, rather than on spouses' and children's failure to bring in enough supplementary income.

Source: Authors' estimations based on household surveys by the National Statistical Institute (INE).

models will be estimated linking exports, imports and FDI to poverty, while controlling for changes in other factors.

According to the economic literature, the effects of RI on poverty are best analyzed through a computable general equilibrium model, where it is possible to include certain provisions that may affect the volume, price and 'poverty focus,' of trade and FDI. This approach not only requires a complete social accounting matrix, but also a microeconomic component based on household surveys, like the IMMPA (Integrated Macroeconomic Model for Poverty Analysis) developed by the World Bank.

The approach that is used in the present study to test the effects of RI on poverty is similar to that used in the Bolivian Poverty Report by the World Bank (2002); but it includes variables on exports, imports and FDI at the individual level according to each individual's sector of work (down to four digits of the ISIC code). The analysis was carried out at the household level, using the work sector of the family member with the highest labour income (see Appendix 6.3 for the full results).

Chart 6.18 summarizes the results of this analysis, indicating that exports tend to reduce poverty, while imports tend to increase it. For example, a doubling of exports to CAN, would result in a reduction in poverty of 1.1 percentage points. Unfortunately, a doubling of imports from CAN would more than cancel out this benefit, as it would cause an increase in poverty of 1.7 percentage points. For all the trade blocs the negative effect of imports is larger than the positive effect of exports, but the difference is smallest in the case of MERCOSUR. This can be explained by the fact that imports from MERCOSUR are mainly capital goods, which do not compete with local production. In contrast, imports from CAN are concentrated in sectors that compete with Bolivian production (food, beverages and tobacco; natural resource-based manufacturing; and labour-intensive industries – see Chart 6.13).

At the aggregate level, FDI was not found to have a significant impact on poverty. However, when analyzed by trade bloc, some FDI was found to be more beneficial than others. For example, a doubling of FDI from CAN was estimated to cause a 0.6 percentage point decrease in poverty, whereas FDI from Chile and MERCOSUR did not have any beneficial impact. The reason for these differences is that FDI from Chile and MERCOSUR was concentrated in hydrocarbons and financial intermediation, which are both highly capital-intensive and have very limited effects on employment, as we shall see below. In contrast, the FDI from CAN targeted more labour-intensive industries.

**Chart 6.18   Estimated impact of a doubling of exports/imports/FDI on the
probability of being poor, 2002**

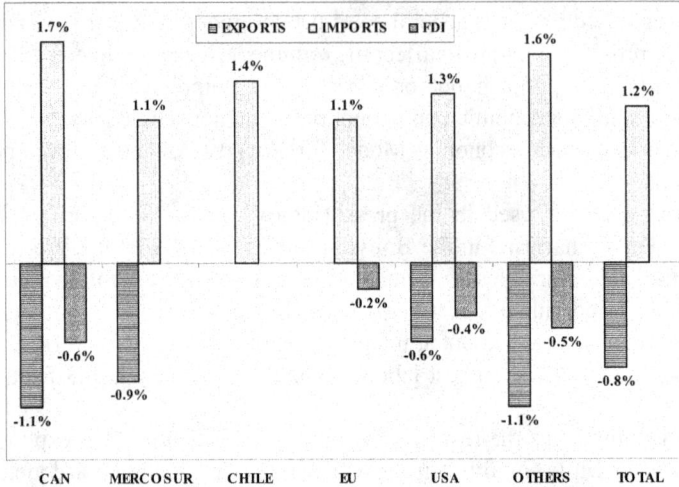

Note: The impacts are calculated as the dF/dX*ln(2), where dF/dX is the marginal effect evaluated at the mean of X (reported by Statas dprobit command) and ln(2)=0.691347 is the change in lnX required to double X.
Source: Authors' estimation. Full probit regression results in Table 3a and 3b in Appendix 6.3.

The relatively small impacts of trade on poverty are due to the structure of labour markets and trade in Bolivia, and in particular to the fact that most poor people are concentrated in traditional agriculture and the non-tradable sectors, which have only very indirect links with trade.

In order to assess the total impact of regional integration on poverty, we would need to multiply the elasticities in Chart 6.18 by the total changes in imports, exports and FDI caused by regional integration. We do not know the latter for sure, but Chart 6.10 suggests that regional integration has caused exports to CAN and MERCOSUR to go up significantly and exports to the US and the EU to go down significantly. The same chart suggests that imports from MERCOSUR have gone up and imports from the EU and the US have gone down. In the case of FDI, Chart 6.15 suggests that it has gone up for MERCOSUR and the EU and down for the US. We can thus construct the following table (Table 6.3) which allows us to assess at least the signs of the impacts on poverty.

Remember that a negative sign is desirable, as it means a reduction in poverty. For example, the increase in exports to CAN and MERCOSUR multiplied by the negative elasticity of exports on poverty, implies a negative (beneficial) effect on poverty. However, this is partially counterbalanced by reductions in exports to the US and by increases in imports which have a positive (adverse) effect on poverty.

In the case of FDI, there appears to be a beneficial effect from more FDI from the EU, but an adverse effect from less FDI from the US. For CAN and MERCOSUR there were no FDI impacts, in the first case because there was no change in quantity and in the second case because the poverty elasticity of FDI was estimated at zero. In total, there may have been a slightly beneficial effect of regional integration on poverty.

Table 6.3   Sign analysis of the poverty impact of regional integration

	change in quantity * elasticity = impact on poverty				
	CAN	MERCOSUR	US	EU	TOTAL
Exports	$+ * \div = \div$	$+ * \div = \div$	$\div * \div = +$	$\div * 0 = 0$	$\div$
Imports	$+ * + = +$	$0 * + = 0$	$\div * + = \div$	$\div * + = \div$	$\div$
FDI	$0 * \div = 0$	$+ * 0 = 0$	$\div * \div = +$	$+ * \div = \div$	0
Total	0	$\div$	$+$	$\div$	$\div$

This poverty analysis is obviously very crude, but it does give an overview of the somewhat mixed effects of regional integration. In the following, we complement it with a more detailed analysis of the impact of trade and FDI on individual salaries and employment.

6.4.2 The structure of production, exports and imports

Although the overall division of economic activity between agriculture, manufacturing and services barely changed during the 10-year period from 1992 to 2002, there were still interesting developments to be observed. For example, Table 6.4 shows that exports from the manufacturing sector increased from 5.6 per cent of GDP in 1992 to 9.9 per cent in 2002. This is hardly due to FDI, of which the manufacturing sector received little, but may have been substantially influenced by trade policies, and especially by the integration agreements with CAN and MERCOSUR.

Table 6.4   Composition of production, exports and imports by economic activity (% of GDP)

Economic Activity	Production			Export			Import		
	1992	1997	2002	1992	1997	2002	1992	1997	2002
Agriculture, Hunting, Forestry and Fishing	15.1	15.2	14.2	0.4	1.3	0.2	0.7	0.7	1.4
Hydrocarbons	4.1	4.4	5.1	2.2	1.2	4.2	0.0	0.0	0.0
Mining	5.8	5.3	4.3	4.9	3.5	2.6	0.0	0.2	0.0
Manufacturing	16.6	16.7	16.5	5.6	8.9	9.9	18.2	21.0	20.9
Food, beverages and tobacco				1.3	3.0	4.8	1.2	1.0	1.4
Basic metals and non-metallic minerals				1.8	2.7	1.9	2.3	2.0	3.3
Other manufacturing industries				0.8	1.1	1.2	4.7	5.8	2.3
Textiles, leather and wearing apparel				0.4	0.6	0.7	0.6	0.5	1.2
Wood and cork				0.9	1.1	0.5	0.0	0.0	0.0
Machinery and equipment				0.3	0.1	0.4	6.3	7.1	6.2
Chemicals, plastics and refined petroleum				0.0	0.2	0.3	2.6	3.6	5.6
Paper, publishing and printing				0.0	0.1	0.0	0.5	0.8	0.9
Services	58.4	58.4	59.9	0.0	0.0	0.0	0.3	0.0	0.0
Total	100.0	100.0	100.0	13.2	15.0	16.8	19.2	22.0	22.3

Source: National Statistical Institute (INE).

The manufacturing sector has become substantially more export-oriented since 1992, when only 30 per cent of production was destined for export; this share is now above 60 per cent. However, the service sector accounts for almost 60 per cent of total economic activity in Bolivia, explaining why trade is likely to have only a limited effect on poverty. Although manufacturing exports have increased impressively, they still account for only about 10 per cent of GDP, and 11 per cent of employment, as will be seen next.

6.4.3 Employment and labour income

The effects of trade and FDI on poverty depend mainly on the labour market. However, Table 6.5 shows that the composition of the labour market hardly changed at all between 1992 and 2002. The service sector still absorbs more than three-quarters of the labour force in the main cities, while the share dedicated to manufacturing has remained constant at just below 20 per cent. At the national level, there were no significant changes, either.

While FDI and regional integration have not apparently affected the structure of the labour market, Table 6.6 shows that they may have had a significant impact on labour incomes in some sectors. For example, the average monthly salary in utilities more than doubled from \$251 in 1992 to \$587 in 2002, while the average in main cities remained constant at \$156. Salaries in the main FDI-receiving sector, hydrocarbons, also increased substantially, from an already high level. In contrast, the average salary in manufacturing fell from \$132/month in 1992 to \$108 in 2002. There thus appears to be a positive relationship between FDI and salary growth.[10]

A large part of the salary increases observed in the sectors receiving FDI appears to be made possible by efficiency gains (or lay-offs in less rosy words). While the average salary in the electricity, gas and water sector, for example, increased by 2.2 per cent per year between 1997 and 2002, the number of people employed in the sector fell by 6.8 per cent per year. Salaries in the hydrocarbon sector also rose at the expense of rapidly falling employment. Indeed, the only sector that managed to raise salaries and employment simultaneously is 'Other services', which mainly covers public services such as education and health.

Chart 6.19 shows the results of a micro-level analysis of exports, imports, and FDI on labour income (see Appendix 6.4 for the full results). The analysis uses individual workers, in contrast to the poverty analysis in Chart 6.18, which used households as the unit of analysis. It thus captures a more direct effect of regional integration. In general, exports have a positive effect on salaries in the exporting sectors, while imports have a negative effect. The effect of FDI is ambiguous.

While exports in general have a positive effect on salaries, the elasticity is largest for the countries with which Bolivia does not have any agreements. This suggests that it is not necessarily an advantage to have trade agreements. It all depends on the type of exports.

Imports have a generally negative effect on salaries in the sectors with which they compete. Imports from CAN and 'Other countries' appear to compete more directly with Bolivian products, as the estimated elasticities are quite large. Imports from the EU, on the other hand, do not appear to have a negative effect on salaries, most probably because these imports are composed mainly of goods which do not compete with Bolivian products.

---

[10] These numbers should be taken as only rough indications because the surveys used were not designed to be representative at the sector level.

Table 6.5   Labour market composition by economic activity: 1992, 1997, 2002 (%)

Economic Activity	Capital Cities			Bolivia		Average Annual Growth	
						Cities	Bolivia
	1992	1997	2002	1997	2002	92–02	97–02
Agriculture	2.1	1.9	3.0	43.2	42.4	8.5	1.0
Hydrocarbons	0.7	0.5	0.2	0.2	0.1	-8.9	-17.0
Mining	1.1	0.8	0.8	1.6	0.9	1.8	-8.2
Manufacturing	19.6	19.8	19.7	11.0	11.4	4.8	2.1
Textiles, leather and wearing apparels	7.7	7.9	6.9	3.9	3.6	3.8	-0.2
Food, beverages and tobacco	4.0	3.1	5.0	2.5	3.3	7.1	7.1
Other manufacturing industries	3.0	3.9	2.9	2.0	1.5	4.3	-4.2
Machinery and equipment	1.4	1.5	1.7	0.7	0.9	6.3	6.7
Basic metals and other non-metallic minerals	1.1	0.9	1.1	0.7	0.9	4.8	6.0
Paper, publishing and printing	1.1	1.4	1.0	0.5	0.4	4.4	-2.1
Chemicals, plastics and refined petroleum	0.8	0.6	0.6	0.3	0.3	1.6	2.4
Wood and cork	0.6	0.6	0.5	0.4	0.5	4.6	5.5
Services	76.5	77.0	76.4	44.0	45.1	4.8	1.9
Electricity, gas and water supply	0.7	0.6	0.3	0.3	0.2	-4.0	-6.8
Construction	9.3	8.9	8.4	5.2	5.5	3.8	2.3
Commerce	25.2	24.4	24.7	14.2	14.4	4.6	1.7
Hotels and restaurants	3.8	5.3	6.9	3.5	4.1	11.2	4.3
Transport, storage and communications	7.1	8.7	7.1	4.8	4.4	4.8	-0.1
Financial intermediation	0.8	1.3	0.8	0.6	0.4	5.3	-3.7
Others services	29.5	27.9	28.0	15.4	16.1	4.3	2.3
Total (millions)	1.0	1.3	1.6	3.6	3.8	4.8	1.4

Source: Authors' estimations based on household surveys by the National Statistical Institute (INE).

Table 6.6   Monthly labour income by economic activity: 1992, 1997, 2002
(Constant 1995 US$)

Economic Activity	Capital Cities			Bolivia		Average Annual Growth (%)	
						Cities	Bolivia
	1992	1997	2002	1997	2002	92–02	97–02
Agriculture	303	389	168	91	54	-5.7	-9.8
Hydrocarbons	359	456	513	445	448	3.6	0.1
Mining	152	214	115	149	118	-2.8	-4.5
Manufacturing	132	143	108	138	101	-1.9	-6.0
Food, beverages and tobacco	99	184	135	153	115	3.2	-5.4
Textiles, leather and wearing apparel	107	94	71	89	66	-4.0	-5.8
Wood and cork	189	138	134	129	124	-3.4	-0.8
Paper, publishing and printing	179	131	131	134	138	-3.1	0.6
Chemicals, plastics and refined petroleum	131	208	233	237	212	6.0	-2.2
Basic metals and other non-metallic minerals	134	259	176	234	141	2.8	-9.6
Machinery and equipment	159	172	97	188	98	-4.8	-12.3
Other manufacturing industries	149	160	96	148	98	-4.3	-8.0
Electricity, gas and water supply	251	483	587	401	447	8.9	2.2
Construction	157	172	129	154	118	-1.9	-5.1
Commerce	131	159	132	151	122	0.0	-4.1
Hotels and restaurants	167	136	111	137	108	-4.0	-4.7
Transport, storage and communications	199	245	172	224	164	-1.5	-6.1
Financial intermediation	338	352	440	321	391	2.7	4.0
Others services	160	181	204	161	182	2.5	2.5
Total	156	180	156	148	118	0.0	-4.4

Source: Authors' estimations based on household surveys by the National Statistical Institute (INE).

Chart 6.19   Estimated impacts of a doubling of exports/imports/FDI on labour income, 2002

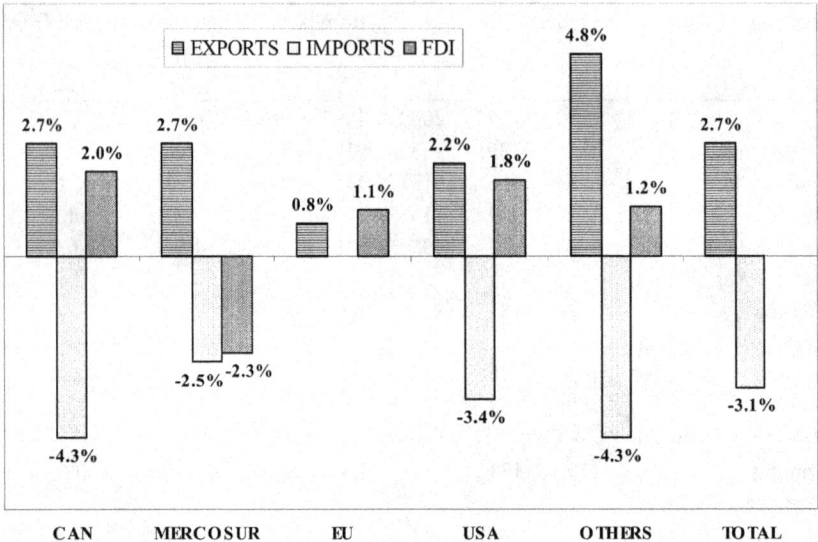

Note: Impact is calculated as $\beta*\ln(2)$, where $\ln(2)$ is the correction factor that should be used for a doubling of X.
Source: Authors' estimation. See full regression results in Tables 4a–4d in Appendix 6.4.

FDI that went into the monopolistic service sectors had a generally positive impact on salaries, but the salary increases were to a large extent made possible by lay-offs in the same sectors. In the case of MERCOSUR, the estimated effect of FDI on salaries is significantly negative. This is because the few employees who enjoyed high salary increases in the hydrocarbons sector were outweighed by the large number of workers in labour-intensive sectors that also received FDI, but which use low salaries as a competitive advantage (manufacturing sectors).

The preceding analysis indicates that it would be very difficult to reduce poverty significantly through trade alone. Although the sectors that have received more FDI, and have increased exports faster, have also seen more rapid reduction in poverty, this has mainly been accomplished by laying off workers in these sectors.

6.5 Conclusion

The present analysis has shown that Bolivia enjoys relatively favourable conditions for access to export markets both in Latin America and in the United States and the

European Union. In practice, however, Bolivia is mainly taking advantage of the regional markets, while exports to the US and the EU have decreased during the past decade or so. Imports have also been diverted away from the traditional suppliers in the US and the EU to new suppliers in MERCOSUR. Thus, while the regional integration processes have contributed to increased trade within the region, overall trade, as a percentage of GDP, has not increased for Bolivia. Even if trade had increased substantially, the effect on poverty would probably have been negligible, since the positive effect of increased exports would be cancelled out by the negative effect of increased imports.

The shift towards regional markets has also implied a change in the composition of exports. Manufacturing products now account for a larger share of exports, and primary goods for a smaller share. This change has an ambiguous effect on workers. The traditional exports to Europe (minerals) had a high content of natural resource rents, which benefited workers. On the other hand, the manufacturing sector tends to use the low wage levels in Bolivia as a competitive advantage, which does not benefit the workers.

Foreign direct investment has concentrated in two main areas: hydrocarbons, to exploit the rapidly growing regional markets, and utilities, to exploit natural monopolies. Very little FDI has gone into manufacturing or agriculture, where most of the poor people are concentrated. Very few people benefited from the rapidly growing salaries in the hydrocarbons sector and in the utilities, implying that FDI had no impact on either salaries or poverty at the aggregate level.

For trade and FDI to have a beneficial effect on household incomes in Bolivia, it would have to concentrate on the labour-intensive sectors that also exploit some natural resource rents. Natural resource rents that are extracted by highly capital-intensive technologies will not benefit the population, while labour-intensive activities without any rents will keep workers on minimum salaries. Examples of sectors that exploit both would be modern agriculture and tourism.

References

Machinea, José Luis, 'Panorama de la inserción internacional de América Latina y el Caribe, 2002–2003' (speech by the Executive Secretary of CEPAL. Santiago, Chile, 12 May 2004).

Nina, Osvaldo and Velde, D.W. te 'Foreign Direct Investment and Development: The case of Bolivia' in *Carta Informativa* 1 (La Paz: Grupo Integral SRL, 2003).

Peñaranda, Carla, 'La Reforma Comercial: Una Evaluación del Caso Bolivianao (1986–1992)' (BA thesis: Universidad Católica Boliviana, La Paz, 1993).

Pöyhönen, Pentti, 'A Tentative Model for the Volume of Trade between Countries', *Weltwirtschaftliches Archiv* 90 (1) (1963): 93–9.

Schiff, Maurice and Winters, Alan, *Regional Integration and Development* (Washington, DC: Oxford University Press for the World Bank, 2003).

Spatz, Julius, 'Creating National Poverty Profiles and Growth Incidence Curves with Incomplete Income or Expenditure Data' (Kiel: Kiel Institute of World Economics, 2004), mimeo.

Uculmana, Peter, *Procesos de Integración* (La Paz: 2003).

Tinbergen, Jan, *Shaping the World Economy: Suggestions for an International Economic Policy* (New York: Twentieth Century Fund, 1962).

World Bank, *Bolivia: Poverty Diagnostic 2000* (Washington, DC: World Bank, 2002)

Appendices

Appendix 6.1 Harmonized Commodity, Description and Coding

Sections	Categories
I	ANIMALS & ANIMAL PRODUCTS
II	VEGETABLE PRODUCTS
III	ANIMAL OR VEGETABLE FATS
IV	PREPARED FOODSTUFFS
V	MINERAL PRODUCTS
VI	CHEMICAL PRODUCTS
VII	PLASTICS & RUBBER
VIII	HIDES, SKINS, LEATHER AND FUR
IX	WOOD & WOOD PRODUCTS
X	WOOD PULP PRODUCTS
XI	TEXTILES & TEXTILE ARTICLES
XII	FOOTWEAR, HEADGEAR
XIII	ARTICLES OF STONE, PLASTER, CEMENT, CERAMIC, GLASS
XIV	PEARLS, PRECIOUS OR SEMI-PRECIOUS STONES, METALS
XV	BASE METALS & ARTICLES THEREOF
XVI	MACHINERY & MECHANICAL APPLIANCES
XVII	TRANSPORTATION EQUIPMENT
XVIII	INSTRUMENTS – MEASURING, MUSICAL
IXX	ARMS & AMMUNITION
XX	MISCELLANEOUS
XXI	WORKS OF ART

Appendix 6.2 Bilateral Investment Treaties

Country	Bilateral Investment Treaty	Entry into force
United Kingdom	Covenant for the Promotion and Reciprocal Protection of Capital Investments, signed in La Paz on 24 May 1988.	16 February 1990
Germany	Treaty on Reciprocal Protection of Capital Investments, signed in La Paz on 23 March 1987.	9 November 1990
Switzerland	Agreement for the Promotion and Reciprocal Protection of Investments, signed in la Paz on 6 November 1987.	13 May 1991

Appendix 6.2 (continued)

Country	Bilateral Investment Treaty	Entry into force
Italy	Agreement for the Promotion and Reciprocal Protection of Investments signed in Rome on 30 April 1990.	22 February 1992
Spain	Agreement for the Promotion and Reciprocal Protection of Investments, signed in Roma on 24 March 1990.	12 May 1992
Sweden	Covenant for the Promotion and Reciprocal Protection of Investments, signed in Stockholm on 20 September 1990.	3 July 1992
People's Republic of China	Covenant for the Promotion and Reciprocal Protection of Investments, signed in Beijing on 8 May 1992.	26 July 1992
Netherlands	Agreement for the Promotion and Reciprocal Protection of Investments, signed in La Paz on 10 March 1992.	1 November 1994
Peru	Covenant for the Promotion and Reciprocal Protection of Investments signed in Ilo on 30 July 1993.	19 March 1995
Argentina	Covenant for the Promotion and Reciprocal Protection of Investments, signed in Buenos Aires on17 March 1994.	1 May 1995
France	Covenant for the Promotion and Reciprocal Protection of Investments, signed in Paris on 25 October 1989.	12 October 1996
Romania	Agreement for the Promotion and Reciprocal Protection of Investments, signed in Bucharest on 9 October 1995.	16 March 1997.
Denmark	Agreement for the Promotion and Reciprocal Protection of Investments, signed in Copenhagen on 12 March, 1995.	23 March 1997
Korea	Covenant for the Promotion and Reciprocal Protection of Investments, signed on 1 April 1996.	4 June 1997
Ecuador	Covenant for the Promotion and Reciprocal Protection of Investments signed in Quito on 25 May 1995.	15 August 1997
Cuba	Covenant for the Promotion and Reciprocal Protection of Investments signed in Havana on 6 May 1995.	23 August 1998

Appendix 6.2 (continued)

Country	Bilateral Investment Treaty	Entry into force
U.S.A.	Covenant for the Promotion and Reciprocal Protection of Investments signed in Santiago de Chile on 17 April 1998.	7 July 2001
Chile	Treaty on Promotion and Reciprocal Protection of Investments signed in La Paz on 22 September 1994.	5 May 1999
Belgium – Luxemburg	Agreement for the Promotion and Reciprocal Protection of Investments, signed in Brussels on 25 April 1990.	The exchange of ratifications did not take place.
Austria	Agreement for the Promotion and Reciprocal Protection of Investments, signed in Vienna on 4 April 1997.	The exchange of ratifications did not take place.
Spain	Agreement for the Promotion and Reciprocal Protection of Investments, signed in Madrid on 29 October 2001.	The exchange of ratifications did not take place.

Source: Ministry of Foreign Trade and Investment.

Appendix 6.3 Probit regression results

Table 3a Impact of regional integration on poverty: 2002

Variable	(1)		(2)		(3)		(4)	
	Coefficient	Standard Deviation	Coefficient	Standard Deviation	Coefficient	Standard Deviation	Coefficient	Standard Deviation
Constant	0.3939	0.2225	0.3418[a]	0.2253	0.3587[a]	0.2245	0.3564[a]	0.2238
Number of children	0.3081	0.0171	0.3115	0.0172	0.3055	0.0171	0.3065	0.0171
Number of children squared	-0.0118	0.0011	-0.0120	0.0011	-0.0117	0.0011	-0.0118	0.0011
Female head	-0.2802	0.0503	-0.2719	0.0504	-0.2691	0.0502	-0.2755	0.0501
Age of the head	-0.0110	0.0013	-0.0107	0.0013	-0.0111	0.0013	-0.0109	0.0013
No spouse for the head	0.6944	0.1996	0.7120	0.2026	0.7122	0.2021	0.7070	0.2015
Native	0.2536	0.0393	0.2513	0.0392	0.2410	0.0390	0.2461	0.0390
Head								
Education	-0.0694	0.0051	-0.0686	0.0051	-0.0686	0.0051	-0.0689	0.0051
Worker	-0.2170	0.0612	-0.1752	0.0625	-0.1918	0.0624	-0.2076	0.0609
Employee	-0.3429	0.0579	-0.3177	0.0588	-0.3258	0.0584	-0.3380	0.0577
Cooperative			0.4856	0.1895	0.4964	0.1920		
Family worker	0.3371	0.1619	0.3300	0.1626	0.3348	0.1607	0.3310	0.1612
Second activity	-0.3240	0.0566	-0.3235	0.0568	-0.3428	0.0561	-0.3343	0.0560

Appendix 6.3 (continued)

Variable	(1) Coefficient	Standard Deviation	(2) Coefficient	Standard Deviation	(3) Coefficient	Standard Deviation	(4) Coefficient	Standard Deviation
Size of firm								
1 to 4 workers	-0.1887	0.0506	-0.1952	0.0509	-0.1962	0.0503	-0.1998	0.0500
5 to 9 workers	-0.1849	0.0738	-0.2005	0.0738	-0.2007	0.0733	-0.2023	0.0730
10 to 14 workers	-0.2630	0.1090	-0.2796	0.1100	-0.2899	0.1087	-0.3089	0.1087
20 to 49 workers	-0.3777	0.0964	-0.3768	0.0958	-0.3883	0.0958	-0.4008	0.0964
50 to 99 workers	-0.4330	0.1496	-0.4375	0.1510	-0.4537	0.1500	-0.4502	0.1489
more than 99	-0.3666	0.1061	-0.4140	0.1151	-0.4146	0.1147	-0.3699	0.1058
Spouse								
Education	-0.0193	0.0054	-0.0193	0.0054	-0.0182	0.0054	-0.0187	0.0054
Employee	-0.3731	0.0816	-0.3680	0.0817	-0.3683	0.0818	-0.3658	0.0816
Family Worker	0.4007	0.0706	0.3951	0.0708	0.3876	0.0692	0.3927	0.0691
Size of firm								
1 to 4 workers	-0.1345	0.0503	-0.1363	0.0505	-0.1339	0.0503	-0.1343	0.0504
Rural	-0.0980	0.0489	-0.1034	0.0489				
Traditional agriculture	0.5433	0.0739	0.5681	0.0741	0.4979	0.0698	0.4956	0.0695
Ln (Total Exports)	-0.0306	0.0116						
Ln (Total Imports)	0.0467	0.0113						
Ln (Exports to CAN)			-0.0408	0.0105				

Appendix 6.3 (continued)

Variable	(1) Coefficient	(1) Standard Deviation	(2) Coefficient	(2) Standard Deviation	(3) Coefficient	(3) Standard Deviation	(4) Coefficient	(4) Standard Deviation
Ln (Imports to CAN)			0.0661	0.0111				
Ln (Exports to MERCOSUR)					-0.0361	0.0121		
Ln (Imports from MERCOSUR)					0.0424	0.0093		
Ln (Exports to Chile)							-0.0069[a]	0.0132
Ln (Imports from Chile)							0.0516	0.0130
Observations	5746		5746		5746		5746	
Pseudo R2	0.2450		0.2473		0.2451		0.2451	

Note: a) Not significant at 10%

Table 3b   Impact of regional integration on poverty: 2002

Variable	(5) Coefficient	(5) Standard Deviation	(6) Coefficient	(6) Standard Deviation	(7) Coefficient	(7) Standard Deviation	(8) Coefficient	(8) Standard Deviation
Constant	0.3810	0.2234	0.3852	0.2225	0.3544[a]	0.2241	0.3379[a]	0.2243
Number of children	0.3082	0.0171	0.3051	0.0171	0.3090	0.0172	0.3087	0.0171
Number of children squared	-0.0117	0.0011	-0.0118	0.0011	-0.0120	0.0011	-0.0119	0.0011
Female head	-0.2782	0.0502	-0.2771	0.0502	-0.2676	0.0502	-0.2757	0.0504

Appendix 6.3 (continued)

Variable	(5) Coefficient	(5) Standard Deviation	(6) Coefficient	(6) Standard Deviation	(7) Coefficient	(7) Standard Deviation	(8) Coefficient	(8) Standard Deviation
Age of the head	-0.0109	0.0013	-0.0111	0.0013	-0.0108	0.0013	-0.0109	0.0013
No spouse for the head	0.7005	0.2010	0.7047	0.2001	0.7020	0.2013	0.7044	0.1999
Native	0.2450	0.0389	0.2454	0.0390	0.2529	0.0393	0.2451	0.0392
Head								
Education	-0.0703	0.0051	-0.0696	0.0051	-0.0684	0.0051	-0.0692	0.0051
Worker	-0.2044	0.0610	-0.2159	0.0612	-0.1860	0.0620	-0.2131	0.0613
Employee	-0.3475	0.0577	-0.3441	0.0576	-0.3130	0.0584	-0.3327	0.0578
Cooperative					0.3964	0.1876		
Family worker	0.3483	0.1619	0.3406	0.1608	0.3462	0.1627	0.3552	0.1627
Second activity	-0.3277	0.0561	-0.3395	0.0560	-0.3298	0.0568	-0.3424	0.0560
Size of firm								
1 to 4 workers	-0.1870	0.0498	-0.1960	0.0501	-0.1879	0.0507	-0.1945	0.0502
5 to 9 workers	-0.1821	0.0730	-0.1891	0.0733	-0.1948	0.0737	-0.1918	0.0737
10 to 14 workers	-0.2769	0.1096	-0.2677	0.1084	-0.2861	0.1090	-0.2462	0.1092
20 to 49 workers	-0.3801	0.0968	-0.3810	0.0961	-0.3929	0.0961	-0.3805	0.0962
50 to 99 workers	-0.4271	0.1494	-0.4424	0.1490	-0.4589	0.1501	-0.4306	0.1504
more than 99	-0.3623	0.1083	-0.3506	0.1066	-0.4480	0.1150	-0.3552	0.1071

Appendix 6.3 (continued)

Variable	(5)		(6)		(7)		(8)	
	Coefficient	Standard Deviation	Coefficient	Standard Deviation	Coefficient	Standard Deviation	Coefficient	Standard Deviation
Spouse								
Education	-0.0189	0.0054	-0.0186	0.0054	-0.0195	0.0054	-0.0184	0.0054
Employee	-0.3711	0.0821	-0.3701	0.0817	-0.3680	0.0817	-0.3667	0.0818
Family worker	0.4143	0.0686	0.3944	0.0689	0.3966	0.0707	0.3939	0.0694
Size of firm								
1 to 4 workers	-0.1388	0.0502	-0.1328	0.0502	-0.1299	0.0503	-0.1333	0.0502
Other urban areas							0.0856	0.0433
Rural					-0.1132	0.0489		
Traditional agriculture	0.4552	0.0674	0.4798	0.0692	0.5713	0.0738	0.5043	0.0700
Ln (Exports to Mexico)	-0.0075[a]	0.0109						
Ln (Imports from Mexico)	0.0820	0.0186						
Ln (Exports to Europe Union)			-0.0074[a]	0.0087				
Ln (Imports from Europe Union)			0.0412	0.0121				
Ln (Exports to United States)					-0.0218	0.0110		
Ln (Imports from United States)					0.0511	0.0112		
Ln (Exports to Others)							-0.0425	0.0119
Ln (Imports from Others)							0.0598	0.0121

Appendix 6.3 (continued)

Variable	(5) Coefficient	Standard Deviation	(6) Coefficient	Standard Deviation	(7) Coefficient	Standard Deviation	(8) Coefficient	Standard Deviation
Observations	5746		5746		5746		5746	
Pseudo R2	0.2447		0.2438		0.2458		0.2456	

Note: a) Not significant at 10%

Table 3c   Impact of regional integration on poverty: 2002

Variable	(1) Coefficient	Standard Deviation	(2) Coefficient	Standard Deviation	(3) Coefficient	Standard Deviation	(4) Coefficient	Standard Deviation
Constant	0.4878	0.2248	0.4049703	0.221674	0.456862	0.223507	0.459711	0.223109
Number of children	0.3089	0.0172	0.3025	0.0168	0.3081	0.0171	0.3081	0.0171
Number of children squared	-0.0118	0.0011	-0.0116	0.0011	-0.0117	0.0011	-0.0117	0.0011
Female head	-0.2911	0.0504	-0.2846	0.0502	-0.2856	0.0504	-0.2865	0.0502
Age of the head	-0.0112	0.0013	-0.0111	0.0013	-0.0111	0.0013	-0.0111	0.0013
No spouse for the head	0.6929	0.2009	0.7058	0.2013	0.6924	0.2005	0.6931	0.2005
Native Head	0.2556	0.0392	0.2515	0.0392	0.2540	0.0392	0.2542	0.0392
Education	-0.0723	0.0051	-0.0722	0.0051	-0.0715	0.0051	-0.0716	0.0051

Appendix 6.3 (continued)

Variable	(1) Coefficient	Standard Deviation	(2) Coefficient	Standard Deviation	(3) Coefficient	Standard Deviation	(4) Coefficient	Standard Deviation
Worker	-0.2067	0.0621	-0.2214	0.0609	-0.2224	0.0622	-0.2201	0.0615
Employee	-0.3544	0.0576	-0.3822	0.0549	-0.3483	0.0575	-0.3493	0.0573
Family worker	0.3342	0.1620	0.2984	0.1611	0.3382	0.1624	0.3379	0.1624
Second activity	-0.3267	0.0564	-0.3338	0.0562	-0.3271	0.0564	-0.3265	0.0564
Size of firm								
1 to 4 workers	-0.1245	0.0514			-0.1309	0.0512	-0.1304	0.0511
5 to 9 workers	-0.1360	0.0736			-0.1447	0.0733	-0.1439	0.0732
10 to 14 workers	-0.2361	0.1083			-0.2466	0.1082	-0.2456	0.1081
20 to 49 workers	-0.3583	0.0957	-0.2545	0.0884	-0.3670	0.0956	-0.3664	0.0956
50 to 99 workers	-0.3981	0.1478	-0.2974	0.1431	-0.4113	0.1478	-0.4101	0.1476
more than 99	-0.3652	0.1026	-0.2950	0.0958	-0.3858	0.1009	-0.3867	0.1008
Spouse								
Education	-0.0180	0.0054	-0.0187	0.0054	-0.0182	0.0054	-0.0182	0.0054
Employee	-0.4019	0.0821	-0.4047	0.0825	-0.3980	0.0819	-0.3981	0.0819
Family worker	0.4154	0.0701	0.3860	0.0693	0.4177	0.0702	0.4180	0.0702
Size of firm								
1 to 4 workers	-0.1241	0.0505	-0.1202	0.0500	-0.1279	0.0506	-0.1277	0.0506
Rural	-0.1062	0.0492	-0.1416	0.0488	-0.1032	0.0492	-0.1029	0.0493
Traditional agriculture	0.4062	0.0729	0.4052	0.0700	0.4347	0.0716	0.4313	0.0700
Trade & commerce	-0.1508	0.0619	-0.1718	0.0596	-0.1275	0.0608	-0.1301	0.0597
Transport	-0.2182	0.0805	-0.2320	0.0790	-0.2056	0.0808	-0.2088	0.0798

Appendix 6.3 (continued)

Variable	(1)		(2)		(3)		(4)	
	Coefficient	Standard Deviation	Coefficient	Standard Deviation	Coefficient	Standard Deviation	Coefficient	Standard Deviation
Ln (Total FDI)	-0.0061[a]	0.0046						
Ln (FDI CAN)			-0.0220	0.0095				
Ln (FDI MERCOSUR)					0.0013[a]	0.0054		
Ln (FDI Chile)							0.0024[a]	0.0165
Pseudo R2	0.2440		0.2431		0.2437		0.2437	
Observations	5746		5746		5746		5746	

Note: a) Not significant at 10%. FDI: Foreign Direct Investment

Table 3d Impact of regional integration on poverty: 2002

Variable	(5)		(6)		(7)		(8)	
	Coefficient	Standard Deviation	Coefficient	Standard Deviation	Coefficient	Standard Deviation	Coefficient	Standard Deviation
Constant	0.459196	0.223158	0.4251798	0.222619	0.4834216	0.224229	0.4294305	0.222754
Number of children	0.3083	0.0171	0.3038	0.0169	0.3095	0.0172	0.3051	0.0169
Number of children squared	-0.0117	0.0011	-0.0117	0.0011	-0.0118	0.0011	-0.0118	0.0011
Female head	-0.2860	0.0502	-0.2828	0.0502	-0.2916	0.0504	-0.2864	0.0502
Age of the head	-0.0111	0.0013	-0.0112	0.0013	-0.0112	0.0013	-0.0112	0.0013

Appendix 6.3 (continued)

Variable	(5)		(6)		(7)		(8)	
	Coefficient	Standard Deviation	Coefficient	Standard Deviation	Coefficient	Standard Deviation	Coefficient	Standard Deviation
No spouse for the head	0.6934	0.2005	0.6972	0.2013	0.6940	0.2006	0.6976	0.2018
Native	0.2547	0.0392	0.2537	0.0392	0.2562	0.0393	0.2515	0.0393
Head								
Education	-0.0715	0.0051	-0.0721	0.0051	-0.0719	0.0051	-0.0723	0.0051
Worker	-0.2201	0.0615	-0.2296	0.0602	-0.2011	0.0621	-0.2074	0.0612
Employee	-0.3479	0.0574	-0.4036	0.0546	-0.3594	0.0579	-0.3945	0.0550
Family worker	0.3366	0.1623	0.3098	0.1611	0.3301	0.1623		
Second activity	-0.3269	0.0564	-0.3345	0.0561	-0.3252	0.0565	-0.3366	0.0563
Size of firm								
1 to 4 workers	-0.1315	0.0511			-0.1261	0.0512		
5 to 9 workers	-0.1431	0.0733			-0.1364	0.0735		
10 to 14 workers	-0.2472	0.1081			-0.2359	0.1084		
20 to 49 workers	-0.3680	0.0956	-0.2240	0.0881	-0.3561	0.0957	-0.2470	0.0884
50 to 99 workers	-0.4114	0.1476			-0.3900	0.1478	-0.2991	0.1420
more than 99	-0.3884	0.1009	-0.2127	0.0972	-0.3613	0.1020	-0.2438	0.0960
Spouse								
Education	-0.0182	0.0054	-0.0187	0.0054	-0.0182	0.0054	-0.0182	0.0054
Employee	-0.3989	0.0819	-0.4121	0.0828	-0.4042	0.0822	-0.4149	0.0823
Family Worker	0.4176	0.0702	0.3786	0.0694	0.4081	0.0703	0.3775	0.0693
Size of firm								
1 to 4 workers	-0.1274	0.0505	-0.1164	0.0500	-0.1223	0.0506	-0.1120	0.0497

Appendix 6.3 (continued)

Variable	(5)		(6)		(7)		(8)	
	Coefficient	Standard Deviation	Coefficient	Standard Deviation	Coefficient	Standard Deviation	Coefficient	Standard Deviation
Rural	-0.1035	0.0492	-0.1404	0.0488	-0.1109	0.0495	-0.1320	0.0485
Traditional agriculture	0.4320	0.0700	0.3928	0.0704	0.4162	0.0707	0.3863	0.0708
Trade & commerce	-0.1262	0.0599	-0.1842	0.0601	-0.1493	0.0609	-0.1855	0.0600
Transport	-0.2081	0.0798	-0.2621	0.0805	-0.2228	0.0809	-0.2471	0.0790
Ln (FDI Mexico)	-0.1132[a]	0.1090						
Ln (FDI United States)			-0.0165	0.0056				
Ln (FDI Europe Union)					-0.0094	0.0052		
Ln (FDI others)							-0.0179	0.0056
Pseudo R2	0.2438		0.2430		0.2442		0.2432	
Observations	5746		5746		5746		5746	

Note: a) Not significant at 10%. FDI: Foreign Direct Investment

Appendix 6.4 Earnings Regression Results

Table 4a   Impact of regional integration on labour income: 2002

Variable	(1)		(2)		(3)		(4)	
	Coefficient	Standard Deviation	Coefficient	Standard Deviation	Coefficient	Standard Deviation	Coefficient	Standard Deviation
Constant	4.7675	0.0950	4.8386	0.0908	4.7552	0.0878	4.7432	0.0890
Age	0.0803	0.0040	0.0798	0.0040	0.0802	0.0040	0.0812	0.0040
Age square	-0.0009	0.0000	-0.0009	0.0000	-0.0009	0.0000	-0.0009	0.0000
Education	0.0529	0.0030	0.0533	0.0029	0.0529	0.0030	0.0536	0.0030
Gender	-0.4118	0.0272	-0.4058	0.0272	-0.4141	0.0272	-0.4136	0.0274
Public institution	0.0907	0.0357	0.0912	0.0356	0.0918	0.0356	0.0917	0.0357
Self-employed	-0.5571	0.0285	-0.5444	0.0286	-0.5532	0.0285	-0.5624	0.0285
Cooperative	-0.2591	0.1077	-0.4128	0.1123	-0.3969	0.1157		
Family worker	-0.5570	0.1030	-0.5415	0.1028	-0.5545	0.1031	-0.5726	0.1033
Native	-0.2881	0.0216	-0.2822	0.0215	-0.2825	0.0215	-0.2834	0.0216
Other urban areas	-0.0778	0.0259	-0.0829	0.0259	-0.0769	0.0259	-0.0785	0.0258
Rural	-0.3078	0.0310	-0.3154	0.0310	-0.3142	0.0310	-0.3137	0.0316
Traditional agriculture	-0.6443	0.0708	-0.7177	0.0634	-0.6316	0.0596	-0.6312	0.0608
Electricity	0.4732	0.1499	0.4263	0.1469	0.5145	0.1458	0.4986	0.1472
Construction	0.2699	0.0647	0.2006	0.0557	0.2804	0.0510	0.2732	0.0541

Appendix 6.4 (continued)

Variable	(1) Coefficient	Standard Deviation	(2) Coefficient	Standard Deviation	(3) Coefficient	Standard Deviation	(4) Coefficient	Standard Deviation
Trade & commerce	0.3142	0.0667	0.2346	0.0589	0.3240	0.0532	0.3209	0.0583
Hotels & restaurants	0.4783	0.0777	0.4008	0.0711	0.4898	0.0664	0.4856	0.0706
Transport	0.4632	0.0705	0.3912	0.0625	0.4729	0.0580	0.4657	0.0615
Banking	0.6036	0.1449	0.5327	0.1414	0.6168	0.1391	0.6025	0.1410
Services	0.1815	0.0643	0.1100	0.0563	0.1941	0.0505	0.1804	0.0562
Ln (Total Exports)	0.0386	0.0076						
Ln (Total Imports)	-0.0451	0.0087						
Ln (Exports CAN)			0.0383	0.0072				
Ln (Imports CAN)			-0.0628	0.0090				
Ln (Exports to MERCOSUR)					0.0383	0.0076		
Ln (Imports from MERCOSUR)					-0.0359	0.0068		
Ln (Exports to Chile)							-0.0124[a]	0.0085
Ln (Imports from Chile)							-0.0132[a]	0.0085
Observations	7941		7941		7941		7941	
F-statistic	249.33		250.96		248.15		259.97	
R-squared	0.4160		0.4184		0.4161		0.4139	

Note: a) Not significant at 10%

Appendix 6.4 (continued)

Table 4b   Impact of regional integration on labour income: 2002

Variable	(5) Coefficient	Standard Deviation	(6) Coefficient	Standard Deviation	(7) Coefficient	Standard Deviation	(8) Coefficient	Standard Deviation
Constant	4.6383	0.0840	4.6678	0.0894	4.7915	0.0893	4.7111	0.0869
Age	0.0803	0.0040	0.0805	0.0040	0.0805	0.0040	0.0794	0.0040
Age square	0.0009	0.0000	-0.0009	0.0000	-0.0009	0.0000	-0.0009	0.0000
Education	0.0525	0.0030	0.0532	0.0030	0.0526	0.0030	0.0532	0.0029
Gender	-0.4208	0.0271	-0.4141	0.0272	-0.4243	0.0271	-0.4066	0.0270
Public institution	0.0932	0.0356	0.0949	0.0357	0.0908	0.0357	0.0962	0.0356
Self-employed	-0.5548	0.0285	-0.5562	0.0286	-0.5519	0.0286	-0.5343	0.0285
Cooperative	-0.3424	0.1167			-0.3365	0.1105	-0.4077	0.1117
Family worker	-0.5509	0.1032	-0.5621	0.1032	-0.5418	0.1030	-0.5349	0.1034
Native	-0.2870	0.0217	-0.2869	0.0216	-0.2863	0.0216	-0.2810	0.0216
Other urban areas	-0.0767	0.0261	-0.0814	0.0258	-0.0749	0.0259	-0.0872	0.0259
Rural	-0.2970	0.0321	-0.3083	0.0313	-0.2927	0.0310	-0.3241	0.0312
Traditional agriculture	-0.5263	0.0516	-0.5480	0.0608	-0.6901	0.0621	-0.5808	0.0597
Electricity	0.6325	0.1442	0.5940	0.1470	0.4740	0.1474	0.5269	0.1441
Construction	0.3969	0.0438	0.3647	0.0538	0.2370	0.0538	0.3365	0.0520
Trade & commerce	0.4465	0.0463	0.4104	0.0559	0.2873	0.0567	0.3662	0.0541
Hotels & restaurants	0.6125	0.0611	0.5756	0.0685	0.4545	0.0692	0.5345	0.0670
Transport	0.5917	0.0519	0.5578	0.0607	0.4313	0.0607	0.5257	0.0589
Banking	0.7380	0.1370	0.6973	0.1402	0.5799	0.1404	0.6703	0.1397

Appendix 6.4 (continued)

Variable	(5) Coefficient	Standard Deviation	(6) Coefficient	Standard Deviation	(7) Coefficient	Standard Deviation	(8) Coefficient	Standard Deviation
Services	0.3132	0.0449	0.2732	0.0537	0.1577	0.0540	0.2467	0.0517
Ln (Exports to Mexico)	0.0379	0.0080						
Ln (Imports from Mexico)	-0.0151[a]	0.0111						
Ln (Exports to Europe Union)			0.0120	0.0060				
Ln (Imports to Europe Union)			-0.0136[a]	0.0085				
Ln (Exports to United States)					0.0313	0.0069		
Ln (Imports from United States)					-0.0491	0.0090		
Ln (Exports to others)							0.0691	0.0079
Ln (Imports from others)							-0.0618	0.0081
Observations	7941		7941		7941		7941	
F-statistic	247.87		259.68		248.23		251.19	
R-squared	0.4151		0.4139		0.4164		0.4199	

Note: a) Not significant at 10%

Appendix 6.4 (continued)

Table 4c   Impact of regional integration on labour income: 2002

Variable	(1)		(2)		(3)		(4)	
	Coefficient	Standard Deviation	Coefficient	Standard Deviation	Coefficient	Standard Deviation	Coefficient	Standard Deviation
Constant	4.6627	0.0833	4.6425	0.0822	4.6953	0.0818	4.6553	0.0821
Age	0.0810	0.0040	0.0809	0.0040	0.0808	0.0039	0.0810	0.0040
Age square	-0.0009	0.0000	-0.0009	0.0000	-0.0009	0.0000	-0.0009	0.0000
Education	0.0531	0.0030	0.0533	0.0030	0.0532	0.0030	0.0528	0.0030
Gender	-0.4188	0.0271	-0.4174	0.0270	-0.4243	0.0269	-0.4172	0.0270
Public institution	0.0920	0.0357	0.0907	0.0357	0.1006	0.0358	0.0954	0.0357
Self-employed	-0.5655	0.0291	-0.5570	0.0285	-0.5687	0.0284	-0.5624	0.0285
Family worker	-0.5719	0.1032	-0.5652	0.1034	-0.5464	0.1031	-0.5695	0.1032
Native	-0.2846	0.0215	-0.2829	0.0216	-0.2816	0.0214	-0.2846	0.0215
Other urban areas	-0.0756	0.0256	-0.0745	0.0256	-0.0726	0.0256	-0.0739	0.0256
Rural	-0.3021	0.0309	-0.2969	0.0309	-0.2830	0.0310	-0.2980	0.0310
Traditional agriculture	-0.5539	0.0503	-0.5452	0.0490	-0.6071	0.0490	-0.5498	0.0490
Electricity	0.5931	0.1444	0.6047	0.1420	0.7186	0.1408	0.5967	0.1423
Construction	0.3657	0.0491	0.2018	0.0564	0.6834	0.0701	0.3660	0.0377
Trade & commerce	0.4110	0.0400	0.4180	0.0394	0.3866	0.0393	0.4143	0.0393
Hotels & restaurants	0.5795	0.0577	0.5885	0.0563	0.5426	0.0564	0.5821	0.0563
Transport	0.5541	0.0462	0.5304	0.0458	0.5309	0.0460	0.5534	0.0461

Appendix 6.4 (continued)

Variable	(1) Coefficient	Standard Deviation	(2) Coefficient	Standard Deviation	(3) Coefficient	Standard Deviation	(4) Coefficient	Standard Deviation
Banking	0.6956	0.1345	0.5986	0.1362	0.7651	0.1373	0.6468	0.1355
Services	0.2698	0.0390	0.2852	0.0376	0.2499	0.0374	0.2761	0.0376
Ln (Total FDI)	-0.0007[a]	0.0037						
Ln (FDI CAN)			0.0289	0.0076				
Ln (FDI MERCOSUR)					-0.0326	0.0056		
Ln (FDI Chile)							0.0149[a]	0.0091
Observations	7941		7941		7941		7941	
F-statistic	273.16		273.97		274		273.53	
R-squared	0.4134		0.4142		0.4164		0.4136	

Note: a) Not significant at 10%. FDI: Foreign Direct Investment

Table 4d Impact of regional integration on labour income: 2002

Variable	(5) Coefficient	Standard Deviation	(6) Coefficient	Standard Deviation	(7) Coefficient	Standard Deviation	(8) Coefficient	Standard Deviation
Constant	4.6599	0.0820	4.6569	0.0820	4.6409	0.0820	4.6406	0.0824
Age	0.0810	0.0040	0.0804	0.0040	0.0805	0.0040	0.0804	0.0040
Age square	-0.0009	0.0000	-0.0009	0.0000	-0.0009	0.0000	-0.0009	0.0000

Appendix 6.4 (continued)

Variable	(5) Coefficient	Standard Deviation	(6) Coefficient	Standard Deviation	(7) Coefficient	Standard Deviation	(8) Coefficient	Standard Deviation
Education	0.0531	0.0030	0.0526	0.0030	0.0522	0.0029	0.0529	0.0030
Gender	-0.4184	0.0270	-0.4155	0.0270	-0.4097	0.0271	-0.4132	0.0272
Public institution	0.0923	0.0357	0.0994	0.0358	0.0978	0.0357	0.1022	0.0357
Self-employed	-0.5641	0.0284	-0.5496	0.0289	-0.5449	0.0289	-0.5453	0.0289
Cooperative					-0.2892	0.1093		
Family worker	-0.5714	0.1032	-0.5601	0.1032	-0.5566	0.1034	-0.5577	0.1034
Native	-0.2847	0.0215	-0.2876	0.0216	-0.2860	0.0216	-0.2861	0.0215
Other urban areas	-0.0756	0.0256	-0.0809	0.0257	-0.0748	0.0258	-0.0838	0.0258
Rural	-0.3021	0.0309	-0.3031	0.0309	-0.2998	0.0309	-0.3086	0.0310
Traditional agriculture	-0.5515	0.0490	-0.5410	0.0491	-0.5372	0.0491	-0.5265	0.0495
Electricity	0.5891	0.1418	0.4478	0.1492	0.3728	0.1477	0.6243	0.1423
Construction	0.3604	0.0375	0.1937	0.0664	0.1367	0.0571	0.2203	0.0565
Trade & commerce	0.4121	0.0395	0.4197	0.0394	0.4176	0.0395	0.4292	0.0395
Hotels & restaurants	0.5775	0.0562	0.5439	0.0571	0.4253	0.0627	0.5871	0.0562
Transport	0.5551	0.0461	0.5580	0.0460	0.5555	0.0464	0.5559	0.0458
Banking	0.6956	0.1344	0.6453	0.1347	0.6353	0.1364	0.6616	0.1349
Services	0.2722	0.0373	0.2866	0.0378	0.2882	0.0378	0.2962	0.0381
Ln (FDI Mexico)	0.0210[a]	0.0274						
Ln (FDI United States)			0.0157	0.0050				
Ln (FDI Europe Union)					0.0267	0.0050		
Ln (FDI others)							0.0166	0.0049

Appendix 6.4 (continued)

Variable	(5)		(6)		(7)		(8)	
	Coefficient	Standard Deviation	Coefficient	Standard Deviation	Coefficient	Standard Deviation	Coefficient	Standard Deviation
Observations	7941		7941		7941		7941	
F-statistic	274.10		273.55		260.68		273.10	
R-squared	0.4134		0.4141		0.4154		0.4143	

Note: a) Not significant at 10%. FDI: Foreign Direct Investment

Chapter 7

Regional Integration and Poverty: The Case of Tanzania

Josaphat Kweka and Phillip Gaspar Mboya

7.1 Introduction

One of the critical challenges facing Tanzania is how to improve the country's economic competitiveness and increase its share of global trade in order to achieve the poverty reduction targets. Among the various strategies adopted to overcome this problem, Tanzania has joined a number of regional economic groupings including the East African Community (EAC), the Southern African Development Community (SADC), the Common Market for Eastern and Central African States (COMESA)[1] and the Cross Border Initiative (CBI).[2] But Tanzania is not alone in adopting this strategy. Many countries have grouped together to form, expand or strengthen various regional integration agreements (RIAs) in the past decade or so. In addition, the efficacy of such agreements in revamping the integration of the developing countries in the global economy and subsequently their impact in reducing poverty have become important subjects of analysis. Many recognize that regional integration forms an important part of the strategy for developing countries to achieve a 'smooth and gradual' integration into the world economy (Kennes, 1997). An ensuing question is whether and how Regional Integration Agreements (RIAs) have affected poverty in a low-income country like Tanzania.

The literature admits that the precise pathways through which the formation of regional groupings affects poverty are somewhat indirect – through trade, investment and other regional socio-economic cooperation. A theoretical framework mapping these links has been proposed by te Velde, Page and Morrissey (2004). The empirical literature has tended to address each channel separately; research on the investment channel, for instance, has examined how the investment and trade-related provisions in the RIAs affect poverty (see te Velde and Fahnbulleh, 2003), the impact of regional integration (RI) on FDI (te Velde and Bezemer, 2004; Bende-Nabende, 2003), and the impact of trade on poverty (Winters, 2000). The literature for Tanzania is limited. A few current studies

---

[1] Tanzania withdrew from COMESA in 2000.
[2] The CBI changed its name in 2000 to Regional Integration Facilitation Forum.

consider the impact of regional integration on the Tanzanian economy more generally and trade in particular, without a focus on poverty (see Musonda, 2000, 2004). Others have examined the impact of trade on poverty (see Booth and Kweka, 2004), or the impact of investment on the economy (see, for example, Madete, 2000; Mboya, 2003; Mashindano, 2004) without reference to RI processes. The study by Wanga and Matambalya (2001) examines the impact of RI on poverty in the SADC economies, with a minor focus on trade and investment provisions.

The present study examines regional integration and poverty in Tanzania. In particular, its objective is to assess how regional integration has affected poverty in Tanzania according to the following links:

- RI can affect poverty through the increased volume and poverty focus of trade

- RI can affect poverty through the increased volume and poverty focus of investment

- RI can affect poverty through other routes.

The regions covered include the EAC and the SADC, but where possible other relevant RI efforts as well.[3] Since the study focuses on the trade and investment provisions of the RIAs of which Tanzania is a member, it is in no way a comprehensive assessment of the link between regional integration and poverty. In addition, Tanzania has implemented a number of policy reforms aimed at improving its trade and investment regime independent of the regional integration process (see Appendices 7.1 and 7.2).

The chapter is organized as follows. The theoretical framework and methodology used for the study are summarized in Section 7.2 (see te Velde *et al.*, 2004). Section 7.3 describes the status of regional integration processes by identifying the challenges and prospects of RIAs for Tanzania, namely, the EAC, SADC, COMESA and others (for example, the CBI and other multilateral initiatives). Section 7.4 examines the investment links between regional integration and poverty, while section 7.5 covers the trade links. Through a survey of a sample of firms, Section 7.5 also provides industry perspectives on the efficacy of intra-regional trade and investment in poverty reduction. Other routes through which RI affects poverty are examined in Section 7.6, paying attention to the various socio-

---

[3]   In some aspects of this analysis, we also cover COMESA for comparison purposes, although Tanzania withdrew from the organization in 2000. This is important for two reasons. First, Tanzania remained in COMESA long enough to warrant examination of its effectiveness in poverty reduction. Second, some members of EAC and SADC are also members of COMESA, which will have an inherent impact on the analysis. And finally, analysts still argue for Tanzania to reconsider its decision to withdraw.

economic programmes implemented in a regional context. Finally Section 7.7 concludes.

7.2 Analytical framework and methodology

7.2.1 The analytical framework

There are both analytical and methodological challenges in examining the impact of RI on poverty for a low-income country such as Tanzania. First, regional integration is still in the formative stages in most aspects; there is therefore a lack of evidence. For instance, the Customs Union (CU) as part of the RI process is less than a year old in the EAC and not yet fully operational, while the SADC plans to establish a free trade area in 2008. Second, low-income countries often suffer from a serious lack of reliable data to perform meaningful analysis. Third, members of a Regional Integration Agreement may choose to cooperate on other aspects of social importance, which are eventually difficult to measure. For instance, Tanzania's objective in joining SADC was based less on economic integration than on socio-political cooperation as compared with COMESA or the EAC. Finally, there are many factors other than RI that affect development or poverty reduction, such as, for example, changes in social norms or behaviours, the increased effectiveness of institutions, and natural resources endowment. These factors impair a credible analysis of how RI has affected poverty in the context of Tanzania. Therefore, the analytical framework (according to Chapters 2–4 in Part 1 of this book) will be applied with caution.

7.2.2 Methodology

In general, due to the limitations identified above, analyses and evidence provided for the link between RI and poverty use a number of approaches; (i) use of both secondary and primary data and information; (ii) interviews with key stakeholders in RIAs (for example, firms and institutions); and (iii) information from the literature and related studies on Tanzania.

Secondary data from published and national sources were used to examine both the performance and the poverty focus of intra- and extra-regional investment and trade. Where data are available, correlations of FDI and trade with poverty indicators are made to examine the impact of RI. Disaggregation of the RI effect is constrained by the limited availability of data, necessitating the use of total (intra- and extra-regional) figures to indicate potential impact. This may not cause problems, given the fact that most RI investment and trade provisions are a long way from being effectively operational. The general impacts are therefore likely to be good proxies for regional impacts. Secondary information from documents was used to identify other routes through which RI affects poverty in Tanzania. Primary data were collected from a sample of 30 firms in three regions surveyed to investigate trade and FDI impact and prospects for Tanzania. We consider it important to have information 'from the horse's mouth' and to evaluate, using semi-structured questionnaires, investors' confidence and opinions on RI and its efficacy for reducing poverty.

We also interviewed a number of stakeholders to obtain a qualitative assessment of how RI affects poverty in Tanzania. Interviews were held with investors and with a number of institutions managing the RI process in Tanzania. These included government departments, the Tanzania Investment Centre, the EAC Secretariat and the SADC coordinating officer, as well as the Bank of Tanzania, beneficiaries and managers of regional socio-economic projects (for example, NGOs, the Fisheries department of Lake Victoria, and the East African Development Bank). Top private sector bodies, such as the Tanzania Chamber of Commerce Industry and Agriculture (TCCIA) and the Confederation of Tanzania Industries (CTI) were also interviewed for similar purposes.

As already noted, there are a number of studies of Tanzania that address different and partial aspects of the analytical framework. The three approaches of the methodology are interdependent in modelling the link between RI and poverty in the circumstances of Tanzania. For instance, stakeholders provided secondary data for analysis, while the literature also reports evidence from survey data.

7.3 Regional integration and the poverty reduction challenge for Tanzania

As a background to the subsequent sections, this section describes the current status and challenges of various Regional Integration Agreements and highlights the Poverty Reduction Strategy (PRS) for Tanzania. A description of RIAs will show their variations in terms of focus, integration process and challenges for poverty reduction. More importantly, and subject to the available information, we shall identify, for each RIA, any trade, investment or other provisions that have implications for poverty reduction. In highlighting the poverty reduction challenge for Tanzania, we first review the macroeconomic performance of the economy to assess the potential of growth of trade and investment to reduce poverty.

7.3.1 Performance of the economy

Tanzania depends substantially on the agriculture sector for export earnings and employment. The economy is characterized by a large traditional rural sector and a small modern urban sector. Agriculture is the primary economic activity, accounting for about 50 per cent of export earnings. The manufacturing sector is small. Infrastructure, particularly the transport sector, is still underdeveloped. Exports comprise a few cash crops, notably coffee, cotton and cashew nuts, but in recent years tourism and mining have become the largest earners of foreign exchange. The level of government spending as a proportion of GDP has been high, albeit growing recently at a slower rate. Donor financing assumed greater importance after the adoption of economic reforms in 1986. The servicing of foreign debt absorbs an increasing share of current revenue, which relies heavily on indirect taxes.

Examination of post-reform economic performance reveals three noteworthy facts. First, economic growth has improved significantly since the adoption of the reforms. In recent years, the economy has been growing at about 5 per cent per annum. Second, and relatedly, an impressive macroeconomic stability has been achieved, illustrated by a significant reduction in the inflation rate to single-digit levels since 2000. Thirdly, although the government has put in place an elaborate policy framework for poverty reduction with its Poverty Reduction Strategy Paper (PRSP), the above macroeconomic achievements have not resulted in the expected reduction in poverty levels.

According to the various Poverty Reduction Strategy (PRS) review reports, little progress has been achieved in poverty reduction, though the prospects for a substantial decline in poverty are still considered feasible. Currently, the government is revising its strategy to emphasize the growth and employment aspects of the PRSP. Private investment has increased following the reforms, compensating for a reduction in public investment. The revival of economic growth has also been accompanied by substantive changes in the structure of the economy. For instance, services and mineral exports have been responsible for most of the increased growth in exports. According to the data published by the Bank of Tanzania, the share of merchandise exports to total exports has declined from over 70 per cent in 1995 to about 54 per cent in 2003.

7.3.2 Overlapping membership of trade agreements

It is a policy choice for a country to join a particular RIA. Tanzania is party to several trade agreements both at the regional and the multilateral level (see Tables 7.1 and 7.2). Multiplicity of membership raises the problem of coordination and commitment for an individual country in terms of the adequacy and efficiency of its human and financial resources. For a poor country like Tanzania with inadequate resources and human capacity and inefficient institutions, this is considered a daunting challenge, which limits the effectiveness and implementation of agreed protocols (Musonda, 2004).

However, it is important to note that RIAs differ in focus. Tanzania might therefore have different reasons for joining or leaving different regional trade groupings and hence may decide to speed up the integration process of one while slowing down on another (variable geometry argument), based on a perceived cost-benefit analysis. The objectives of different RIAs range from purely market/economic integration to socio-political cooperation agreements. The market integration model is based on Viner's (1950) customs union theory associated with increasing trade flows amongst member states. The theory predicts two possible outcomes of eliminating trade barriers in a regional context: *trade creation* (increased flow of trade from efficient producers in the region) and *trade diversion*

Regional Integration and Poverty

Table 7.1 Overlapping membership of selected trade agreements

Country	WTO	COMESA	SADC	SACU	IOR	EAC	RIFF
Angola	*	*	*				
Botswana	*		*	*			
Burundi	*	*					*
Comoros					*		
DRC	*	*	*				
Djibouti	*	*					
Egypt	*	*					
Eritrea			*				
Ethiopia			*				
Kenya	*	*				*	*
Lesotho	*		*	*			
Madagascar	*	*			*		
Malawi	*	*	*				*
Mauritius	*	*	*		*		*
Mozambique	*		*				
Namibia	*	*	*	*			*
Rwanda	*	*					*
Seychelles		*	*		*		*
South Africa	*		*	*			
Sudan		*					
Swaziland	*	*	*	*			*
Tanzania	*		*			*	*
Uganda	*	*				*	*
Zambia	*	*	*				*
Zimbabwe	*	*	*				*

Source: Various documents from the reference list.
* Membership

(increased flow of trade from inefficient producers in the region). The development integration model of RIAs follows a deliberate intervention by member states to pursue certain benefits of cooperation. This is particularly relevant when there are barriers to realizing the economic benefits of trade and investment. The model includes the common provision of regional public goods such as regional infrastructure and other public utilities. However, one of the criticisms of the development integration model is that the need for flexibility may entrench backwardness since there are no specific timeframes or quantifiable benchmarks for the achievement of targets.

Tanzania withdrew from membership of COMESA in 2000 because the government perceived fewer benefits in it compared with the EAC and SADC, and believed that the agendas of these latter organizations were incompatible with that of COMESA. The fact that Tanzania's leading trade partners are members of the EAC (Kenya) and recently SADC (South Africa) makes it unlikely that Tanzania can benefit significantly from COMESA. We corroborate this argument in Section 7.5 by noting the marginal level of trade with COMESA members that are not also members of SADC or the EAC. The desire to further promote an economic relationship with South Africa was another deciding factor.[4] However, the private sector in Tanzania still believes that COMESA is beneficial to Tanzania and has opened the debate as to whether the country should reinstate its membership. Part of the problem is that no efforts are made by the authorities to disseminate information about private sector opportunities available in the SADC market. The motives for forming SADC, however, were also about socio-political cooperation (for example, the then liberation struggle for independence in Zimbabwe and the fight against apartheid policies in South Africa). In all cases Tanzania has been a committed member in advocating the fraternity objectives of SADC states.

7.3.3 Trade, investment and other provisions in RIAs

Table 7.2 gives a summary of the status of various regional and multilateral agreements in which Tanzania is involved. Below we describe and discuss each in turn.

Table 7.2   Summary of Tanzania's international trade agreements

No.	Agreements	Membership for Tanzania (year)	Nature of Agreements	Current Status
1	COMESA	• 1995 – endorsed • 2000 – withdrew	Started with FTA and now in progress to a Customs Union	Working towards a Customs Union
2	SADC	• 1992 signed the	Establish a Free Trade	Preparing for

---

[4]   South Africa has been one of the significant sources of Tanzania's FDI in the recent years (see Kabelwa, 2004).

No.	Agreements	Membership for Tanzania (year)	Nature of Agreements	Current Status
		declaration and treaty • 1996 – adopted SADC protocol on Trade	Area in SADC region between 2008 to 2012	implementation of various protocols
3	EAC	• 1999 – signed the treaty • 2000 – ratified by parliament	Regional trade integration with Customs Union as the entry point	Customs Union signed in March 2004. EALA unanimously approved Customs Management Bill in December 2004.
4	Cross-Border Initiative (now RIIFF)	• 1999 – signed • 2002 changed into Regional Investment Facilitation Forum	Facilitating forum to remove tariff and non-tariff barriers across the countries	Not active. Donors withdrew their support in December 2003
5	ACP-EU Cooperation	• 1975 – First Lomé Convention • Eligible for EBA initiative • 2000 – Cotonou Agreement	Reciprocal EPAs compatible with WTO regulations may be negotiated EBA provides duty-free access to EU market for Tanzania	Still in the preparation process
6	AGOA (extension of US GSP)	July 2002, eligible	Bilateral, conditional upon meeting all the criteria set by the US	Tanzania has qualified in all the criteria
7	WTO	1995	Multilateral rules on various issues	Tanzania like other LDCs benefits from SDT options
8	Indian Ocean Rim	March 1995	Regional cooperation to strengthen trade and business cooperation among the members	Is not very active in inter-regional cooperation
9	NEPAD Initiatives	July 2001	Try to implement what is agreed within AU	Tanzania has not been active participant
10	Bilateral initiatives	There are more than twenty bilateral treaties	Most of them are for technical or cultural cooperation	Most of them are not active

Source: Various documents from the reference list.

7.3.4 The East African Community (EAC)

One of the most important achievements of the new EAC is the establishment of a Customs Union. The Protocol was signed on 2 March 2004, and the East African Legislative Assembly (EALA) unanimously approved the EAC Customs Management Bill in December 2004. In addition, the integration process in the EAC has succeeded in putting in place a strong institutional base and programmes which determine the effectiveness of this RIA. The EAC institutional framework was taken over from the old EAC with a few changes (see Musonda, 2004:82). The Treaty establishing the new EAC was signed in 1999 and in 2000 the community came into force again after its collapse in 1977. The failure of the old EAC was due to differing political and economic ideologies among its members, a change of government in Uganda (1971), a sustained perception of unequal sharing of benefits and a compensation mechanism inadequate to address this situation. The main objective of the Community is the development of policies and programmes aimed at widening and deepening cooperation among its members in various fields of development.

Having achieved a strong institutional base upon which to implement the integration agreement, the Community must still meet a number of challenges before becoming a fully operational RIA. First, the EAC needs to maintain the political will towards implementation of the treaty as a whole. Second, the EAC should ensure agreement on implementing a transfer mechanism that allows the less developed members to catch up with the richer ones. Third, alternative sources of revenue must be identified to compensate for the immediate but short-term losses arising from the elimination of intra-regional tariffs. And finally, adequate sources of funding must be secured for the regional secretariat to implement the various programmes identified in its development strategy. The second and third challenges are particularly important for Tanzania and Uganda, whose duties on imports from Kenya are relatively substantial. This is why it is important to examine the trade and investment provisions that may have serious implications for the efficacy of RI on poverty reduction.

The EAC has formed a committee on Trade, Industry and Investment to undertake various initiatives relating to trade and investment. These initiatives have culminated in the establishment of a Protocol for the East African Customs Union, the objectives of which are (i) to further liberalise intra-regional trade in goods on the basis of mutually beneficial trade arrangements among the partner states; (ii) to promote efficiency in production within the Community; (iii) to increase domestic, cross-border and foreign investment in the region, and (iv) to promote economic development and diversification by supporting the industrialization process (for a detailed description, see www.eac.int.).

Trade and investment provisions

The Protocol for establishing a Customs Union (CU) provides for the elimination of all tariffs within the Union and the establishment of a three-band common external tariff with a minimum rate of zero (for capital goods), a middle rate of 10 per cent (for intermediate goods) and a maximum rate of 25 per cent (for final consumption goods) on all products imported into the Community. The protocol also includes immediate removal of all existing non-tariff barriers to imports from other partner states and the adoption of the East African Community Rules of Origin. Other provisions cover national treatment, anti-dumping measures, subsidies, countervailing and safeguard measures, competition, restrictions and prohibitions to trade and re-exportation of goods.

Under the CU, Kenya will reduce its internal tariffs to zero on all products upon the coming into force of the Protocol, whereas Tanzania and Uganda will gradually over a period of 5 years remove the internal tariffs for a small list of products deemed to be sensitive by the partner states. Tanzania has included over 800 goods on the sensitive list and Uganda 149 goods. Thus the majority of products will be duty-free from the first year, since, in the case of Tanzania, the residual products on which the duty is to be phased out gradually account for only 15 per cent of Kenya's total exports to Tanzania. Trade between Uganda and Tanzania will be duty-free on the coming into force of the Protocol. The products on which duties will be phased out gradually are those that are deemed to have a substantial revenue impact/loss and serious industrial development consequences.

Two issues are of immediate concern for Tanzania and the other partner states. First, as the Protocol is signed, agreement on which goods fall within the CET and which outside the CET bands (sensitive) has still to be achieved. The products which are within the CET and on which agreement has yet to be reached include palm oil, tyres, paper and paper products, iron and aluminium products and motor vehicles, spare parts, etc. There is also a list of products considered sensitive from both sides on which each country still maintains high tariffs (textile products, for example, *Kitenge*). Secondly, there is the issue of multiple memberships. This is likely to remain unresolved for some time, as a broad integration vision of the three schemes (SADC, EAC and COMESA) is not yet feasible and may be complicated further by the differing rules of origin. Another important investment provision under the EAC is the model investment code that is being developed (but has not yet been agreed) for the EAC as described in Box 7.1.

In addition, the EAC has provided for cooperation in the development of the capital markets of the three member countries. Capital market development is one of the most important strategies for achieving higher rates of investment in general, and one of the factors behind attracting FDI. As part of the broader cooperation in the financial and monetary sectors, efforts to develop capital markets in the regional blocs have been made in the EAC as discussed in its development strategy. This includes harmonization of the regulatory and legislative framework, promotion of cross-border listings, and development of a regional rating system for securities. For instance, the Ugandan Capital Markets Authority allowed East African Breweries to cross list on the Uganda Securities Exchange in addition to its initial listing on the Kenyan Stock Exchange (Musonda, 2004:101). One of the benefits expected from this cooperation is to enable companies in the member

Box 7.1 The EAC model investment code (2002)

The EAC model investment code – 2002 (hereafter 'the code') is in an advanced stage of preparation after the consultant (see Ruhindi, 2002) completed the drafting and a workshop to discuss it in 2002. The code is now going through the usual process of adoption and ratification within the regional and national bureaucracy. The Code is composed of 5 parts. The first is the preliminary part highlighting the title, interpretation and scope of the code. The second part is a more substantive section of the code, dealing with the rights to establish and the benefits and other operational investment incentive procedures. Part three describes the rationale and objectives for establishing a regional investment promotion agency. Part four covers the establishment, operation and incentives for the special economic zones. Finally, part five contains miscellaneous clauses/issues and regulations of the code. For a region trying to hasten its integration process for growth and poverty reduction, the code is a very welcome idea, although reading the code, one comes to the conclusion that its content and structure are not substantially different from the Tanzanian investment policy/code.

The code outlines the key benefits of establishing a regional investment code/agency as follows: improving the investment climate in the region by advocating policies and regulations favourable to foreign investment; harmonizing national investment policies/agencies in order to achieve the regional development goals; and finally, the code is envisaged as providing the international best practices in investment promotion and practice that will enhance the flow and impact of foreign investment in the region. Establishment of the regional investment agency and code do not replace but rather complement the respective national codes/agencies. It should also be noted that the investment code is not intended to be a legal instrument, but rather a guiding document for a particular member state that, in turn, may want to incorporate it into its national investment policies or laws. In the interim before harmonization of investment policies and laws, investors are obliged to access the incentive packages from their respective national investment agencies.

The code provides for national treatment and non-discrimination, and the facilitative services of the investment agency of a partner state to any eligible investors. Eligible investors for investment incentive certificates are only those meeting the minimum threshold and those intending to invest in the permissible areas/sectors (see section 5(5) and section 8 of part (I). The investment laws of the respective partner states cover the minimum thresholds for portfolio investment for foreign and local investment.

Furthermore, the code includes several provisions relating to eligibility and granting of incentive certificates, incorporation and registration of investment, transfer and retention of funds, compensation in case of expropriation and settlement of disputes etc. The investment is allowed to employ only four or fewer foreigners but can employ more if deemed necessary and approved by the immigration department. Other incentives for investors include a uniform corporation tax of 30%, exemption from import duty for all machinery and raw materials, duty drawback for all exporters, 100% deduction allowance on training, research and mineral exploration expenditures and loss carried forward to be offset against future taxable profits. The code also provides for the establishment of (and conditions thereof) special economic zones including export processing zones, free trade zones, technology parks and tourism centres and virtual zones. The special economic zones are given specific fiscal and non-fiscal incentives according to specific investment activities. These are shown in Annexure I of the code.

countries to diversify their funding sources for investment. Savers would also benefit from a variety of investment opportunities. The East Africa Securities and Regulatory Authority (EASRA), comprising the capital market authorities of Kenya, Tanzania and Uganda, has emerged. However, of the three, the Kenyan market is the most advanced, and is likely to take the lead in the integration process (Masinde and Kibua, 2004).

In the case of Tanzania, the Capital Market and Securities Authority (CMSA) was established under the Capital Markets and Securities Act of 1994 as a regulatory body of the stock and securities exchange. The Dar es Salaam stock exchange (DSE) is expanding, but the number of listings and share transactions is growing at a slow rate. So far only six business establishments are listed by the CMSA on the DSE, and of these, only two are flexible and can sell shares to foreign investors; the remaining four are already above the ceiling (65 per cent or more) for foreign ownership (Mashindano, 2004:13).[5] Nevertheless, the CMSA has succeeded in educating and engaging the public about the importance of trading shares on the stock exchange.

Table 7.3 provides a summary of the status of major projects under EAC auspices.

Table 7.3   Summary of major projects/programmes under the EAC

S/N	Elements to be contained in the Protocol	Current Status	Remarks/Further work envisaged
1.	The elimination of internal tariffs and other charges	In December 2003, the relevant Permanent Secretaries re-aligned the list of category B products with the proposed EAC CET. Tanzania substituted tariffs on tea for the proposed special arrangement.	With the earlier arrangements, there are no outstanding issues.
2.	Establishment of EAC Common External Tariff	Extraordinary meeting of heads of state of 20 June 2003 approved the EAC CET as: 0%, 10%, and 25%. The partner states have categorized and classified products within the CET structure, albeit some matters are outstanding including: unresolved tariff lines within the EAC–CET, proposed	The Custom Union started its operation in January 2005 with the application of the CET.

---

[5]   The rules governing capital markets in Tanzania allow foreigners to purchase shares at the DSE with certain restrictions. For example, foreigners can only purchase shares if the company is less than 65% foreign-owned. The objective is to protect the Tanzanian capital account from financial instability that is hazardous to the economy. However, the 65% foreign ownership restriction is considered too high to provide the opportunity of financial liberalization to Tanzanians, and it also limits the extent of the supply response from foreigners, as the prevailing demand for stocks is probably too low.

S/N	Elements to be contained in the Protocol	Current Status	Remarks/Further work envisaged
		EAC–CET tariff splits, criteria for selection of sensitive products on the basis of impact on public revenue, issue of sensitive products, national measure to be applied to the sensitive products already adopted by the council.	
3.	Simplification and harmonization of trade documentation and procedures	Customs documentation to be used once the Protocol on an EAC customs union comes into force, have been simplified and harmonized. Pending work includes review of other customs forms such as the F- and P- series, review of registers, financial procedures, reporting and returns, procedures for customs preventive services, cross-border transfer of duty-paid goods and all other customs procedures, harmonization of the different computer systems (ASYCUDA and BOFIN)	Remaining work will be addressed within the context of the on-going drafting of EAC common customs law. However, the outstanding work is not substantive and cannot therefore hinder conclusion of the Protocol
4.	Harmonization of commodity description and coding system	Work on the EAC commodity description and coding system has been completed and draft EAC customs nomenclature has been produced	Outstanding work is in respect of developing explanatory notes to the customs nomenclature. This will be undertaken following finalization of categorization of imports
5.	Harmonization of exemptions regime	A matrix of harmonized EAC exempting regimes and a text of the proposed harmonized exemption regime for the EAC have been produced. However, consensus has not been reached in respect of harmonization of the Armed Forces and NGOs.	Consultations in respect of outstanding exemptions are ongoing
6.	Establishment of EAC rules	At their meeting of 27–28 November 2003, the sectoral council on legal and judicial	Work on the EAC Rules of Origin

S/N	Elements to be contained in the Protocol	Current Status	Remarks/Further work envisaged
	of origin	affairs approved the annex on the EAC rules of origin, which was adopted by the Council at its 6th meeting. Work on the EAC rules of origin has therefore been successfully adopted.	including drafting of the users' notes has been completed.
7.	Harmonization of duty drawback and other export promotion schemes	Harmonization of duty drawback and other export promotion schemes has been completed. Draft regulations have been developed in respect of: - duty drawback scheme - duty/ value added tax remission scheme - refund and remission of duty and taxes - manufacturing under bond (MUB) and - export processing zones (EPZs) The draft regulations on export promotion schemes have been referred to the Working Group on the EAC common customs law for incorporation.	The Working Group is expected to incorporate the draft regulations in the EAC common customs law.
8.	Anti-dumping practices and subsidies and countervailing measures	The (anti-dumping measures) regulations have been drafted and considered by the sectoral committee on legal and judicial affairs and are awaiting consideration and adoption by the sectoral council in the legal and judicial affairs.	Work on the regulations has been completed and adopted by the sectoral council on legal and judicial affairs
9.	Application of the principle of asymmetry	The principle of asymmetry has been applied in the modalities and the programme for elimination of internal tariffs and other charges of equivalent effect. Final study report on the application of the principle was completed and presented to the Permanent Secretaries on implementation of Article 75(7) of the Treaty.	The final study report on application of the principle of asymmetry has been completed and considered by the Permanent Secretaries
10.	Elimination of non-tariff barriers to trade	Article 75(5) of the Treaty provides for removal by partner states of all existing non-tariff barriers on the importation into their territories of goods originating from	The secretariat is formulating a mechanism for monitoring

S/N	Elements to be contained in the Protocol	Current Status	Remarks/Further work envisaged
		the other partner states and thereafter to refrain from imposing any further non-tariff barriers.	removal of non-tariff barriers. The draft proposal was submitted to the trade/industry committee in March 2004.
11.	Customs cooperation	The relevant text with respect to customs cooperation has been included in the draft protocol.	This matter is completed
12.	Re-exportation of goods	The relevant text with respect to re-exportation of goods has been included in the draft protocol.	This matter is completed
13.	Security and other restrictions to trade	The relevant text with respect to security and other restrictions has been included in the draft protocol.	This matter is completed
14.	Formulation of EAC competition policy and law.	EAC competition policy and law have been completed. Enactment of the EAC competition law by the East African Legislative Assembly was envisaged to take place by 15 May 2004	The EAC competition law is pending enactment.
15.	Formulation of legal, institutional and administrative structure of an EAC customs union	The council at its 6th meeting approved an institutional and administrative structure for the EAC customs union. The preparation and adoption of EAC Customs Law is in an advanced stage of completion by the EAC working Group on Customs Law.	Outstanding is the on-going work on the EAC common customs law.
16.	Preparation of a draft protocol on the establishment of an EAC customs union	Except for Articles 12(2) and 15(4) awaiting consultation by the summit and council respectively, draft protocol No. 5 has been completed and approved by the council for signature by the Heads of State	Outstanding work relate to Articles 12(2) and 15(4), which await further consultation.

Source: EAC Secretariat – Report of the Council, 2004.

7.3.5 The Southern African Development Community (SADC)

Trade and investment provisions
As part of its objectives, the SADC encourages intra-SADC cross-border flows of investment to bring about diversification and industrialization in the region. More importantly, SADC intends to establish a fully-fledged Free Trade Area (FTA) by 2012. The implementation of tariff elimination schedules, rules of origin and dispute settlement mechanisms have now begun.

The SADC trade protocol came into effect in 2000 and is aimed at removing tariff and non-tariff trade barriers within eight years. Up to now, eleven SADC countries have been implementing the Protocol through their schedules of tariff cuts and special agreements for various sectors. By 2001, about 47 per cent of goods traded in the region were at zero tariffs. Preparations are under way to carry out a mid-term review of the implementation of the Protocol. An agreement has been reached on rules of origin for most products. These rules have been designed to encourage regional manufacturers to make use of regional raw materials and to boost investments in processing and manufacturing industries. Substantial work has been done to harmonize documentation and procedures in the area of customs cooperation. The Integrated Committee of Ministers (ICM) developed and approved a code of conduct for customs officials, with the aim of improving the performance and efficiency of customs border clearance systems and reducing transaction costs for traders. In line with this, a lot has been done to ensure that regional products are competitive and comply with internationally accepted standards, quality assertion and accreditation. Substantial work has also been done on the harmonization of sanitary and phytosanitary measures that will enhance intra-SADC trade in agricultural products. Non-tariff barriers have been removed except for a few barriers related to administrative systems, which are also being dealt with.

The member states are implementing macroeconomic policies that encourage the development of a sound investment climate, enhance savings, and stimulate investment flows, technology transfer and innovation in the region. Efforts are being made to ensure that national investment legislation and guidelines facilitate foreign direct investment and that investment policies promote the free movement of capital in the region. Emphasis has also been put on mobilizing domestic investment resources. In this respect, a network of development finance institutions (DFIs) has been created to mobilize resources for financing development projects, and a feasibility study is under way for the establishment of a SADC Development Fund (SDF) to mobilize both domestic and international resources for investment in the region. This fund will play a catalytic role as a promoter and thus raise confidence levels among other potential investors. The EU/SADC Investment Promotion Programme (ESIPP), worth Euro 18 million, has been established to improve the overall investment climate in the region. The programme will carry out sectoral studies and organize face-to-face fora at which the project promoters from SADC will meet potential investors from the EU and other third countries, and is expected to substantially improve the investment climate. In December 2004, agreement on the Mtwara Development Corridor was signed by Presidents of four of the SADC countries, namely, Tanzania, Malawi, Zambia and Mozambique, in Lilongwe. This is a multi-billion-dollar regional project aimed at enhancing economic cooperation and developing jointly the cross-border resources and infrastructure of the four countries. Investment projects identified for the Mtwara Development Corridor are at advanced stages of preparation.

The key challenge facing SADC is to establish a free trade area within a reasonable timeframe, given the problem of the overlapping membership of SADC countries in other different regional bodies, and the conflicting obligations arising therefrom. Conducting trade according to more than one regional provision can prove difficult and may mean choosing one out of a number of conflicting sets of rules of origin. Another challenge is to formulate new policies and strategies that will target vulnerable groups, especially the poor, to ensure that they benefit from regional policies. The 14 member countries are expected to sign a free trade area agreement by 2008 and to implement the Customs Union Protocol by 2010 and the Common Market by 2012 (SADC Secretariat, 2004).

The EU–EPA challenge

The countries in the African Caribbean and Pacific (ACP) group are due to negotiate Economic Partnership Agreements (EPAs) with the European Union in a number of regions. All the countries that are members of both COMESA and SADC have already chosen to negotiate jointly with the EU as the Eastern and Southern African (ESA) group.[6] SADC has lagged behind in this and been overtaken by events. The fact that COMESA members have chosen the ESA would suggest that SADC is fragile. And, given that COMESA is relatively more experienced in market integration than SADC, it may benefit trade-wise more readily with the EU. Botswana, Namibia, Lesotho, and Swaziland do not need to negotiate anything because they are implicitly bound by the South African–EU agreement. It is therefore Tanzania, Angola and Mozambique that will effectively constitute the SADC–EU EPA, but Mozambique may join the Southern African Customs Union, leaving Tanzania desperate if it really wants to negotiate an EPA. The SADC Secretariat is taking a lead in the preparation for negotiations about how SADC can improve its access to the EU market.

7.3.6 The Common Market for East and Southern Africa (COMESA)

The Treaty establishing COMESA was signed in 1993 and ratified in 1994, and progressed to a Free Trade Area (FTA) in 2000 through annual reductions in tariffs. The region's main aims are to cooperate in exploiting member countries'

---

[6]   There are 16 countries forming the ESA group, namely: Burundi, Comoros, DR Congo, Djibouti, Eritrea, Ethiopia, Kenya, Madagascar, Malawi, Mauritius, Rwanda, Seychelles, Sudan, Uganda, Zambia and Zimbabwe.

natural and human resources and to maintain peace and security for the common good of all its people. COMESA objectives are to remove the structural and institutional weaknesses in the member states by pooling their resources in order to sustain their development efforts both individually and collectively. The member countries are as shown in Table 7.1. Tanzania withdrew its membership in 2000 for reasons discussed earlier. However, there has been mixed opinion regarding this decision. Some members of the business community are opposed to it, while others find no reason to complain in the absence of supporting evidence as to whether the membership was beneficial to the country. It is unlikely, however, that the government will rejoin the institution. There are also opinions that the debate on rejoining COMESA is being stirred up by a few industrialists with particular interests in COMESA, but we found this difficult to corroborate.

Trade and investment provisions
To expand trade and investment opportunities, nine members of COMESA (Djibouti, Egypt, Kenya, Madagascar, Malawi, Mauritius, Sudan, Zambia and Zimbabwe) launched the COMESA Free Trade Area (FTA) on 31 October 2000. These countries are trading on quota-free and duty-free terms for all goods originating from their territories, but continue to impose their own national tariffs on goods imported from the rest of the world. Meanwhile, COMESA is working to establish the COMESA Common Investment Area (CCIA) in order to attract larger and sustainable levels of investment – an objective that is expected to be achieved by creating an international competitive investment area that allows for free movement of capital, labour, goods and services across the borders of the member states. CCIA is expected to enhance operations in the Free Trade Area and thus increase intra-COMESA trade. Further details in relation to COMESA trade and investment arrangements are not relevant for this study, since these arrangements began after Tanzania had withdrawn its membership.

7.3.7 Regional Integration Facilitation Forum (RIFF)

RIFF (formerly known as the Cross-Border Initiative) is a programme for stimulating cross-border trade and investment amongst countries of the Eastern, Central and Southern African regions, with the objective of accelerating the process of trade liberalization and curbing food insecurity. The programme was launched in 1993, funded by the African Development Bank, the World Bank, the International Monetary Fund, and the European Union. The sponsors awarded financial incentives to the CBI members whose measures with regard to tariffs and non-tariff barriers had performed above the agreed targets. The donors have withdrawn their support since December 2003, following the change of name in 2000 to the Regional Integration Facilitation Forum (RIFF).

RIFF was signed in 1999 with the aim of reducing import duties and statutory exemptions. According to the assessment conducted for the IMF by José Fajgenbaum and others (1999), the CBI initiative started in 1993 had made tremendous (but uneven) progress in trade liberalization (reducing tariffs and non-tariff barriers) by the end of 1998, although none of the members had fully eliminated intra-regional tariffs. In 1993, about 93 per cent of the CBI member countries had a highly restrictive trade regime but by 1999 only 43 per cent had maintained this regime, 36 per cent (compared with 22 per cent for non-CBI countries) had established an open regime and 21 per cent had a moderate regime in sub-Saharan Africa.

Almost all RIIF member countries have eliminated the state monopoly of trade and harmonized road transit charges (as part of trade facilitation targets). Progress was also made in the area of investment deregulation by instituting one-stop investment centres in almost all member countries. With the exception of a few countries, most of the investment codes included some form of tariff exemptions, on which little or no progress is evident, nor is there much agreement on double taxation or labour mobility. While its objectives are laudable, RIFF seems much weaker in terms of policy influence than the regional integration efforts of the EAC and SADC.

7.3.8 Multilateral trade and investment provisions

As a least developed country, Tanzania receives numerous trade preferences in the current multilateral trade system (MTS) under the World Trade Organization in the form of the Generalized System of Preferences. In addition, it benefits from specific bilateral initiatives notably by the US (the familiar African Growth and Opportunity Act programme is an extension of the GSP to products such as textiles and clothing) and the EU (under the Everything But Arms Programme, and recently EPAs). Our coverage of these initiatives is relatively limited, given the focus of the study on the specific RIAs mentioned above. However, three points are particularly worth noting. First, the traditional focus of the MTS on trade issues has shifted to cover other issues including investment issues such as trade-related investment measures (TRIMs), which may affect the ability to attract FDI to developing countries. Second, although Tanzania has qualified for many of the trade preferences at the multilateral level, the performance in terms of access to these markets for Tanzanian exports has been dismal. The problem lies not only in the obviously low productive capacity of the economy and the inefficiency of the market and supporting institutions, but also in the policy response. For instance, despite all the opportunities offered under successive EU arrangements, Tanzania's total exports to the EU declined during the 1990s. The new EU–ACP partnership under the well-known Cotonou Agreement entails much longer-term cooperation in the EPAs. EPAs can include trade and investment provisions in addition to development assistance, but Tanzania does not seem abreast of the opportunities. How much of a problem an EPA presents depends on how much Tanzania wants to be in an EPA. Purely from the point of view of access to the EU market, the permanent privileges it enjoys as a least developed country under the EBA initiative mean that it does not need to sign an EPA.

7.3.9 Poverty reduction challenge for Tanzania

Tanzania is one of the poorest countries in the world, with about 36 per cent of its population lacking sufficient income to meet their basic human needs. The income and non-income indicators shown in Table 7.4 provide evidence of the depth of poverty. The table indicates that Tanzania is poorer than the average developing country in terms of under-five mortality rate, maternal mortality, literacy rate, primary school enrolment, average life expectancy, doctor–patient ratio, etc.

Table 7.4   Comparison of poverty between Tanzania and developing countries as a whole

Indicators	Tanzania	Developing Countries
GDP per Capita (US$)	270	970
Population below poverty line (%)	51.1	n.a.
Under-five mortality rate (Per 1000 live births)	165	88
Maternal mortality (Per 1000,000_	530	384
Literacy rate (%)	76	85.5
Primary school enrolment (%)	63	77
Secondary school enrolment (%)	6	35–47
Doctor–patient ratio (Patients per doctor)	23000	5767
Severe malnutrition (%)	29	30
Average life expectancy (Years)	44	63.3
Families with water supply at home (%)	11	70
People living in temporary settlements (%)	60–70	30-60

Source: World Bank, *World Development Indicators*, 2003.

The 2000/01 *Household Budget Survey* reveals that (i) 19 per cent of the total population cannot meet their basic food requirements; (ii) 87 per cent of all poor people live in the rural areas; (iii) 51 per cent of poor people are in households whose head had not attained primary education; (iv) households that depend on subsistence agriculture have high levels of poverty; (v) a high level of poverty is in households with a larger number of members and whose heads have neither fulfilled economic activities nor followed primary education; (vi) a low proportion of children from poor families attend primary school; (vii) poor people have declining access to health services especially since the introduction of a cost-sharing system; (viii) the poorest people have a long distance to go to find water sources, and 54 per cent of them depend on unprotected water sources.

As a response to this situation, the government embarked on a National Poverty Eradication Strategy in 1998 aimed at providing a framework to guide poverty eradication initiatives. Goals were set to halve absolute poverty by 2010 and to eradicate it completely by 2025. Subsequently, the drawing up of the PRSP[7] involved broad-based participation by civil society and the private sector in all stages. Tanzania's first PRSP was finalized in 2000 and since then, a series of poverty reduction initiatives have been undertaken. Progress on poverty reduction is updated on an annual basis in the PRS progress reports. The third of these reports notes that divergent efforts have been made to improve delivery of social services such as education, health and water supply, but argues that greater attention has to be paid to quality and equity issues in the delivery of these services (URT, 2004). The private sector (in growth issues and trade) has become the subject of attention due to its critical role in poverty reduction. As a result, the new PRS framework (2004) is entitled the 'National Strategy for Growth and Reduction of Poverty' (in Swahili, *MKUKUTA*).[8] Since increased trade and investment are considered crucial for Tanzania's efforts to achieve the growth rate needed for poverty reduction, regional integration is assuming an important role in the poverty reduction strategy, because RI is expected to increase intra-regional trade and investment. It is against this background that we assess, in the following two sections, the extent to which RI has affected poverty in Tanzania via trade and investment channels.

7.4 Regional integration and poverty reduction through FDI

The literature offers little guidance on how or whether regionalization increases FDI in developing countries (see te Velde and Bezemer, 2004; OECD, 2001; Hartzenberg, 2000; Collier and Pattillo, 2000). However, for a country like Tanzania, the answer to this question may be further complicated by the fact that most RIAs in sub-Saharan African countries are at an infant stage of implementation, thus limiting a quantitative analysis. The issue for the present study is whether the investment provisions in the RIA are conducive to an environment favourable to attracting FDI, especially when it is extra-regional. And

---

[7]   Poverty Reduction Strategy Papers are to provide the basis for assistance from the World Bank and the IMF as well as debt relief under the HIPC initiative. PRSPs are country-driven, comprehensive in scope, partnership-oriented, and participatory. A country only needs to write a PRSP every three years. Changes are made to the content of a PRSP using an Annual Progress Report.

[8]   As part of the first PRS, a number of sectors have been identified as key, including education, health, agriculture, infrastructure (rural roads), water, judiciary and cross-cutting issues (governance, HIV/AIDS, environment and gender).

if so, to what extent is this FDI poverty-reducing? We address these questions first by examining the performance of FDI flows to Tanzania both intra- and extra-regionally. We then discuss the poverty focus of FDI flows by examining the sectoral and regional (sub-national) distribution of FDI in order to determine the extent to which key sectors for poverty reduction (for example, agriculture, health, education, and manufacturing) have received increased FDI. In addition, we correlate indices of FDI flows to the poverty (for example, Human Development) index to examine the potential relationship between the two variables.

7.4.1 Global and African trends in FDI inflows

Trends in global FDI flows (see Chart 7.1) show a small share of FDI going to Africa, whereas the EU, the US and Japan have been the focal centres for FDI. During the 1980s, approximately 81 per cent of FDI outflows originated from the EU, the US and Japan, while 71 per cent was destined for the same regions (UNCTAD, 2002). Africa as a location for FDI has been unfavourable because the continent is often associated with factors that discourage FDI – for example, civil

Chart 7.1   Global FDI inflow by major regions

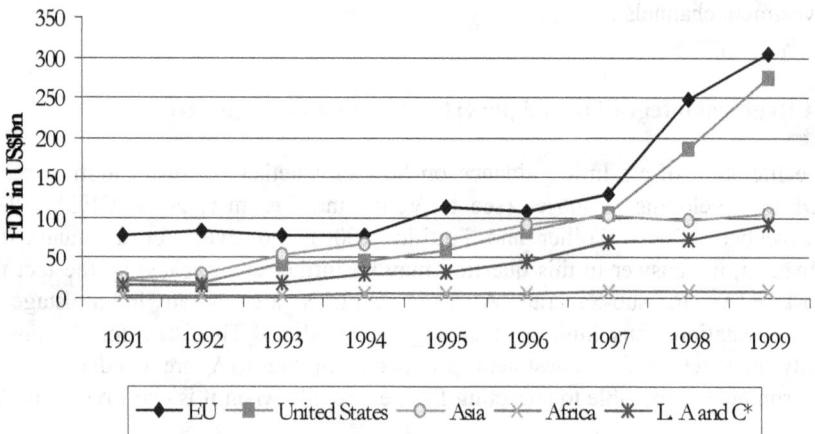

* L. A and C – Latin America and Caribbean
Source: Data from UNCTAD (various years).

unrest, deadly diseases and economic disorders. This raises the challenge for African countries to support regional initiatives that can tame such negative factors and also encourage intra-regional FDI. Most African countries have formed regional groupings and, sometimes as part of structural reforms, have liberalized their investment and trade regimes in the past two decades or so in order to attract more FDI. However, the direction of FDI flows has been determined more by the growth potential and level of productivity of the host economies than by the liberalization agenda.

While Africa's share of global FDI has been minimal, the pattern of FDI flows has been unevenly distributed across African countries, with oil-rich countries (Angola and Nigeria) in the lead (see Chart 7.2). FDI in Africa has traditionally concentrated in the primary sector but, of late, the manufacturing and service sectors are becoming key sectors for FDI inflows.

Chart 7.2   Composition of FDI in sub-Saharan Africa

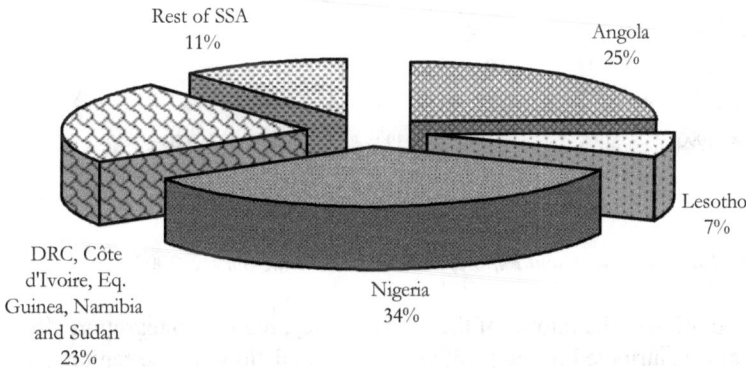

Rest of SSA
11%

Angola
25%

Lesotho
7%

DRC, Côte
d'Ivoire, Eq.
Guinea, Namibia
and Sudan
23%

Nigeria
34%

Source: UNCTAD (2001).

7.4.2 Trend of FDI inflow to Tanzania

Tanzania is quickly becoming an FDI front-runner in Africa with the inflow increasing from less than US$2 million in 1992 to about US$250 million in 2002 (see Chart 7.3), attributable to the implementation of comprehensive national reform policies (UNCTAD, 2002). The stock of FDI in 1995–2000 amounted to US$1 billion compared with less than US$2 million during 1986–92. Tanzania's share of FDI inflows into least developed countries doubled from 2.7 per cent in

1991–5 to 5.3 per cent in 1996–9 and more than doubled in the case of sub-Saharan African countries from 1.5 per cent to 3.3 per cent respectively. Aware of the benefits associated with it, the government has made concerted efforts to attract FDI since the mid-1980s. These efforts included economic liberalization towards a market-oriented economy, the restoration of macroeconomic stability and the implementation of various institutional reforms such as the establishment of the Tanzania Investment Centre (TIC),[9] the Parastatal Sector Reforms Commission (PSRC) and the Tanzania Revenue Authority, and the formulation of sector-specific policies.

Chart 7.3   FDI inflows to Tanzania, 1991–2002

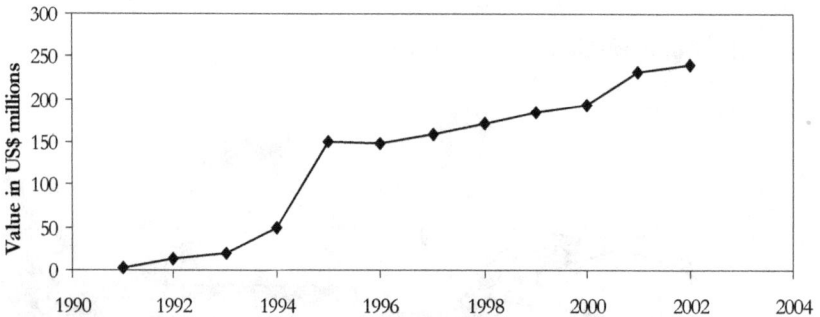

Source: Tanzania Investment Report, 2001 and *Economic Survey,* 2002.

In addition to the impact of the reform policy, regional integration efforts in the EAC also contributed to the positive trend of FDI flows to the region, particularly for Uganda and Tanzania. Parallel with the impressive performance of Tanzania, the three East African countries increased their total FDI inflows tenfold from less than $50 million in 1985 to over US$500 million in 2002. Comparison of the three countries shows that, from 1970 to 1991, the region received a total of US$270 million in FDI inflows, with 90 per cent of it going to Kenya, 10 per cent to Tanzania and hardly any for Uganda.[10] The picture changed completely during the

---

[9]   Established in 1997, TIC is a primary agency of the government to coordinate, encourage, promote and facilitate investment in Tanzania and to advise the government on investment-related matters. It is a 'one stop facilitative center for all investors' engaged in the business of marketing Tanzania as an investment destination.

[10]   Anecdotal evidence shows that some Kenyan firms (which used to supply/export to Tanzania) have decided to establish plants in Dar es Salaam to take advantage of the market

1990s so that by 2000 total FDI inflows to the three countries amounted to US$500 million; half of this went to Uganda and 40 per cent to Tanzania, and Kenya attracted only 10 per cent.

7.4.3 FDI distribution by country of origin

We can report on data on the distribution of FDI by country of origin, by sector and by region for Tanzania. Table 7.5 shows FDI flows by country of origin. The leading countries that have invested in Tanzania during the period 1998–2001 are the UK, Ghana and South Africa. It is widely believed that the dominance of the UK is based on historical reasons. Of late, the mining sector has become an important source of FDI attraction, and it has drawn in new investors from Ghana, South Africa, Australia, Canada and the United States.

As is shown in Table 7.5, the top six countries account for 63 per cent of the FDI inflows. South Africa and Kenya are the only two African countries that are important sources of FDI inflows to Tanzania accounting for 13 per cent and 3 per cent of total FDI respectively. This indicates that they are best positioned to take advantage of trade investment provisions in the SADC and the EAC respectively.

Table 7.5   **FDI inflows by country of origin, 1998–2001 (US$ m., except % of total)**

ORIGIN	1998[a]	1999	2000	2001	Total	% of Total[b]
EAC						
Kenya	53.7	21.1	6.5	12.5	93.8	3.2
Uganda	0.4	1.8	0.4	0	2.6	0.1
Sub-total	*54.1*	*22.9*	*6.9*	*12.5*	*96.4*	*3.3*
SADC						
South Africa	32.4	44.3	133.5	174.5	384.7	13.2
Mauritius	70.4	16.5	4.6	3.7	95.3	3.3
Swaziland	0.2	8	1.2	2.8	12.2	0.4
Malawi	10.5	1.1	0	0	11.6	0.4
Zambia	8.6	0.6	0	0	9.2	0.3
Sub-total	*122.1*	*70.5*	*139.3*	*181*	*513*	*17.6*
America and Australia						
Canada	96.7	78.9	0	20.6	196.2	6.8
US	122.2	24	27.6	27.6	201.4	6.9
Australia	106.3	48.5	4	3.9	162.7	5.6
Sub-total	*325.2*	*151.4*	*31.6*	*52.1*	*560.3*	*19.3*

but also the fiscal incentives offered to FDI; and especially since the avenues for corruption in importing have been closed.

ORIGIN	1998[a]	1999	2000	2001	Total	% of Total[b]
Europe						
United Kingdom	313.8	30.7	24.4	82.2	451.2	15.5
France	30.2	13.1	2.3	2.2	47.8	1.6
Switzerland	28.3	9	30.8	23.8	91.9	3.2
Germany	35.1	8.5	12.2	1.2	56.9	2.0
Denmark	24	6.3	0.4	0.1	30.8	1.1
Norway	31.5	5.5	1.6	4.6	43.2	1.5
Netherlands	106.4	5.5	1.7	58.5	172.2	5.9
Italy	68.1	3.5	1.5	1.2	74.3	2.6
Sweden	24.5	3.5	4.1	5.4	37.5	1.3
Luxembourg	16.5	0.6	0	2.4	19.4	0.7
Japan	6.5	0.4	16.8	0	23.7	0.8
Isle of Man	13	0.1	0	1.6	14.7	0.5
Sub-total	*697.9*	*86.7*	*95.8*	*183.2*	*1063.6*	*36.7*
Rest of Africa and world						
Ghana	265.1	162.7	0	1.5	429.3	14.8
Lebanon	1	6.4	0	0.9	8.3	0.3
Saudi Arabia	4.1	6.1	0	0	10.2	0.4
Bermuda	61.2	5.3	0	0	66.5	2.3
Foreign – not specified	3.7	4.1	0.2	1.3	9.3	0.3
Malaysia	40.5	3.7	0.1	1	45.4	1.6
Panama	1	2.4	0	5	8.4	0.3
China	9.9	0.8	1.9	1.5	14.2	0.5
United Arab Emirates	2.2	0.6	2.2	0.3	5.4	0.2
India	4.7	0.5	1.5	1.8	8.5	0.3
Sub-total	*393.4*	*192.6*	*5.9*	*13.3*	*605.5*	*21.0*
Grand total	1592.7	524.1	279.5	442.1	2838.8	97.9

Notes: a) 1998 represents FDI stock, and the subsequent years are flows
b) Total does not add because of rounding-off errors and the fact that our calculation omitted countries with insignificant value of FDI to Tanzania.
Source: TIC (2002).

7.4.4 Distribution by sector

Table 7.6 indicates that most FDI in Tanzania has gone to the mining and quarrying sector (about 31 per cent), followed by manufacturing (20.3 per cent), wholesale and retail trade, catering and accommodation services (14.8 per cent) and transport, storage and communication (11 per cent). These four sectors alone accounted for about 77 per cent of total FDI inflows at the end of 2001. The agriculture sector received a low share of 7.7 per cent of the total inflows in spite of its importance to the economy and to poverty reduction (as the largest employer and source of export revenue).

Examination of the key sectors for growth (namely agriculture, manufacturing and services) and the priority sectors for poverty reduction shows that the types of FDI inflows to Tanzania are not well poverty-focused. For instance, the mining sector has fewer sectoral linkages and multiplier effects compared with the cash-crop sector such as cotton or a service sector such as tourism (Kweka *et al.*, 2003). The revealed structure of FDI inflows is more a testimony to FDI preferences and opportunities available in the high concentration sectors than to promotion efforts in these sectors. In addition, the social sectors identified as crucial for poverty reduction (in the first PRS) have attracted only a small share of total FDI. This implies that the direct impact of FDI on poverty in Tanzania is limited. The small share of total FDI in the agriculture sector is also attributed to the adverse conditions in that sector (including adverse weather condition, low prices of agricultural products in the world market, insufficient domestic markets and other supply-side and institutional bottlenecks).

Table 7.6   Distribution of FDI inflows by sector, 1998–2001 (US$ m.)

Sector	1998[a]	1999	2000	2001	Total	% of total
Mining and Quarrying	568.2	293.6	9.5	37.7	908.95	30.9
Manufacturing	407.1	94.0	47.0	48.5	596.57	20.3
Wholesale & Retail trade, catering & accommodation services	251.5	64.7	58.8	58.4	433.34	14.8
Construction	93.02	28.1	5.9	6.2	133.22	4.5
Agriculture, hunting, forestry and fishing	105.34	23.1	50.4	47.5	226.43	7.7
Transport, storage & communications	47.7	15.6	100.7	158.1	322.07	11.0
Financing, insurance, real estate, and business services	132.5	14.9	3.5	8.9	159.84	5.4
Community, social and personal services	1.4	2.1	3.5	1.8	8.79	0.3
Utilities	35.36	0.0	0.2	83.0	118.56	4.0
Others	29.36	0.0	0.0	0.0	29.36	1.0
Total	1671.48	536.2	279.4	450.1	2,937.12	100.0

Note a) Figures for 1998 are FDI in stock.
Source: TIC (2001).

There have been insufficient policy efforts to establish an environment that encourages FDI to the agriculture sector. The government needs to make deliberate efforts to attract more FDI to the sector as a way of enhancing its efforts to alleviate poverty by, among other things, expediting land ownership reforms and addressing the infrastructure and other supply-side bottlenecks to rural enterprises.

7.4.5 Distribution by region

The regional distribution of FDI in Tanzania is also highly skewed in favour of a few regions, namely Dar es Salaam, Mwanza, Shinyanga, Arusha and Morogoro (see Table 7.7). By the end of 2001, these five regions accounted for about 87 per cent of FDI inflows to the country, with Dar es Salaam alone accounting for 53 per cent. However, this is not surprising, since most of the privatized manufacturing companies are located in Dar es Salaam while most mining activities are concentrated in Mwanza, Arusha and Shinyanga. Also, Dar es Salaam is more advantaged than other regions due to its being the main commercial centre, with a diverse social structure and more advanced economic infrastructure which are more conducive to business activities as compared with other areas of the country.

Table 7.7   Stock and flow of FDI by region, 1998–2001 (US$ m.)

Region	1998[a]	1999	2000	2001	Total	% of Total
Dar es Salaam	649.8	358.2	175.0	343.0	1526.0	52.69
Shinyanga	111.2	84.5	0.0	24.2	219.9	7.59
Arusha	159.2	23.6	17.1	12.7	212.6	7.34
Mwanza	327.4	21.4	5.0	15.5	369.3	12.75
Kilimanjaro	25.3	13.9	42.4	12.4	94.0	3.25
Morogoro	119.3	12.0	31.9	30.7	193.9	6.69
Mara	66.7	11.5	1.2	0.0	79.4	3.25
Tanga	50.3	5.8	0.7	9.5	66.3	2.29
Iringa	88.9	4.7	0.1	0.5	94.2	3.25
Mbeya	10.9	0.3	0.0	0.1	11.3	0.39
Pwani	1.9	0.1	0.3	0.1	2.4	0.18
Dodoma	5.3	0.0	0.0	0.0	5.3	0.18
Tabora	21.7	0.0	0.0	0.0	21.7	0.75
Ruvuma	0.0	0.0	0.0	0.0	0	0.00

Note: a) Figures for 1998 are FDI in stock.
Source: TIC (2001).

Other regions that have attracted a substantial amount of FDI are Arusha, Mwanza, Morogoro, Kilimanjaro, Mara and Iringa, while Pwani, Dodoma and Ruvuma have the lowest concentrations of FDI. These latter are the regions least endowed with natural resources and with poorer infrastructure. Unfortunately, there are few if any production and economic linkages between the regions with most and least FDI. Government efforts to attract FDI into the country should work concomitantly with the improvement of the rural infrastructure and productive utilities. However, little FDI involvement in agriculture seems typical of general least developed country experience rather than peculiar to Tanzania.

7.4.6 Impact of FDI on poverty

We have observed that the flow of FDI to Tanzania has been growing rapidly, especially in the late 1990s. The stock of FDI as a percentage of GDP grew from 2 per cent in 1990 to 36 per cent in 2002. Also, the share of FDI inflow in total capital formation increased from 0.5 per cent in 1991 to 13 per cent in 2002. The overall impact of FDI performance on poverty reduction has been limited, however, due to its concentration in a few sectors and regions and the fact that these sectors have low linkages with or multiplier effects on the rest of the economy (see Kweka, *et al.,* 2003). For instance, while agricultural projects accounted for only 5 per cent of the total value of investment approved by the TIC between 1999 and 2000, they were the most efficient projects in creating employment (estimated at 37 per cent – see Chart 7.4). This is not to imply that FDI going to other sectors is not important for poverty reduction. In fact, FDI in the manufacturing sector has huge prospects for reducing poverty through the creation of employment and backward linkages with other sectors of the economy. The latter impact will spur entrepreneurship and increase the employment multiplier in the economy overall. In general, sectors differ in the extent to which additional investment will reduce poverty directly, depending on the linkage effect with the other sectors (especially agriculture) and employment generation capacity.

While FDI can have great potential for reducing poverty, it is the actual conditions in a particular sector/economy that will determine the eventual outcome. In this case, the poverty challenge (mostly a rural phenomenon) and existing conditions in the rural agricultural sectors (unfavourable business environment, unskilled labour force) in Tanzania do not permit a significant impact of FDI on poverty reduction.

Anecdotal evidence finds that some Kenyan firms have set up in Tanzania as a result of regional integration. More importantly, given South Africa's accession to the SADC bloc, Tanzania has witnessed a lot of incoming South African investment with measured economic benefits such as in skills, employment, technology, tax revenue, trade and entrepreneurship. A study by George Kabelwa (2004) found that South African companies have a significant potential to improve the country's low technological base, thereby contributing to entrepreneurship and industrial development.

There is also a spatial aspect to the FDI-poverty nexus. Regions with a better investment climate because of better infrastructure and natural resource endowment have performed better in terms of trade and investment, and are also less poverty-stricken. As mentioned earlier, the distribution of FDI in Tanzania is skewed towards a few regions with Dar es Salaam and Mwanza attracting the highest level of FDI inflows (more than US$500m. each, about 57 per cent of total FDI inflows, in 1999), leaving only 43 per cent for the remaining regions. With this kind of distribution, a very small section of the country has benefited directly from the improved performance in FDI inflows. Column three of Table 7.8 reflects regional achievements in three dimensions of human development: long and healthy life, knowledge and decent standard of living. It is interesting to note that the regions with relatively higher concentrations of FDI also have the highest performance in terms of the Human Development Index (HDI). However, although Mwanza and Shinyanga are among the worst HDI performers, the two regions have rich mineral deposits (gold) and are among the top five with the highest stock of FDI. This implies that FDI inflows to the mining sector have so far had only a limited impact on poverty reduction.

Chart 7.4   Employment of approved FDI in Tanzania by sector, 1999–2000

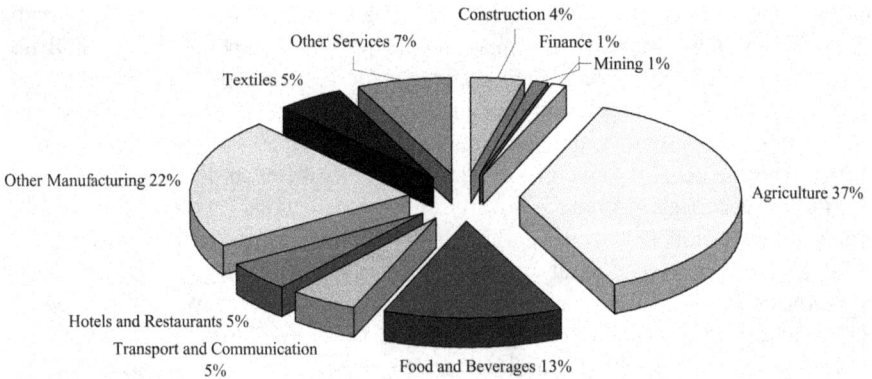

Construction 4%
Finance 1%
Mining 1%
Other Services 7%
Textiles 5%
Other Manufacturing 22%
Agriculture 37%
Hotels and Restaurants 5%
Transport and Communication 5%
Food and Beverages 13%

Source: TIC (various years).

The important role of domestic investment is acknowledged but is not analyzed here. One question is whether regional integration increases FDI inflows to a member country such as Tanzania. Another question which we address here is whether FDI will affect poverty reduction generally. As shown in Chart 7.5, we observe a clear correlation between the FDI share of GDP and the primary school enrolment rate, suggesting a possible positive impact of FDI on poverty. Similarly, from Chart 7.6 one notes a positive relationship between investment and GDP growth, signifying a positive association between investment and growth (or vice versa).

Table 7.8   Regional distributions of FDI, trade and poverty

Region	FDI	HDI	CC exports	
Arusha	◉◉◉	□□□	◇◇	**Key**
Coast	◉	□□	-	FDI =Foreign Direct Investment
Dar es Salaam	◉◉◉◉	□□□	-	◉◉◉◉ $501m. and above
Dodoma	◉	□□	-	◉◉◉ $101m.–500m.
Iringa	◉◉	□□□	◇◇	◉◉ $11m.–100m.
Kagera	◉	□	◇◇◇	◉ $0m.–10m.
Kigoma	◉	□□	-	
Kilimanjaro	◉	□□□	◇◇◇	HDI= Human Development Index
Lindi	◉	□	-	□□□ High HDI
Mafia	◉	□□	-	□□ Medium HDI
Mara	◉◉◉	□□	-	□ Low HDI
Mbeya	◉	□□□	◇◇	- Missing data
Morogoro	◉◉◉	□□	-	
Mtwara	◉	□□	◇◇◇	CC exports = share of cash crops available
Mwanza	◉◉◉◉	□	◇◇◇	◇◇◇ 50–100%
Pemba	◉	□□	-	◇◇ 10–50%
Rukwa	◉	□	-	◇ Below 10%
Ruvuma	◉	□□	◇	- No cash crop for export
Shinyanga	◉◉◉	□	◇◇	
Singida	◉	□□	-	
Tabora	◉◉	□□	◇	
Tanga	◉◉	□□	◇◇	
Zanzibar	◉	□□	-	

Sources:FDI – TIC (2001); HDI – URT (2002a); CC – Mkenda (2003).

Chart 7.5 FDI share of GDP and primary school net enrolment rate, 1990–2002

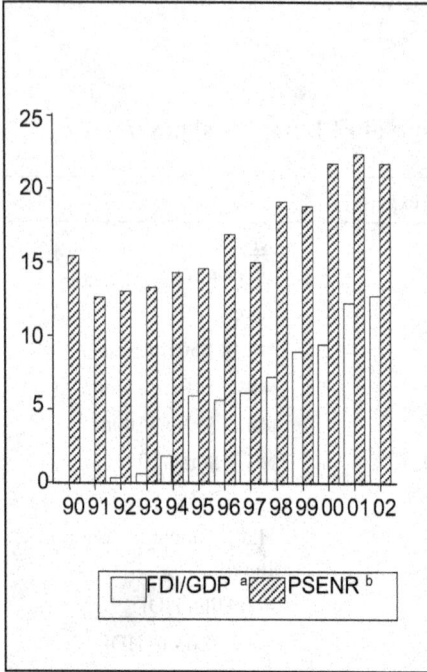

Chart 7.6 GDP growth and investment share of GDP, 1990–2002

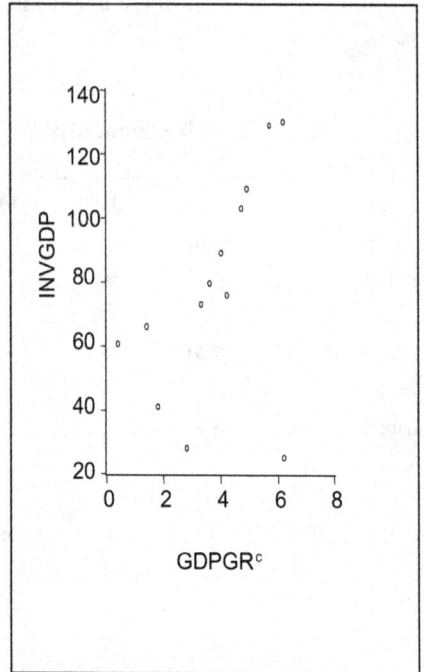

Notes a) *FDI/GDP* is ratio of FDI Inflows to GDP expressed as percentage share.
b) *PSENR* is Primary School net Enrolment Rate (i.e. number of enrolled pupils of a particular age as percentage of total population of children in that age group).
c) *GDPGR* is GDP growth rate, and *INVGDP* is ratio of investment to GDP expressed as percentage share.
Source: Authors' calculations.

7.5 Regional integration and poverty reduction through trade

One of the key benefits and expectations of a RIA is to enhance the trade performance of the participating member countries. The literature has tended to examine whether RI is trade creating or diverting, or to estimate the impact of RI on the economy of the member country, in particular the implications for the loss of government revenue. In contrast, our focus will be to assess the efficacy of regional trade on poverty reduction in Tanzania.

Given the various trade provisions (such as those under the customs union of the EAC, the trade Protocol of SADC and other trade preferences), the first question we investigate is whether regional integration has led to increased trade performance for Tanzania. Regional markets are considered important remedies for the failure of least developed countries to achieve significant market access in the global economy, since the market access conditions are expected to be easier because of lower transport costs, due to the proximity of markets, the favourable rules of origin and the joint promotional measures for investment and trade. In addition, regional markets may be considered useful stepping-stones to gaining the competitiveness needed for least developed countries to access the global market.

Secondly, we aim to assess the poverty focus of regional trade so as to estimate the extent to which regionalization has contributed or will contribute to poverty reduction. This is analyzed by examining the trend and share of the agricultural exports in regional markets, given the importance of the agricultural sector in poverty reduction and the multiplier effects it has on the economy. Thirdly, the impact of trade on poverty reduction is examined by linking trade performance to a set of poverty indicators over time (to demonstrate the likely effect of regionalization) and by regions. Finally, we discuss the factors limiting the poverty focus of trade and the stumbling-blocks for the poor to benefit from enhanced trade performance.

7.5.1 Regional trade performance in Tanzania

Examination of the trend and structure of Tanzania's trade performance in the past decade or so reveals three interesting features. First, total exports have been increasing, in particular due to the rising share of non-traditional exports (mainly exports of minerals, fish and tourism services). Second, imports have grown faster (with a negative trade balance), although at a decreasing rate in recent years, signifying potential for improvement in the trade balance. Finally and more importantly, trade (exports in particular) with the regional markets is picking up fast with the progress in regional integration. Clearly this indicates better prospects for some of Tanzania's non-traditional exports to the regional markets, a favourable change in a trade regime that is dominated by traditional exports of agricultural raw materials to traditional markets.

For instance, total exports to the regional markets increased to US$125 million in 2002 from US$43 million in 1995; over the same period, the regional share of total exports increased from 6 per cent to 14 per cent. This demonstrates that Tanzania's exports to regional markets are growing faster than extra-regional exports (see Chart 7.7). Notable variation exists in the performance of Tanzania's exports among regional blocs, as can be seen in Chart 7.8

The rise in export performance indicates that certain export products have increased in value and/or volume as a result of regional integration. For instance, most of the informal cross-border trade in cereals and other agricultural/food crops has been formalized following lifting the ban on exporting food crops in 1999 and 'opening up' the borders as part of the process of regional integration. SADC and EAC combined have accounted for over 80 per cent of Tanzania's regional

Chart 7.7   Growth of regional and non-regional exports (1995–2002)

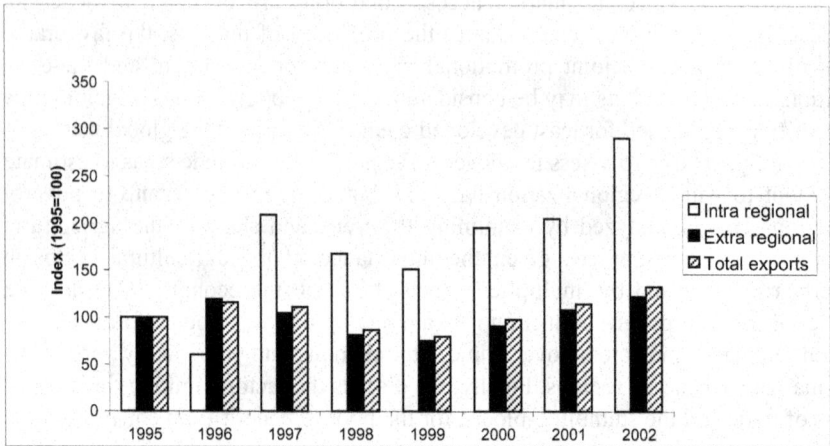

Source: UN Commodity Trade Statistics Database.

Chart 7.8   Tanzania's exports by RTA (1995–2002)

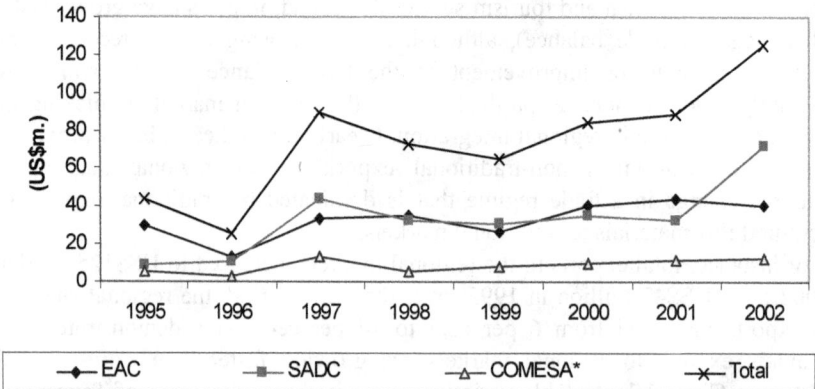

Source: Ibid.

exports and almost all of its regional imports. Chart 7.8 demonstrates two striking features of Tanzania's regional trade. First, after netting out the overlapping membership with SADC and EAC, COMESA's trade with Tanzania has been insignificant and in EAC and SADC's favour since Tanzania's withdrawal in 2000. Clearly the regional trade provisions have affected trade performance with the region. Secondly, although the pace of trade integration is faster in the EAC, the

SADC share of Tanzania's trade is peaking faster, mainly due to the accession of South Africa to the region in 1994. The two points clearly show that Tanzania is not losing as much as was feared by withdrawing from COMESA, so long as the SADC and EAC blocs continue to exist. A follow-up question (not analyzed here) is whether the trade provisions in COMESA are necessarily better/more effective than those of EAC or SADC.

Tanzania has also achieved a reasonable diversification of its exports. Chart 7.9 shows that the number of products exported to its regional markets has increased in parallel with the value of exports. The types of products range from natural resources (bees wax, honey, wild life), new cash crops (such as vanilla, spices, paprika and horticulture – cut flowers) to manufactures and artistic objects (textiles, electrical equipment, etc.). For instance, the AGOA scheme has led to the establishment of new textile and clothing mills. The main trading partners have been South Africa and Kenya for the SADC and EAC regional markets respectively. The two countries accounted for over 40 per cent of all Tanzania's exports to the three regions in 2002. Although the balance of payments between Tanzania and the other countries in the region has been generally unfavourable, it had improved from a deficit of US$223m. in 1995 to US$ 67m. by June 2003.

Chart 7.9   Range and value of products exported to the regional markets

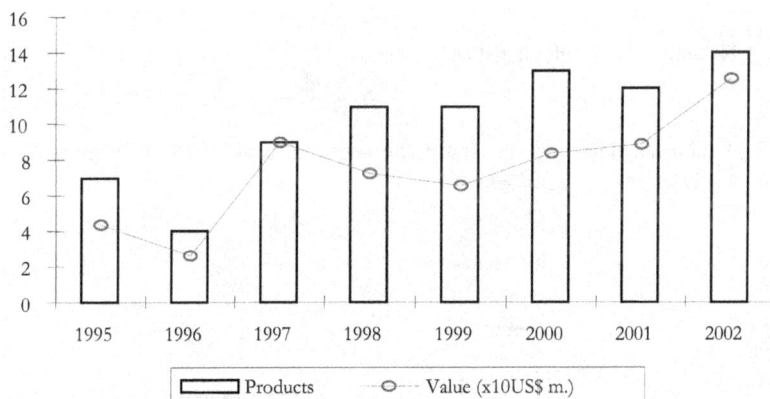

Source: Authors' computation using export data from Tanzania Revenue Authority (TRA).

Chart 7.10 shows that Tanzania's imports from the regional markets have increased slightly faster than those from non-regional markets. Regional variation in terms of growth of imports to Tanzania is shown in Chart 7.11. The share of Tanzania's imports from COMESA, SADC and EAC in total imports increased from 17 per cent in 1995 to 18 per cent in 2002 (Appendix Table 7.4.2). Like regional exports, most regional imports come from South Africa and Kenya, with the share of the two countries in total regional imports increasing from 70 per cent in 1995 to over 90 per cent in 2002. Imports from South Africa alone amount to almost half of Tanzania's total regional imports. Unlike exports, the share of regional imports in total imports of agricultural products has stabilized at around 10 per cent.

Chart 7.10   Growth of regional and non-regional imports (1995–2002)

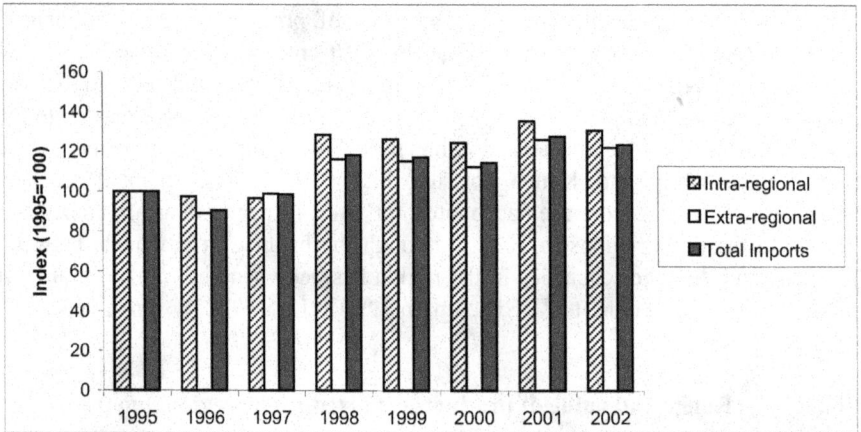

Source: UN Commodity Trade Statistics Database.

Chart 7.11   Tanzania's imports from the regional market (% of regional imports)

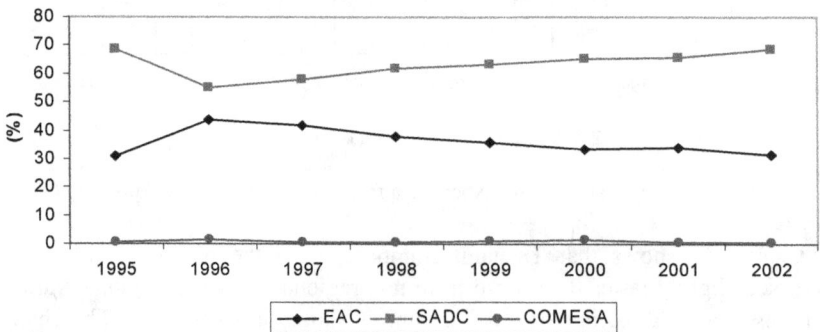

Source: UN Commodity Trade Statistics Database.

7.5.2 Poverty focus of regional trade

Regional integration can affect poverty if its provisions change the poverty focus of trade. One way to examine the poverty focus of trade (or investment) in regional integration is to discuss the share of the agriculture sector in regional trade. This is because of the role that this sector can play in poverty alleviation directly or indirectly through the high linkage it has with the rest of the economy. As noted earlier, emphasizing trade in agricultural goods does not demean the importance of trade in other sectors such as manufacturing and services in alleviating poverty. Instead, we emphasize the following two points. First, Tanzania's comparative advantage continues to lie in the agricultural sector, despite the country's notable failure to transform this comparative advantage into a competitive one (reasons for this failure are beyond the scope of this study). Associated with this failure is the slow (if any) strategic transformation of this sector for growth and poverty reduction. Second, poverty in Tanzania is basically a rural phenomenon, particularly since the implementation of the economic reforms and the adoption of a market economy obliged the government to abandon most of the state-led agricultural activities. Unfortunately, the expected takeover by the private sector has not been forthcoming, given the small amount (and interest) of FDI in this sector. Given these two points, agricultural trade plays an important role in reducing poverty relative to trade in other goods/sectors.

Tanzania's regional exports of agricultural and agro-processed products (mainly food products) as a share of its total regional exports increased from 50 per cent in 1995 to 60 per cent in June 2003. Unlike most of its neighbours, Tanzania suffers few food shortages due to its diverse and favourable agro-ecological climate, contributing to a positive trade balance as shown in Table 7.9. Chart 7.12 (see also Appendix Table 7.4.3) shows the share of the value of agriculture/ agro-processed products in total exports, distinguishing between exports to and outside regional markets. It is found that the share of the value of agricultural products in total intra-regional exports has been increasing, while that of extra-regional and total exports has been declining steadily from 1999 onwards. This is a good sign that the process of regional integration has significant potential for agricultural exports and hence for increases in the welfare of those in the rural sector.[11]

Chart 7.13 shows trends in the value of agricultural exports to the regional markets, while Chart 7.14 shows the share of agriculture in total regional exports by region. Both the value and share of agricultural exports have been increasing

---

[11]   According to interviews conducted for this study with various stakeholders, there has been a significant increase in the export of food crops (including cereals) to the neighbouring countries of Kenya, Uganda, DR Congo, Zambia and Malawi. This positive move is a response to the government's decision to lift the export ban on cereals/food products, but also to the regional trade agreements that alleviated most other non-tariff barriers to trade.

Chart 7.12   Share of agriculture in the value of exports (1995–2002)

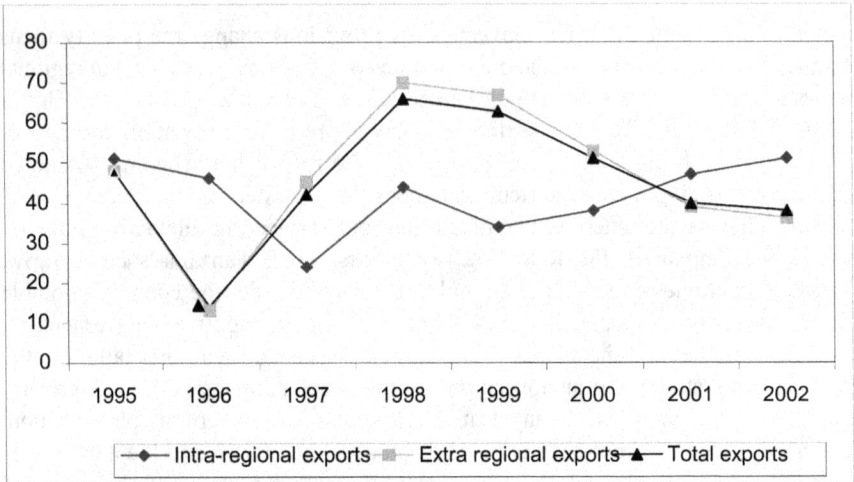

Source: Authors' own calculations.

Chart 7.13   Exports of agricultural products to regional markets (US$ m.)

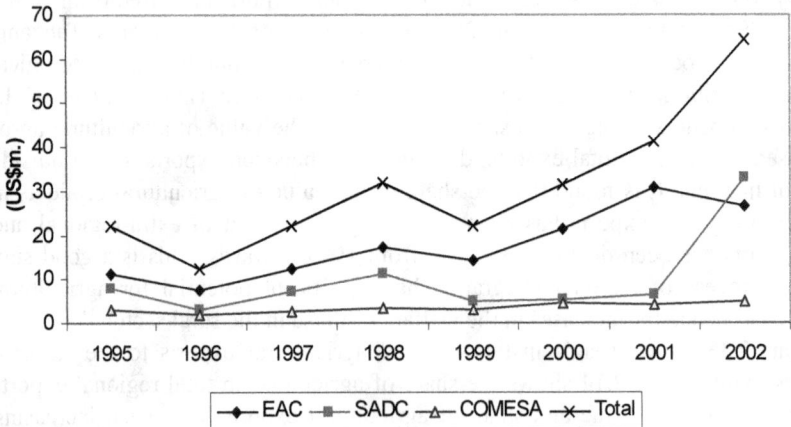

Source: Own computation based on data from Customs Department.

consistently for the EAC market. Between 2001 and 2002, the share of agriculture in total exports to the SADC region has increased sharply alongside that of total (overall) exports, while total exports to the EAC declined slightly. The sharp increase in the case of the SADC market may reflect the impact of South Africa's imports of agro-raw materials from Tanzania, but more importantly the massive exports of cereals from Tanzania following the famine in the neighbouring SADC countries (especially DR Congo, Zambia and Malawi).

Chart 7.14   Share of agriculture in total regional exports (%)

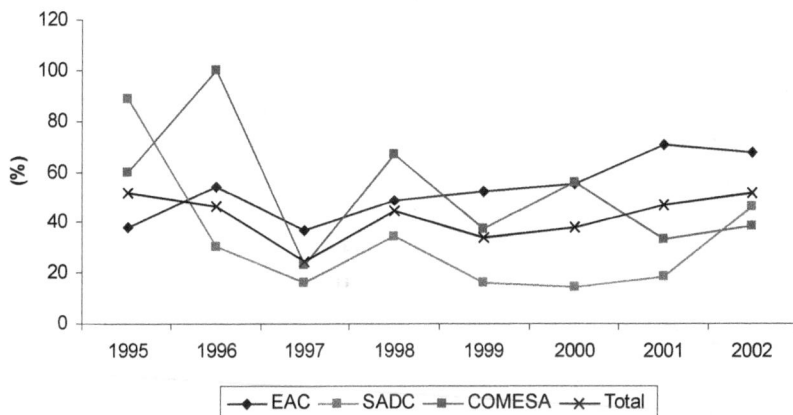

Source: Own computation based on data from Customs Department.

Table 7.9   Trade balance between Tanzania and regional members

| Year | 1995 | | | 2002 | | |
Indicator	X	M	B	X	M	B
Total trade	679	1340	-661	903	1658	-755
Extra-regional trade	641	1114	-473	790	1362	-572
Intra-regional trade	38	226	-188	113	296	-183
o/w Agriculture products	19	24	-5	60	33	27
o/w South Africa (SADC)	0.5	97	-97	35	177	-142
o/w Kenya (EAC)	24	70	-46	16	90	-74

Note: X = exports; M = Imports; B = Trade Balance; o/w = of which.
Source: Calculated from Tanzania Customs data.

Furthermore, regional trade offers significant potential for Tanzania to improve its trade account. Although the trade deficit has increased for total trade, that for regional trade has declined, particularly due to the positive balance in agricultural trade. Notably, the agricultural trade balance with regional markets improved from a deficit of US$5 m. to a surplus of US$27 m. However, the trade balance with the main trading partners in the region (Kenya and South Africa) remains negative, although the South African market shows greater prospects for increased exports compared with the Kenyan market. As shown in Table 7.9, most imports come from SADC, especially from South Africa whose exports to Tanzania have increased markedly since South Africa's accession to the SADC.

7.5.3 Relating trade to poverty indicators

According to Table 7.8, there is a close association between the distribution of poverty by regions and the distribution of cash crops (indicator of availability of tradeable crops). Regions producing cash crops for export also have a lower level

Chart 7.15 Export share of GDP and primary school enrolment rate, 1990-2002

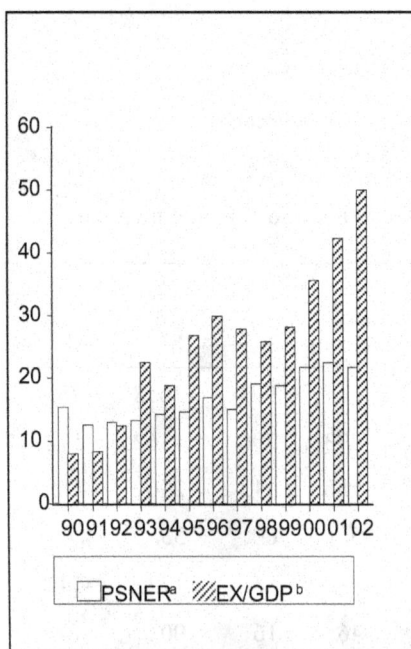

Chart 7.16 Export import ratio and investment share of GDP, 1990-2002

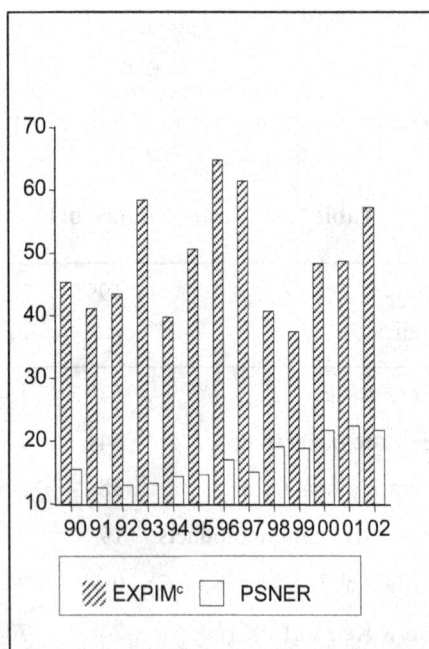

Notes: a) PSNER is Primary School Net Enrolment Rate (i.e. number of enrolled pupils of a particular age as percentage of total population of children in that age group).

b) EX/GDP is ratio of total exports to GDP expressed as percentage share.

c) EXPIM is ratio of export value over import value expressed as percentage share.

Source: Authors' own calculations.

of poverty (higher HDI score), suggesting that trade in agricultural products is likely to be poverty-reducing. Plots of trade and poverty indicators suggest a close positive relation. For instance, Chart 7.15 shows a positive link between the exports share of GDP and the primary school net enrolment rate (PSNER). The correlation between terms of trade and PSNER is positive, albeit less significant. One may need additional econometric analysis to discover the causality between the two, but even for these 'rough and ready' indicators it is clear that trade performance and poverty reduction are not contradictory in the case of Tanzania.

7.5.4 Constraints on trade and investment–poverty link

In a recent study by Booth and Kweka (2004) it was noted that the potential for trade-oriented economic development to reduce poverty in Tanzania is considerable, and that this potential is being seriously undermined. The study highlighted lack of competition in domestic agricultural marketing and inadequate assets available to farmers as the most critical challenges for Tanzania's trade to reduce poverty:

> . . . the poverty profile and production structure of Tanzania create large opportunities for poverty to be reduced through trade-related economic growth. However, this would require rapid agricultural growth oriented towards exports, where the direct impacts and income multipliers would be particularly strong. That has not occurred: Tanzania's agricultural exports have performed very much worse in aggregate than those of Ethiopia, Kenya and Uganda – countries that have a crop mix and natural environment comparable to Tanzania's. This helps to explain why rural poverty rates did not decline significantly during the 1990s, and sets a big challenge to policy makers who hope to do better for the country's poor in the present decade. . . (Booth and Kweka, 2004:iv).

To get a better understanding of how firms are coping with a number of constraints on enhanced trade performance at a regional level and prospects for poverty reduction, we surveyed a few exporting and non-exporting firms to evaluate their prospects for increased regional trade. In this section we report the results of this survey. Although the number of firms interviewed is quite small by research standards, they revealed important information that will supplement our understanding of the challenges limiting the poverty-impact of regional integration in Tanzania.[12] In addition, we considered it necessary to solicit industry perspectives on how Tanzania can effectively realize the benefits of regional integration, given the serious supply-side constraints faced by the productive sectors. We therefore surveyed 30 firms to examine information on production, regional trade/market, employment, and training and skills development issues.

---

[12]   The information revealed by the firms interviewed is, in most cases and based on the recent World Bank-ESRF Investment Climate (RPED) Survey (see World Bank, 2004), consistent with the national average behaviour and concerns of Tanzanian manufacturing firms in the selected sub-sectors.

The sampled firms were sourced equally from the three major industrial regions of Tanzania (numbers in brackets), namely, Dar es Salaam (10), Mwanza (11) and Arusha (9). As noted earlier in the introduction, these firms were carefully selected to target the production sectors that are considered crucial for growth (for example, manufacturing and agriculture) and also have (and a few that do not have) high export potential in the regional markets. All the sectors are privately owned, but are varied to include foreign-owned firms (19 per cent), domestic firms (41 per cent), and joint ventures (37 per cent).[13] Most firms fall between medium-sized and large enterprises, covering the manufacturing, agricultural and fishing sectors. Although we cannot state with certainty the differences in behaviour between regional and non-regional firms, we can make somewhat general conclusions about the domestic versus foreign firms.[14]

Export potential in the regional markets
Almost half of the firms interviewed also export to the regional markets of COMESA, EAC and SADC (in addition to exporting outside these regions). About 30 per cent export mainly to the regional market, 15 per cent to Europe and America, 11 per cent to Japan and Australia, 8 per cent to Asia including India, and 14 per cent to the rest of the world, while 22 per cent sell principally to the domestic market (see Chart 7.17).

Chart 7.17   Export destination for the selected firms

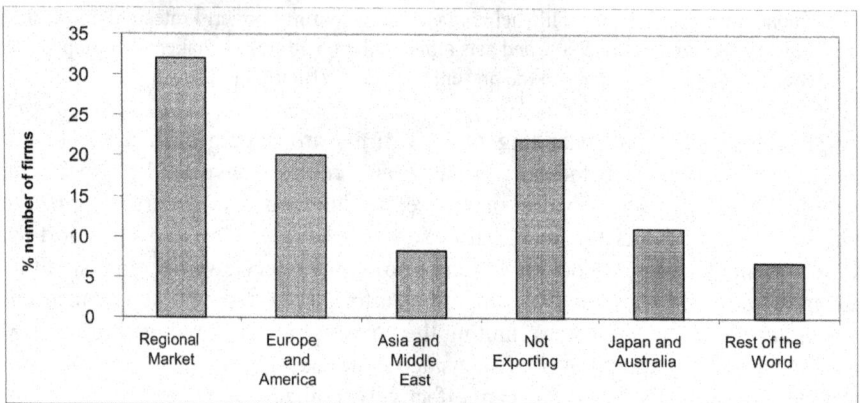

Source: Computed based on data from selected firms.

---

[13] Throughout the text, the percentages may not add up to 100 due to missing values.

[14] Given our limited sample, it was not possible to distinguish firms supplying in or originating from the regional markets from those supplying or originating from outside. However, the important distinction in the context of Tanzania is between behaviours and type of constraints facing the exporting and non-exporting firms (see Chart 7.20).

Chart 7.18 reports the reasons why some of the firms do not export to the regional market. About half of the selected firms do not target this market because they think that the type of goods they produce have no demand in the regional market (for instance, fish fillets), and they fear strong competition and protective tariffs in the importing countries of the regions. This may suggest that firms have failed to diversify their production structure to exploit the regional market because of a perception gap. For instance, although demand for fish fillets is small in the EAC/SADC, there could be a market for products such as sausages, etc. Secondly, some firms seem unaware of changes in regional trade policy. Finally, a number of non-exporting firms are implicitly lacking the confidence or entrepreneurship zeal to venture into the regional export market. However, as is shown in Chart 7.19, exporting to the regional market is not unfeasible. Close to 50 per cent of the firms exporting to the region do not face any substantial barriers to exporting to the regional market. Clearly, this implies that confidence building and entrepreneurship capacity-building by the regional body can make a big difference, and should be one of the appropriate interventions to promote regional exports.

Chart 7.18   Reasons for not exporting in the regional market

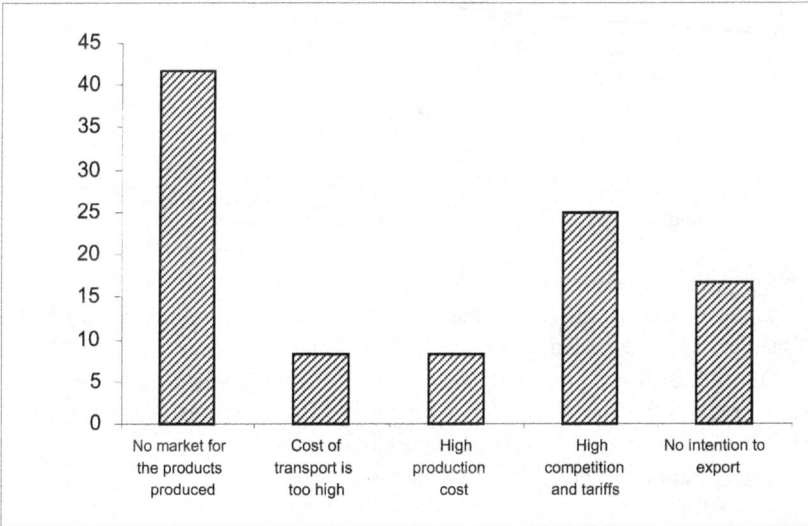

Source: Own computation based on data from selected firms.

Given the infancy of regional integration, firms have yet to realize the impact of the trade reforms arising from regionalization. Over 50 per cent of the selected firms responded that they had not been affected in any way by the signing of the Customs Union for the EAC, but most hope that it is likely to increase production if tariffs are harmonized. The only advantage cited by firms exporting to the regional market is proximitys to the market. When asked whether Tanzanian products can compete with imports from the regional markets of the EAC and SADC after fully fledged integration, firms were ambivalent – 52 per cent were positive and 48 per cent sceptical. For the latter category, high production and energy costs (also see Musonda, 2000), bureaucratic delays in implementing trade agreements, and infrastructure limitations were cited as the most important factors (also see Chart 7.20).

Chart 7.19   Challenges faced by firms in exporting to the regional market

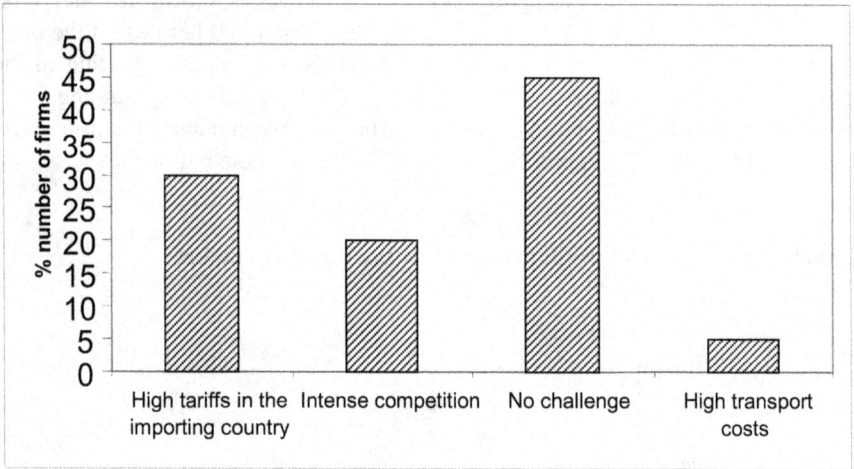

Source: Own computation based on data from selected firms.

Foreign firms are relatively better placed to reap the trade opportunities of liberalization compared with domestically oriented firms. Overall, only 45 per cent of the selected firms regarded regional integration as beneficial to increased export trade, while 55 per cent (most of them domestic) were cynical about the trade benefit of regionalization. Over 80 per cent of the firms that regard regional integration as a trade opportunity are foreign or joint venture companies. This raises a challenge in that policy-makers have not adequately encouraged the wider business community to recognize the opportunities inherent in regional integration. Perhaps there is an ingrained mindset in the business community that regards the export market beyond their neighbours as more important (Amani *et al.*, 2003).

Potential impact of regional FDI
One of the ways in which FDI can be useful in poverty reduction is through its impact on incomes by creating jobs directly and indirectly through its spill-over effects on skill and technology transfer. We investigated the orientation in training, skill development and capacity for technology transfer of the firms interviewed. In

general, the selected firms (almost all) were optimistic that they have sufficient capacity to absorb the technology embodied in FDI. This reflects their quest for technology and skill acquisition as a means of enhancing quality and competitiveness. Associated with this quest, most firms (over 90 per cent) offer regular training to their employees, most of which is done in-house (on the job training). Over time, firms have increasingly demanded skilled labour to support their adherence to quality and modern technology. As shown in Table 7.10, the numbers of skilled and unskilled workers declined between 1998 and 2001 but picked up more recently, while that of semi-skilled workers increased consistently throughout. Clearly, as trade liberalization increases (with the process of regionalization), firms strive to be more competitive, although some (particularly domestic) firms find it a challenge to sustain their output levels and productivity.

Table 7.10   Number of employees in the sampled firms by skill levels (1998=100)

Year	Skilled	Semi-skilled	Unskilled
1998	100	100	100
1999	100	106	104
2000	106	117	94
2001	92	120	112
2002	196	218	170
2003	260	277	252

Source: Computed based on data from selected firms.

Table 7.11   Productivity index (output per worker, 1998=100)

Year	Production (volume)	Total no. of employees	Productivity
1998	100	100	100
1999	114	104	110
2000	162	108	150
2001	168	116	145
2002	175	186	94
2003	185	264	70

Source: Computed based on data from selected firms.

To examine the trend in productivity of the selected regional exporting firms, we computed the output per worker (volume of production/total number of employees) expressed as indices (1998=100), as shown in Table 7.11. The indices show that productivity increased by about 50 per cent from 1998 to 2001 but declined in 2002–3 owing to a faster increase in number of employees relative to output. Presumably, in recent years the increase in competition from imports due to liberalization has negatively affected the rate at which firms' output grows.

Comparative strength of Tanzania as FDI destination
Information from various policy documents and interviews with a number of selected foreign firms suggest that three main factors attract FDI to Tanzania relative to its peers in the EAC and SADC. These are political stability, commitment to reform and endowment of untapped natural resources. We asked the selected firms to identify the three most important factors motivating their investment in Tanzania. Over 40 per cent of them considered political stability to be a prime factor for their investment in Tanzania, while 45 per cent considered trade opportunity (the various trade concessions available for Tanzania) as the second most important factor; and finally, 65 per cent gave incentives from the TIC as the third most important factor. Only a few firms (less than 12 per cent) thought that the regional export market was a strategic reason for their investment in

Chart 7.20   Constraints to exporters and non-exporters

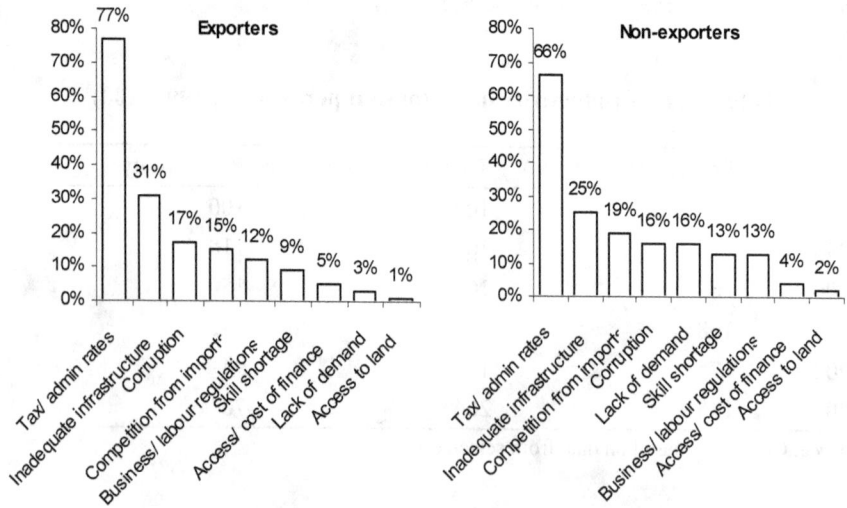

Source: Authors' own calculations.

Tanzania. In addition, many firms in Tanzania are neither aware nor convinced that there are regional-specific incentives for attracting investment – compared with those from the investment centres such as TIC. Eighty-five per cent of the firms reported that there was no incentive from either the EAC or SADC to support their investment. Such scepticism may be expected, since most of the incentives associated with regional integration (for instance, flow of factors of production across boundaries) have yet to be implemented.

Tanzania has probably one of the lowest productivity and competitiveness indicators in the region. It will be difficult to evaluate all the factors limiting productivity and competitiveness, given the scope of this study. The World Bank report (2004) on the Investment Climate Assessment for Tanzania shows a number of constraints faced by exporting (and non-exporting) firms in Tanzania (see Chart 7.20). The highest-ranked constraint is taxation, followed by inadequate infrastructure, corruption and competition from imports. Tanzanian enterprises pay a myriad of taxes – sometimes at exorbitant rates that discourage compliance and enforce rent-seeking behaviour. Although harmonization of fiscal policies is being undertaken within the EAC, Tanzania has the highest VAT rate of 20 per cent compared with 17 per cent in Kenya and 16 per cent in Uganda. In addition, local government taxes are another hurdle for exporters.

7.6 Other regional cooperation for poverty reduction

As noted in Section 7.3, the focus and orientation of the integration process of Regional Integration Agreements may follow a market integration model or a development cooperation model or a combination of the two. In Africa (perhaps in the developing world in general) development cooperation has been a primary objective in many RIAs, given their various development challenges other than trade integration. One such development challenge is poverty reduction. This section reviews the link between RI and poverty in Tanzania via development cooperation. Our concern is to identify regional cooperation programmes for the EAC and SADC that are likely to have an important impact on poverty, and then to evaluate their efficacy using case examples.

For simplicity, we can categorize two ways in which development cooperation takes place: development programmes or projects, and development (management) policy on a particular issue/sector of common interest. The former demonstrates the need for the regional members to pool their resources to meet a particular development objective (for example, the provision of public goods such as infrastructure development). The latter includes non-trade and non-investment regional policy. We shall review some cases of regional development cooperation that have notable implications for poverty in both the EAC and SADC. However, given the scattered nature of the various programmes/projects, it is not easy to access and evaluate all of them. For instance, in the case of SADC, the organization of most programmes is not centralized, but is usually put under the custodianship of the relevant government ministry/department, which may not always be willing to share such information. In the case of the EAC, many programmes are still in the pipeline and have yet to materialise.

7.6.1 Socio-economic programmes in the EAC

Several non-trade/investment initiatives have been undertaken by the EAC that have important bearing on poverty reduction. Due to unforeseen circumstances in the regional organizations in Africa, many of the programmes set by many RIAs were never pursued by the member states, posing the challenge of lack of credibility (Musonda, 2004:61). One of the most successful projects is the East African Development Bank, which mobilizes resources to finance various social/ economic projects in the region. Box 7.2 provides a case study showing how the EADB has strengthened trade and investment relations between the EAC member states, and its potential for poverty reduction. As explained the box, the bank has played an important role in long-term lending for productive sectors of the economy such as manufacturing, agriculture and energy development. This is particularly important for Tanzania where commercial lending to the rural sector is seriously lacking.

Box 7.2 The East African Development Bank (EADB)

The EADB started operations in 1967 following the establishment of the EAC. The bank did not collapse with the Community in 1977 because its assets were in the hands of various shareholders. The ownership structure of the EADB is as follows: EAC – 72.21 per cent; FMO (Netherlands), – 10 per cent; DEG (Germany) – 2.7 per cent. The supervision of credit allocation is controlled by the bank's management and is on a purely commercial basis. The main objective of the bank is to encourage industrial balance by advancing loans to key growth sectors that are not attractive to lending by the commercial banks. The bank's main focus is on financing projects that are regional in nature. The bank is currently involved in regional energy and fishing projects. It has also started issuing bonds to the capital markets of the three member states.

The bank has the capacity to mobilize substantial amounts of resources from other partners and development banks to finance regional projects. Its loans range from US$20,000 to US$10 million and can be short-term (less than two years), medium-term (1–5 years) and long-term (up to 25 years). Most loans have been directed to the manufacturing sector. Loans are awarded in accordance with the commercial viability of specific projects. The bank is comparatively well-placed to reduce poverty, as it accords priority to value adding and agriculture-based projects, with a low interest rate (14 per cent) compared with most commercial banks. However, the practice of extending relatively fewer loans to the agriculture sector emanates from the lack of collateral to support loan applications. This lack of collateral is due to the practice, until recently, of

---

not accepting land as collateral. The government addressed this constraint in 2002 by amending the Land Act to allow land to have a commercial value for investment. The governments of the three member states have not provided a good environment conducive to bankers extending credit to poor farmers. The bank is nevertheless trying to work with the Small Industry Development Organization (SIDO) and micro-finance institutions to help farmers and small to medium-sized enterprises obtain financing, since these institutions have the infrastructure to reach the poor in the rural areas.

Source: EADB, *Annual Report,* 2003

The sectoral distribution of the approved projects (for 1999–2003) is shown in Chart 7.21. The share of agriculture increased from 25 per cent in 1999 to over 40 per cent in 2003. Interviews with EADB officials confirmed their focus on agriculture and fisheries (because of the EAC's Lake Victoria), which reflects the EADB's and EAC's commitment to poverty reduction. Another important recipient of EADB loans is the services sector, notably the financial sector (a couple of banks) and tourism. Currently, the bank does not lend to construction companies. The share of the manufacturing sector has also increased over time.

Chart 7.21   EADB sectoral distribution of investment approvals

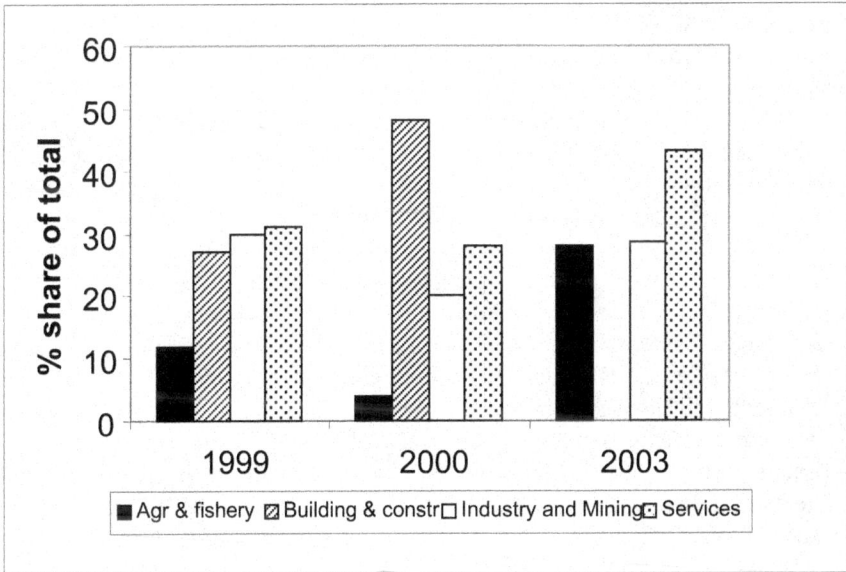

Source: TIC.

Lake Victoria Development Project

Lake Victoria is one of the biggest lakes in Africa covering an area of 68,800 sq. km. The lake is the most important source of livelihood for many people in the EAC, as it has the cleanest water for human consumption and is a source of Nile perch, one of the most popular fish in the world and hence an important source of export revenue for the EAC member countries. In this sub-section, we describe the Lake Victoria Development Project as an important instrument for regional integration in the EAC, and examine its effectiveness in poverty reduction.

The lake is a source of food (fish), safe drinking water, means of transport (marine) and a good climate that enables the region to grow a variety of food and cash crops. As a shared resource, it is instrumental in the EAC's regional integration prospects, but with a number of managerial challenges. First, it presumes the existence of capable regional institutions to oversee its utilization and regulation. Second, it has some environmental effects that need to be alleviated/ tamed. Thirdly, given the fact that the level of the fish stock is subject to depletion, the regional body will require substantial resources to ensure the sustainability of the lake's benefits, including investment in aquaculture, marine research and infrastructure. Finally, it requires the harmonization of social and economic policies and regulation to govern/ promote investments in the lake or exploitation of its downstream benefits. To obtain answers to these issues, the study team visited a couple of institutions and stakeholders responsible for the management of the lake including the Lake Victoria Environmental Management Project – LVEMP (see Box 7.3).

Interviews and a review of the documentation indicate that most of the organizations involved in different aspects of the management of Lake Victoria have adopted a regional approach and, as such, the existence of a shared resource has deepened further the need for regional cooperation and harmonization of policies. This has enhanced the potential use of the lake for poverty reduction that would otherwise have been difficult. However, although poverty reduction is identified as a key objective, a regional integration framework is not yet sufficiently implemented to benefit the poor. This is because most of the regional institutions are too much in their infancy and too under-resourced to implement poverty-reducing programmes. The LVEMP is geared towards regulating fishing methods to ensure a sustainable fish stock. These tasks have resource implications that will be too difficult for a single (poor) country like Tanzania to meet. Pooling resources and capacity at the regional level will reduce the burden on individual countries and ensure sustainable use of the lake. Conversely, the possibility of joint intervention in the management and exploitation of the lake may be held back by the pace at which the integration process is taking place. For instance, while LVEMP has successfully gone through its first phase of operations, the EAC has not yet secured the resources necessary to sustain the LVEMP despite the fact that it is scheduled to assume management responsibility for the organization.

Box 7.3 Lake Victoria Environmental Management Project (LVEMP)

The LVEMP was established in 1997 in Tanzania for the three countries as one of the projects to implement the 1992 Rio Conference Agenda 21. It is supported by a grant from the World Bank and the Global Environmental Facility (GEF) to the tune of $70 million for the three East African countries. Of this, Kenya and Uganda have received US$24.3 m. and US$25.3 m. respectively, and Tanzania has received US$20.4 m.

The philosophy behind LVEMP is to avoid the establishment of parallel institutions. One of the initial tasks of the project was to control the seaweed, which posed a serious environmental problem to the lake and limited its use (it makes water treatment very costly, limits the penetration of light in the lake and obstructs movement in the water). The fishing aspect of the project addresses the regulation of fishing methods and guards against illegal fishing techniques. However, enforcement is still a challenging problem, as there is only a small workforce in Tanzania (193 people) compared with 611 employees in Kenya. Furthermore, the project establishes fish sites and Beach Management Units (BMUs); regulates deforestation and conducts/supports fishery research (to increase the fishing stock and maintain aquaculture). So far the LVEMP has managed to establish over 500 BMUs across Lake Victoria, which the government is keen to maintain and strengthen. In fact, the EAC has embraced the idea of developing the BMUs. In addition, the project has undertaken soil and water conservation and micro-projects that address priority needs of the communities surrounding the lake zone. Finally, it undertakes water quality management, and supports fishery departments in the riparian universities as well as capacity-building initiatives.

The project's achievements include the following. About 90 per cent of the area covered by the weed has been controlled (most of the remaining part is in the Burundi and Rwandan part of the Lake where there is a lack of government commitment); fish quality and safety assurance has been substantially improved; the law enforcement mechanism to curb illegal fishing has been strengthened; new species of fish feared extinct have been discovered and strategies to conserve them have been developed. Many more initiatives are aimed at conserving the biodiversity and genetic resources of the lake for the benefit of the riparian and the global community.

The project was scheduled to fall totally under the management of the EAC, whose role was to coordinate the activities of LVEMP, solicit for funds and provide institutional support. It should be noted that LVEMP is a government project, owned by the three governments. Before the establishment of the EAC, the project was managed under a tripartite agreement with no legal framework; hence the regional integration has helped to consolidate the regional effort. This poses a big challenge to the sustainability of the project, as the EAC does not have its own resources for funding the project's second phase. Phase 2, scheduled for 10–15 years, focuses on the environmental aspects of the lake, applied fishery research, water movement due to climatic changes, and the regulation of water quality. It is thus likely to be less ambitious and smaller in focus than Phase 1, implying that some of the established programmes (such as the micro-project, capacity-building, soil conservation and forestry) may cease or receive little attention. However, in the future, cooperation with the other neighbouring countries of Rwanda and Burundi is essential to enhance the effectiveness of the LVEMP project.

- *Income-generating capacity of the lake.* Lake Victoria's role in poverty reduction can be analyzed by examining the income and employment impact of artisanal fishing. Interviews with various stakeholders revealed that there are some factors that limit the extent to which the lake can be used as a tool for fighting poverty with or without the regional institutions. The artisanal fishermen hold a weak position in the fishing value-addition chain; they lack the capacity to organize themselves and the negotiating capacity to achieve a fair price for their produce. Large-scale fishermen have dominated some fishing sites, often limiting any possible opportunity for artisanal fishermen. Also, the latter have been victims of robbery and piracy in the lake. Some of them have been caught in interlocking contracts, with the fish processing factories supplying nets and other fishing facilities on condition that they sell their total catch to the factories at pre-arranged prices.

   Over-dependence on fishing as a sole source of income/employment is yet another setback. Factories in the last few years have been cutting jobs as a result of declining catches/ fish stock. In total, the number of people employed in the fishing industry increased from 300,000 in 2000 to 500,000 in 2002, including fishermen, traders and factory workers. The lake has also brought in a number of regional NGOs to address the poverty reduction aspects, but their collaboration is somewhat inconsistent and in some cases institutional conflicts arise, limiting the effects for the beneficiaries. For instance, there are notable conflicts between the LVEMP and some smaller watchdog type NGOs, in particular EcoVic, which claim to be concerned with the common good's interests in the lake and its sustainability.

- *Marine transport on the lake and intra-regional trade.* Lake Victoria offers an effective means of transporting cargo and passengers across the three countries. The main service provided by the Marine Company (MSCL) is to transport transit cargo between the three countries via the lake. This makes the lake and the MSCL strategic tools for enhancing intra-regional trade in East Africa. There is tripartite cooperation between the railway companies in the three countries. The tripartite agreement is intended to allow the three countries to cooperate in transporting transit goods across the lake, irrespective of whether the cargo originates in or is destined for the respective member country.

   A few problems limit the significant role of marine transport on the lake. These include (i) lack of adequate rail wagons compared with Kenya, denying Tanzania much business opportunity; (ii) increased competition from road transport; (iii) discrimination and an unduly nationalist attitude on the part of Kenya against Tanzanian business people (for instance, Kenyan customs giving preferential duty rates to fellow Kenyan businesses); and finally, (iv) the soaring oil prices which have reduced Tanzania's competitiveness compared with Kenya. The EAC is keen to cooperate more effectively in infrastructure development and has committed itself to maintaining cooperation in marine environmental management through the LVEMP.

- *Performance of the fisheries sector.* Fishing in Lake Victoria is principally a private sector activity, and a number of export-processing firms have been established around the lake. These firms export processed fish largely to the EU, the US, Australia, the Middle East and Central and Northern America. Tanzania has taken the fishing industry more seriously than the other countries in the region and has therefore greater potential for poverty eradication (for example, development of beach fishing communities, fisheries research and quality, sustainable fishing, an export ban on traditional species for domestic consumption, a ban on the use of fish trolleys). Tanzania was also the first to get on to List 1 of the EU's quality certification. The country's fish fillets are of high quality, due to adherence to international (EU) quality standards.[15] However, the government Fisheries Department is concerned about rising fishing levels as this may compromise the sustainability of the fish stock. Much of the current government effort is directed towards seeking alternative value-adding industry within the fisheries sector to discourage over-reliance on fish exports and to promote downstream benefits.

- *Fish export royalty.* Tanzania is the only one of the three EAC countries to charge a royalty on fish exports (20 cents per kilogram). Coupled with higher petrol and power prices, this additional tax on exports has made Tanzanian fish fillets less competitive. An interview with the Fisheries Department revealed that the royalty has been used to develop the fisheries sector including the fishing beaches, the fisheries division, research, landing sites, etc. So far there has been considerable improvement in these aspects. Firms complain about the size and multiplicity of taxes including the royalty because they see hardly any tangible benefit from the taxes they are paying. The tax collected is not earmarked for expenditure in the local area, and other benefits derived from such taxes are not easily visible or tangible to the firms.

Agricultural and environmental programmes

A study to elaborate a comprehensive East African Agricultural and Rural Development Strategy has been undertaken by the EAC Secretariat. A committee

---

[15] Tanzania lost its market significantly in 1998 following an EU ban on imports of Nile Perch due to the occurrence of dead bodies in Lake Victoria in 1994, the outbreak of cholera in Uganda and the traces (in Spain) of salmonella in the fish fillets in 1997. After the lifting of the EU ban in 2000, the export volume and value nearly doubled and this increased the fishing effort to almost 100% of the 1999 level.

on agriculture and food security has been set up, which has prepared a report on agriculture and rural development policy and sanitary and phytosanitary measures as well as guidelines regarding farm inputs. The report was presented and approved by the Council of Ministers in 2005. A joint project for the control of trans-border livestock diseases and trade in livestock and livestock products is also being developed by the Secretariat. As a basis for these programmes, a Memorandum of Understanding on environmental management and cooperation was signed on 22 October 1998 by the three states. Subsequently, the development of a Protocol on Environmental and Natural Resource Management has begun. Currently, the Secretariat is facilitating study on the importation, manufacture, utilization, disposal and re-cycling of polyethylene material in the region.

Social affairs and human development programmes
Tanzania and Uganda are in the process of issuing national identity cards in order to enhance security control in the region and facilitate the implementation of decisions relating to the free movement of people in the region. On gender issues, a Regional Gender and Community Development Strategy and Programme have been elaborated. The East African Integrated Disease Surveillance Network (EAIDSNet) will facilitate disease surveillance and collaboration in health research in communicable diseases. Funding has been secured from the Rockefeller Foundation to finance a three-year health project. In line with this, a regional programme for the control of cholera, yellow fever and HIV/AIDS has been developed.

7.6.2 Socio-economic programmes/ projects in SADC

Owing to a lack of good detailed case studies of projects and cooperation programmes in SADC, we give a short annotated list of projects for which information was made available.

Maintenance of peace and conflict resolution
Maintaining peace and security in the region is one of the basic SADC objectives. Various initiatives have been undertaken; including an end to the armed conflicts in Angola and Democratic Republic of Congo. In addition, SADC has a Memorandum of Understanding with the UN High Commission for Refugees for solving refugee problems within the member states.

Disaster management and humanitarian crises
SADC and the UN have launched an appeal fund amounting to US$611 million to avert food crises in Zambia, Zimbabwe, Malawi, Lesotho, Swaziland and Mozambique. The member states are also working to manage carefully the Genetically Modified (GMO) food grains supplied to them by donors (in response to their appeal), in order to safeguard cultural and health considerations associated with the consumption of GMO foods. These concerns are critical for poverty

alleviation in the region. A strategy to address systematically the problems of floods and droughts in the region was developed and approved by the Council of Ministers in 2001. Six SADC member countries, namely, Angola, Namibia, the DRC, Mozambique, Zambia and Zimbabwe, have landmine problems, which have exacerbated the poverty situation. The cost of mine removal is very high and these countries face constraints in financing these operations. SADC has responded to the problem by creating a regional Mine Action Programme for devising strategies for mutual assistance. A Regional Mine Action Database linking the affected states has been created to assist the mobilization of resources from potential donors.

Crop, livestock and natural resource development
The most pressing problems facing the agrarian sector in the region include loss of genetic biodiversity, insufficient inputs, poor technology, and inadequate control and containment of plant diseases and pests. SADC, through its Food, Agriculture and Natural Resource Development Unit (FANR), is developing regional programmes to promote crop production, plant protection, processing, storage and monitoring plant diseases, including migratory pests such as the Larger Grain Borer. The SADC Seed Security Network has also developed a five-year action plan to ensure the availability of quality seeds for smallholders in the region. Livestock products also play an important role in poverty reduction and food security in the region. Having recognized this, the Farm Animal Genetic Resource Network programme (FAGRN) aims to support the member states at regional and national level in developing the sustainable use and management of indigenous and local breeds in order to improve income generation and household food security. To ensure animal health in the region, the SADC Animal Health Surveillance Network (SADC–AHSN) has been formed, with staff specialists in veterinary epidemiology, animal disease outbreak investigations, and food inspection and research. These programmes will focus on policies related to the safety of food for domestic consumption and export, the control of Transboundary Animal Diseases (TADs), and the adoption of legislation that stipulates the role of the public sector in food safety.

The Protocol on Forestry was signed in October 2002. The protocol emphasizes the development of an appropriate forestry industry and trade within the SADC region. The project's objective is to improve rural livelihoods through the sustainable utilization of selected indigenous fruit trees in the semi-arid areas of the region. The SADC heads of state also signed a Protocol on Wildlife Conservation and Law Enforcement in 1999, which seeks to establish common approaches to the conservation and sustainable use of wildlife resources. However, the Protocol has yet to be ratified by all the member states.

SADC has also instituted a strategy for environmental protection and sustainable development, aiming to accelerate the economic growth of the poor majority and to ensure equitable and sustainable use of natural resources. Furthermore, a SADC Protocol on the Environment that will commit the member states to cooperation on all issues relating to environmental protection and sustainable use of natural resources is being developed. In 1995, SADC drew up a Protocol on a Shared Watercourse System with the aim of developing and managing shared watercourses in the region. The SADC Fisheries Protocol came into force in September 2003 to stimulate action by the member states to utilize monitoring, control, and surveillance tools and to address Illegal Unreported and Unregulated (IUU) fishing, and to address the negative effects of IUU fishing in their national Exclusive Economic Zones (EEZ).

Social and human development programmes

A number of initiatives are also being pursued in the area of social and human development. In order to combat high illiteracy rates in the member states, a Protocol on Education and Training has been signed. In addition, SADC is considering the establishment of a Regional Centre specializing in lifelong learning to address the problem of illiteracy among older people. A regional proposal is being formulated to solicit funds from the Global Fund to Fight AIDS, TB and Malaria to fight pandemics of these diseases. Other initiatives against these diseases include the launch of the SADC Malaria Strategy by three SADC health ministers, and SADC's revision and reinforcement of its Multi-sectoral HIV/AIDS Strategic Framework and Programme of Action 2003–7. The latter programme aims at intensifying measures to tackle the destructive impact of the HIV/AIDS pandemic in a comprehensive manner in order to promote sustainable human development in the member states. The SADC region is facing problems of illicit drug trafficking and abuses which are usually associated with the spread of infectious diseases, as well as corruption and money-laundering. In reaction to this, a Protocol on Combating Illicit Drugs has been signed, and drug committees have been formed to facilitate the exchange of drug-related information between member governments. SADC provides funding and technical advice for these strategies.

7.7 Conclusion

While regional integration agreements have existed in many parts of the world for a long time, their efficacy in changing the nature of the integration of developing countries into the global economy and, subsequently, their impact in reducing poverty have become an important subject of analysis and policy in the last decade or so. In most parts of Africa, a new wave of regionalization is taking place. Whereas some regional agreements are expanding and others are being strengthened, new ones are also being formed. In this report, we present a case study of Tanzania as part of the larger study that is aimed at identifying the linkages between regionalization and poverty either directly or indirectly through trade, investment or development cooperation channels.

While the overall conclusion is that regional integration is useful for enhancing trade performance, it should be noted that the process of regional integration in the case of Tanzania is in most respects in its initial stages (there is little evidence to attribute most of the post-regionalization trade and investment performance to the respective regional provisions). The EAC was re-established recently (the Customs Union was signed in March 2004), the SADC trade protocol was ratified in 2000 and Tanzania withdrew from the much longer-established COMESA in the same year. Hence, only broad conclusions can be drawn on the impact of regional integration on poverty in Tanzania.

The findings show that regional integration has increased intra-regional trade for Tanzania, but not inward FDI. Regional integration can reduce poverty particularly by increasing exports of agricultural products. While the regional blocs (SADC and EAC) have not been a significant source of FDI to Tanzania, the efficacy of FDI in poverty reduction in general has been limited, among other factors, by its concentration on sectors that have few linkages to the rest of the economy (in particular, FDI in the mining sector). Regional integration can also address poverty reduction through cooperation in development projects/programmes, which we find to have a significant impact on poverty but to be limited in scope.

The limited impact of regional integration on poverty can be explained, *inter alia*, by the infancy of the integration process and the fact that the poverty challenge in Tanzania transcends the role of regional integration *per se*. For instance, since poverty in Tanzania is basically a rural phenomenon, the unfavourable economic conditions in the rural sector (lack of functioning markets, low level of skills and reliance on subsistence agriculture with constrained tradeable crops) limit the benefits of regional integration for the poor. Nevertheless, the realization of the potential for regional integration to reduce poverty depends greatly on how these conditions are addressed, more than on the efforts to hasten the regional integration progress.

Tanzania has a notable comparative advantage over its neighbours in the export of food and agricultural products, but a competitive advantage is required in order to maintain the current positive trends. Economy-wide competitiveness can be achieved by a combination of various initiatives, including measures to improve taxation and the infrastructure to reduce high energy tariffs and the bureaucracy, and to speed up the establishment of, and compliance with, quality standards. The private sector should be made conversant with the modalities and opportunities of regionalization, as part of the government's measures (if any) to support export entrepreneurship.

References

Amani, H.K., Nyange, D., Kweka, J.P. and Leyaro, V., 'Trade Policies and Agricultural Trade in the SADC Region: Challenges and Implications' (Dar es Salaam: Preliminary Report for Tanzania, 2003).

Bende-Nabende, A., *Globalization, FDI, Regional Integration and Sustainable Development* (Aldershot: Ashgate, 2002).

Blomström, M.A. and Kokko, A., *Regional Integration and Foreign Direct Investment*, NBER Working Paper No. 6019 (Cambridge, MA: National Bureau of Economic Research, 1997).

Bank of Tanzania, *Tanzania Investment Report* (Dar es Salaam: Bank of Tanzania, 2001).

Booth, D. and Kweka, J., 'Priorities for National Trade Policy and PRSP Review: The TTPP Trade–Poverty Linkages Study' (report prepared for the TTPP project, Dar es Salaam, 2004).

Collier, P. and Pattilo, C., *Investment and Risk in Africa* (Oxford: Centre for the Study of African Economies, University of Oxford, 2000).

EADB, *Annual Report, 2003* (Nairobi: EADB, 2003).

ESRF, *Tanzania: Current Trade Liberalization study of Tanzanian Firms* (Dar es Salaam: ESRF, 2001).

Fajgenbaum, J., Sharer, R., Thugge, K. and DeZoysa, H., *The Cross-Border Initiative in Eastern and Southern Africa*, IMF Staff Paper (Washington, DC: IMF, 1999) www.imf.org/external/np/cross.

Hartzenberg, T., *What are the Major Trends and Determinants of Foreign Direct Investment in SADC Countries?* (Nairobi: Development Research, 2000).

Kabelwa, G., *Technology Transfer and South African Investment in Tanzania*, Globalization and East Africa Working Paper Series No. 10 (Dar es Salaam: ESRF, 2004).

Kennes, W., 'Developing Countries and Regional Integration', *The Courier*, 165 (1997): 64 –7. www.euforic.org/courier/165e_ken.htm.

Kweka, J., 'Regional Economic Integration in East Africa and its Impact on the Tanzanian Economy' (paper prepared for seminar for members of Parliament, Dodoma, 2003).

Kweka, J., Morrissey, O. and Blake, A., 'Economic Potential of Tourism in Tanzania', *Journal of International Development*, 15 (2003): 335–51.

Madete, L., 'Foreign Direct Investment and Public Policy in Tanzania' (unpublished MA thesis, Economics Department, University of Dar es Salaam, 2000).

Masinde, R. and Kibua, E., *Capital Market Development Policy in Kenya*, IPAR Discussion Paper No. 58 (Nairobi: IPAR, 2004).

Mashindano, O., 'Private Foreign Investment and the Poorest Countries: The case of Tanzania', in North–South Institute, *Investing in Poor Countries* (Ottawa: North–South Institute, 2004).

Mboya, P.G., 'Foreign Direct Investment, Financial Development and Economic Growth in Tanzania' (unpublished MSc. thesis, Economics Department, University of Zimbabwe, 2003).

McKay, A., Milner, C. and Morrissey, O., *The Trade and Welfare Effects of a Regional Economic Partnership Agreement*, CREDIT Research Paper (Nottingham: Department of Economics, University of Nottingham, 2000).

Mkenda, B., *Globalization and Rural Household Welfare in Tanzania*, Globalization, Working Papers No. 15 (Dar es Salaam: ESRF, 2003).

Musonda, F., *Intra-Industry Trade Between Members of the PTA/COMESA Regional Trading Arrangements*, AERC Paper No. 64 (Nairobi: AERC, 1997).

Musonda, F., *The Impact of East African Integration on Tanzania's Economy*, Occasional Paper (Nairobi: Konrad Adenauer Foundation, 2000).

Musonda, F., *Regional Integration in Africa: A Closer Look at the East Africa Community* (Fribourg: Swiss Institute of Federalism, 2004).

Musonda, F., Rajara, A., Yeast, A., Ng'eno, N. and Mwau, G., 'Putting the Horse Before the Cart: On the Appropriate Transition to an East African Customs Union' (a report prepared for the East African Community Secretariat, 1999).

OECD *Regional Integration: Observed Trade and Other Economic Links* (Paris: OECD, 2001).

Ruhindi, Freddie, 'Final Draft Report on the East African Model Investment Code, 2002' (Arusha: Ruhindi & Co. Advocates, 2002).

TIC, *Tanzania Investment Report* (Dar es Salaam: TIC, 2001).

UNCTAD, *Investment Policy Review* (Geneva: United Nations, December 2001).

UNCTAD, *Investment Policy Review: The United Republic of Tanzania* (New York: United Nations, 2002).

United Republic of Tanzania (URT), *Poverty and Human Development Report* (Dar es Salaam: Government Printers, 2002a).

United Republic of Tanzania (URT), *Trade and Poverty Programme: Institutional Review* (Dar es Salaam: Ministry of Industry and Trade, 2002b).

United Republic of Tanzania (URT), *Poverty Reduction Strategy. The Third Progress Report* (Dar es Salaam: The Vice President's Office. 2004).

United Republic of Tanzania (URT), *National Trade Policy for Competitive Economy and Export-Led Growth* (Dar es Salaam: MIT Press, 2003).

Velde, D.W. te and Bezemer, D., *Regional Integration and Foreign Direct Investment in Developing Countries* (London: Overseas Development Institute, 2004).

Velde, D.W. te and Fahnbulleh, M., *Investment-related Provisions in Regional Trade Agreements* (London: Overseas Development Institute, 2003).

Velde, D.W. te, Page, S. and Morrissey, O., 'Regional Integration and Poverty: Mapping the Linkages', Report prepared as part of the EC-PREP funded Project on Regional Integration and Poverty (London: Overseas Development Institute, 2004) (http://www.odi.org.uk/iedg/projects/ec_prep1.pdf).

Viner, J., *The Customs Union Issue* (New York: Carnegie Endowment for International Peace, 1950).

Wanga, G. and Matambalya, F.T., (2001) 'Southern African Development Community and Poverty Alleviation: An Overview' (Paper for the Southern African Regional Integration Conference, St George's Hotel, Johannesburg, 19 and 20 July 2001).

Winters, L.A., *Trade, Trade Policy and Poverty: What Are the Links?* CEPR Discussion Paper No. 2382 (London: Centre for Economic Policy Research, 2002).

World Bank, *Investment Climate Assessment for Tanzania* (Washington, DC: World Bank, 2004).

World Trade Organization, *Trade Policy Review for Tanzania 2000* (Geneva: World Trade Organization, 2000).

Appendices

Appendix 7.1 Some investment-related policy reforms implemented by Tanzania since mid 1990s

Nature of activities implemented	Financial year
The National Investment Protection and Promotion Act 1990 was reviewed to grant tax exemption upon commencement of production.	1994–5
Minimum qualifying investment ceiling for any venture set at US$10 million.	1995–6
Investment Promotion Policy and Act 1992 were reviewed to eliminate bottlenecks hampering steady flow of investments.	1996–7
Government promotes local/foreign investors through provision of conducive investment environment.	1996–7
Agreement reached by EAC to promote East Africa as a single Investment Centre destination.	1996–7
Investment incentives in East Africa harmonized.	1997–8
Investors in petroleum and gas exploration not to be charged customs duty and sales tax on machinery and equipment.	1997–8
Investors in agriculture, infrastructure construction, telecommunications and human resource development to be charged only 5% customs duty and 5% sales tax.	1997–8
Investors in all other sectors than the above to be charged 10% sales tax/ customs duty.	1997–8
Investment Act 1997 transfers tax exemption administration to TRA to enhance efficiency.	1998–9
Investment Promotion Centre changed to Tanzania Investment Centre.	1998–9
Tanzania grants 100% deduction on investment costs to be on a par with Kenya/Uganda.	1998–9
Income tax regime for investors with TIC certificates and those without certificates harmonized by allowing full capital expenses when computing tax relief.	1999–2000
Establishment and review of SADC protocol on trade to spearhead harmonization and cooperation of member states in investment and trade sectors.	2000–1
Withholding tax rate on dividends harmonized at 10% for TIC and non-TIC certificate holders.	2000–1
Withholding tax rates on interest harmonized at 15% for TIC and non-TIC certificate holders.	2000–1
15% Capital Allowances to mining companies on unredeemed expenditure limited to existing investors only.	2001/2
Deferment of royalty limited to existing investors only.	2001/2
Immigration Act and Business Licensing Act harmonized to facilitate investment and speed up activities.	2001/2

Source: ESRF (2001).

Appendix 7.2 Some important trade policy measures implemented in Tanzania since mid-1990s

Nature of activities implemented	Financial year
Government committed to trade liberalization by providing conducive environment for security of bank credit.	1994–5
Government through Bank of Tanzania starts buying gold and countering smuggling of minerals.	1994–5
Export of traditional crops by private sector allowed.	1994–5
To encourage export trade government advises introduction of hire purchase schemes.	1995–6
Government authorizes reciprocal arrangements for Kenya and Uganda businesses to set up local agencies in Tanzania.	1995–6
Consensus for enhancing cooperation amongst East African countries reached by agreeing on intra-regional trade and removal of barriers to facilitate cross-border trade.	1996–7
Presidents of Kenya, Uganda and Tanzania signed Treaty for revival of East African Community.	1996–7
Government pledges to enhance trade liberalization by further lowering of tariff rates while protecting the country from becoming dumping ground of substandard and harmful commodities.	1996–7
Local beer industry accorded protection to stimulate production volumes and employment. COMESA beer tariffs rise.	1997–8
Polished and cut mineral stones not to be charged royalty.	1997–8
Duty drawback scheme sets up 'special account' for deposit of exporters' funds. Exporters to be refunded from this account.	1998–9
Export of scrap metal reintroduced.	1998–9
A number of measures introduced for protection of industries.	1998–9
Pre-shipment inspection extended to cover Zanzibar imports.	1998–9
Promotion of external sector and export strategy devised, targeting agriculture, tourism, minerals and fisheries.	1996–7
Government abolished export tax on traditional agricultural goods, e.g. cotton, coffee, tea, sisal, cashew nuts, pyrethrum and tobacco.	1999–2000
Tanzania resigned from COMESA, effective September 2000.	2000–1
Export tax on scrap metals abolished with effect from 1 July 2000.	2000–1
To encourage cross-border trade with East African member states, import duties between member countries to be reduced substantially.	2001/2
Government abolished all taxes on drugs used by those affected by HIV/AIDS, malaria and TB.	2001/2
Stamp duty on sale proceeds from agricultural produce abolished.	2001/2
District Councils to register and license small-scale traders.	2001/2
Maximum stamp duty on lease agreement to be at lower rate of 0.96% on Tshs. 10 million.	2001/2
Importation of powdered milk banned.	2001/2

Source: Ibid.

Appendix 7.3 Flow of FDI by country of origin: 1998–2001(US$m. except [b])

Origin	1998[a]	1999	2000	2001	Total	% of Total[b]
EAC						
Kenya	53.7	21.1	6.5	12.5	93.8	3.2
Uganda	0.4	1.8	0.4	0	2.6	0.1
Sub-total	*54.1*	*22.9*	*6.9*	*12.5*	*96.4*	*3.3*
SADC						
South Africa	32.4	44.3	133.5	174.5	384.7	13.2
Mauritius	70.4	16.5	4.6	3.7	95.3	3.3
Swaziland	0.2	8	1.2	2.8	12.2	0.4
Malawi	10.5	1.1	0	0	11.6	0.4
Zambia	8.6	0.6	0	0	9.2	0.3
Sub-total	*122.1*	*70.5*	*139.3*	*181*	*513*	*17.6*
America and Australia						
Canada	96.7	78.9	0	20.6	196.2	6.8
USA	122.2	24	27.6	27.6	201.4	6.9
Australia	106.3	48.5	4	3.9	162.7	5.6
Sub-total	*325.2*	*151.4*	*31.6*	*52.1*	*560.3*	*19.3*
Europe						
United Kingdom	313.8	30.7	24.4	82.2	451.2	15.5
France	30.2	13.1	2.3	2.2	47.8	1.6
Switzerland	28.3	9	30.8	23.8	91.9	3.2
Germany	35.1	8.5	12.2	1.2	56.9	2.0
Denmark	24	6.3	0.4	0.1	30.8	1.1
Norway	31.5	5.5	1.6	4.6	43.2	1.5
Netherlands	106.4	5.5	1.7	58.5	172.2	5.9
Italy	68.1	3.5	1.5	1.2	74.3	2.6
Sweden	24.5	3.5	4.1	5.4	37.5	1.3
Luxembourg	16.5	0.6	0	2.4	19.4	0.7
Japan	6.5	0.4	16.8	0	23.7	0.8
Isle of Man	13	0.1	0	1.6	14.7	0.5
Sub-total	*697.9*	*86.7*	*95.8*	*183.2*	*1063.6*	*36.7*

Origin	1998[a]	1999	2000	2001	Total	% of Total[b]
Rest of Africa and World						
Ghana	265.1	162.7	0	1.5	429.3	14.8
Lebanon	1	6.4	0	0.9	8.3	0.3
Saudi Arabia	4.1	6.1	0	0	10.2	0.4
Bermuda	61.2	5.3	0	0	66.5	2.3
Foreign – not specified	3.7	4.1	0.2	1.3	9.3	0.3
Malaysia	40.5	3.7	0.1	1	45.4	1.6
Panama	1	2.4	0	5	8.4	0.3
China	9.9	0.8	1.9	1.5	14.2	0.5
United Arab Emirates	2.2	0.6	2.2	0.3	5.4	0.2
India	4.7	0.5	1.5	1.8	8.5	0.3
Sub-total	*393.4*	*192.6*	*5.9*	*13.3*	*605.5*	*21.0*
Grand total	1592.7	524.1	279.5	442.1	2838.8	97.9

Notes: a) 1998 represents FDI stock, and the subsequent years are flows. b) Total does not add up because of rounding-off errors and omission of countries with insignificant value of FDI.

Source: TIC (2002).

Appendix 7.4.1 Exports to COMESA, SADC and EAC countries: 1995–2002 (US$ m.)

Country	1995	1996	1997	1998	1999	2000	2001	2002
Angola	0.04	0.00	0.16	0.03	0.23	0.35	0.51	1.38
Botswana	0.02	0.03	0.07	0.27	0.21	0.09	0.23	0.04
Burundi	0.03	0.58	0.85	0.34	3.88	6.24	6.75	6.92
Comoros	0.00	0.01	0.00	0.05	0.01	0.05	0.02	0.35
DRC	3.32	4.12	8.75	4.69	8.10	4.87	8.66	15.64
Eritrea	0.00	0.00	0.40	0.00	0.00	0.03	0.34	0.23
Ethiopia	0.24	0.00	3.77	0.51	0.38	0.39	0.73	0.37
Kenya	23.47	8.99	25.49	27.96	21.59	31.53	38.41	34.90
Lesotho	0.00	0.00	0.00	0.00	0.00	0.00	0.00	0.00
Madagascar	0.01	0.01	0.04	0.00	0.04	0.10	0.67	0.68
Malawi	0.01	1.51	5.53	3.54	7.65	7.52	5.87	17.54
Mauritius	0.40	0.11	1.37	0.00	0.16	0.20	0.33	0.29
Mozambique	0.12	0.01	0.29	0.13	0.74	1.51	1.50	1.61
Namibia	0.01	0.00	0.01	0.06	0.35	0.15	0.04	0.03
Rwanda	3.93	1.48	6.25	4.23	3.15	2.10	2.85	3.82
Seychelles	0.00	0.00	0.00	0.58	0.03	0.05	0.03	0.28
South Africa	0.51	2.10	8.38	6.23	6.75	11.52	8.95	16.32
Sudan	0.78	0.20	1.60	0.34	0.17	0.29	0.24	0.27
Swaziland	0.00	0.06	0.24	0.03	0.20	0.21	0.00	0.37
Uganda	5.94	4.04	7.38	6.59	5.00	8.39	5.64	5.42
Zambia	4.12	1.50	2.17	3.62	3.45	5.59	6.09	17.23
Zimbabwe	0.47	0.93	16.71	13.06	2.80	2.68	0.44	1.39
Total	43.44	25.70	89.47	72.26	64.88	83.84	88.29	125.08
Overall exports	679.20	785.20	752.50	588.50	543.20	663.20	776.40	902.50

Source. Authors' own computation based on customs data from Tanzania Revenue Authority (various years).

Appendix 7.4.2 Imports from COMESA, SADC and EAC countries: 1998–2002 (US$ m.)

Country	1995	1996	1997	1998	1999	2000	2001	2002
Angola	0.00	0.00	0.00	0.00	0.00	0.00	0.00	0.00
Botswana	0.33	0.10	0.05	0.22	0.18	0.70	0.16	0.26
Burundi	0.26	1.91	0.55	0.05	0.02	0.01	0.01	0.01
Comoros	0.00	0.01	0.00	0.00	0.00	0.00	0.00	0.00
DRC	0.00	0.00	0.00	0.47	0.14	0.11	0.21	0.37
Eritrea	0.00	0.00	0.00	0.01	0.02	0.19	0.14	0.06
Ethiopia	0.13	1.21	0.26	0.81	0.87	3.12	0.54	0.68
Kenya	69.91	92.82	89.42	108.20	102.93	89.49	92.63	90.08
Lesotho	0.01	0.21	0.23	0.38	0.03	0.00	0.00	0.00
Madagascar	0.01	0.01	0.00	0.00	0.00	0.00	0.00	0.00
Malawi	2.50	2.85	2.06	2.30	3.73	1.80	2.04	1.44
Mauritius	0.64	3.00	0.48	0.74	3.31	2.43	3.14	1.73
Mozambique	6.48	10.10	3.77	5.41	0.03	0.13	0.43	0.03
Namibia	0.00	0.03	0.13	0.18	0.26	0.20	0.19	0.62
Rwanda	0.07	0.52	0.39	0.29	0.01	0.14	0.08	0.04
Seychelles	23.08	20.65	17.28	0.02	0.10	0.01	0.01	0.00
South Africa	96.80	71.56	85.19	127.35	189.68	159.42	180.16	177.17
Sudan	0.01	0.00	0.03	0.17	0.02	0.34	0.05	0.11
Swaziland	0.40	1.64	8.95	11.44	12.89	12.74	12.68	15.48
Uganda	0.33	3.65	2.02	2.17	8.12	5.52	11.34	2.38
Zambia	7.68	8.94	4.07	16.97	7.57	2.39	1.60	4.30
Zimbabwe	17.82	2.08	4.12	14.43	6.33	4.22	3.00	1.99

Appendix 7.4.2 (continued)

Country	1995	1996	1997	1998	1999	2000	2001	2002
Total	226.46	221.31	219.01	291.63	336.25	282.96	308.42	296.75
Overall imports	1340.95	1210.95	1320.30	1588.70	1572.80	1533.90	1714.40	1658.40

Source: Authors' own computation based on customs data from Tanzania Revenue Authority (various years).

Appendix 7.4.3 Trends in intra- and extra-regional exports (1995–2002)

Year	1995	1996	1997	1998	1999	2000	2001	2002
(A) Value of total exports (US$ m.)								
Intra-regional exports	43	26	90	72	65	84	88	125
Extra-regional exports	636	760	663	516	478	579	688	777
Total exports	*679*	*785*	*753*	*589*	*543*	*663*	*776*	*903*
(B) Share of the value of total exports (%)								
Intra-regional exports	6	3	12	12	12	13	11	14
Extra-regional exports	94	97	88	88	88	87	89	86
Total exports	*100*	*100*	*100*	*100*	*100*	*100*	*100*	*100*
(C) Value of agricultural exports (US$ m.)								
Total intra-regional agric. exports	22	12	22	32	22	32	41	64
Extra-regional agric. exports	303	99	296	359	318	309	270	280
Total agriculture export	*325*	*111*	*318*	*391*	*340*	*341*	*311*	*344*
(D) Share of agriculture products in total exports (%)								
Intra-regional exports	51	46	24	44	34	38	47	51
Extra-regional exports	48	13	45	70	67	53	39	36
Total exports	*48*	*14*	*42*	*66*	*63*	*51*	*40*	*38*

Source: Authors' own computation based on customs data from Tanzania Revenue Authority (various years).

Chapter 8

Regional Integration and Poverty: Conclusions

Dirk Willem te Velde

Regional integration can affect poverty in a variety of ways (see Chart 1.1). In order to assess how regional integration (RI) affects poverty, te Velde, Page and Morrissey presented a theoretical framework in Part 1 of this book. The starting point of this was that trade, investment, migration and other provisions can each affect poverty.

RI can affect poverty at country level in a number of ways:

- *1* through the volume and poverty focus of trade
- *2* through the volume and poverty focus of investment
- *3* through the volume and poverty focus of migration, and
- through other routes.

We found that there were four basic steps to assess each route:

- *Step 1* identifying the relevant provisions on trade, investment and migration
- *Step 2* identifying the effect on the volume and poverty focus of trade, investment and migration
- *Step 3* identifying how this change in volume and poverty focus maps onto poverty
- *Step 4* identifying how complementary conditions affect the relationship between the change in volume and poverty focus and poverty.

There are a number of expected and sometimes actual effects of the above links which provide a better understanding of how regional integration affects poverty. Empirical findings from the literature include the following:

- RTAs boost intra-regional trade through tariff reductions; several studies find that many regions are trade creating, but regions such as the EU and EFTA may have been trade diverting.

- Standards and very strict rules of origin may reduce intra-regional trade because the region may not have the appropriate processing capacity. It may also fail to take up the tariff preferences available because obtaining the relevant certificates may be too costly. Overlapping membership of more than one region may add to the confusion. Effects can also interact: rules of origin are likely to be more relevant if intra-regional tariff rates are substantially lower than extra-regional tariffs.
- RTAs are likely to lead to increased FDI from outside the region; various RTAs have led to net investment creation.
- The effects of increased trade and FDI depend on complementary conditions such as the provision of education.
- Despite these positive indications, any effect through trade, investment or migration provisions in developing country regions is likely to be small in the aggregate for various reasons. This is because the share of intra-regional trade in total trade in developing regions is small (for example, 15 per cent) and trade (average of export and imports) usually amounts to no more than 30 per cent of GDP. Regional trade therefore amounts to only around 5 per cent of GDP. In addition, of the 21 percentage point cuts in average weighted tariffs of all developing countries between 1983 and 2003, unilateral reforms accounted for the majority followed by multilateral commitments, leaving only 2 percentage points (10 per cent of the 21 percentage points) attributable to regional agreements.
- Similarly, intra-regional inward FDI is low; although it is 'only' 25 per cent in SADC, several SADC countries depend for more than 50 per cent of their FDI on South Africa. While intra-regional migration as a share can be high in MERCOSUR (26 per cent) or ANDEAN (53 per cent), migration as such is usually (except for small 'migration countries') low and migrants account for less than 1 per cent of the population.
- On the other hand, there can be non-static effects. Increased trade and investment can lead to faster economic growth and poverty reduction, particularly when trade leads not only to increased allocative efficiency but also to increased competition and productivity in the long run. These dynamic effects of regional integration are difficult to measure, but equally they should not be assumed away. There is some limited evidence that trade and investment induced by regions boost productivity (for example, regional exporters pay higher wages than domestic firms in Tanzania) and product variety and availability (for example, at times of country-specific droughts). While such dynamic effects are more likely when liberalizing multilaterally, to the extent that regional integration drives up productivity it might help firms to prepare for multilateral liberalization.

The regional integration effects through merchandise trade are thus likely to remain limited in regions amongst poor countries with similar production structures; expectations that this would lead to large development benefits should therefore be tempered. While there may well be dynamic effects and these can be more important than static effects, the evidence of this remains up to now limited, and it needs to be shown whether dynamic effects from regional integration support dynamic effects from multilateral integration.

Chapter 5 by te Velde and Fahnbulleh in Part 2 shows that regions differ in two fundamental respects:

- *over time* when one region can change or add investment-related provisions
- *across regions* when investment-related provisions differ at one single point in time.

Evidence shows that investment-related provisions in key regions differ significantly, including differences in:

- the extent of regional tariff preferences
- the restrictiveness of Rules of Origin
- investment rules, including national treatment for pre- and post- establishment and the presence of effective dispute settlement mechanisms
- regional coordination on investment
- type of membership: North–North, South–South, North–South, South–South–North.

The effects of regional integration on investment (from outside the region) are positive, but the benefits are likely to be distributed unequally across the region. The poverty effects through trade and investment depend not only on the depth of the integration process, but more probably on the complementary conditions that countries put in place.

Case studies of Bolivia and Tanzania in Part 3 tested the mapping structure set out in Part 1, moving beyond effects at regional level to poverty effects at country level. For Bolivia, new evidence by Nina and Andersen shows that regional integration has affected the country's trade composition, geographically towards more trade with ANDEAN and MERCOSUR, and sectorally in a shift from minerals towards vegetable fats, food and beverages. However, total trade as a percentage of GDP has not increased, mainly due to supply constraints in Bolivia, so that capacities to trade are important in benefiting from regional integration. This demonstrates the importance of complementary conditions. Lower regional tariffs have led to cheaper imports, but since only 8 per cent of the consumption of the poorest part of the population consists of imported goods (and some of this is not from the region) the impact on poverty through a trade price effect has been weak. On the contrary, data on the pattern of employment across sectors and over time support the idea that regional integration may have damaged domestic producers. This is because a large proportion of imports from ANDEAN and MERCOSUR compete with local producers. On the other hand, while increased exports may not have led to higher wages in the manufacturing sectors, they did raise incomes in the mining, hydrocarbon and modern agriculture sectors.

Kweka and Mboya argued in Chapter 7 that regional integration has increased trade in Tanzania. Regional trade has a better poverty focus than other trade; in other words, it comprises products that involve the poor more directly. Regional integration may not have affected FDI, but conversely FDI may actually have affected RI processes: Tanzania is part of the EAC and SADC, not COMESA, and has important commercial links with South Africa. The effects of RI on poverty through trade and investment have been limited. This is not necessarily due to limited progress in the regional integration process, but rather to capacity constraints, particularly in areas where the poor live. On the other hand, the East African Development Bank has provided regional public goods including socio-economic and environmental projects related to Lake Victoria. These projects reduce poverty, but while the initiatives are significant they remain limited in scope. While it is too early to evaluate such initiatives fully, they are an encouraging sign that regional integration can benefit the country through non-trade/investment/migration routes.

In conclusion, while this book remains cautious about the first three routes to the way poverty could be affected (trade, investment and migration), there might be important effects in the fourth route (direct route from regional integration to poverty – the curved arrow in Chart 1.1). Regional integration can affect poverty by including regional socio-economic projects and other types of integration, for example, in providing infrastructure or regional public goods generally. Regions also seem well placed to tackle the liberalization of the sensitive services sectors. In this sense, the type and scope of the regional integration process may matter a lot for poverty reduction. Several regions have widened their scope beyond trade and investment. SADC, for instance, has created a Southern Africa Transport and Communications Commission to implement its transport protocol.

A final note of caution relates to negotiating capacities and incentives to engage in multilateral liberalization. Regional integration processes affect the incentives to engage in multilateral integration (particularly North–South, but also South–South). Countries which have acquired tariff preferences may well like to retain these, and perhaps understandably may prevent further multilateral liberalization which would erode the preference margin. More attention should therefore focus on what areas fall within the competences of regions (for example, regional public goods) and how to ensure that a country does commit to and benefit from regional integration in a way that does not oppose multilateral trade liberalization later on. Regional integration processes, just like other integration processes, require government capacity. Normally, national policy is more important than any trade policy in development, so countries should avoid being diverted excessively to trade, especially to a small portion of total trade, as in most developing country regions. There therefore needs to be a better understanding of which negotiating capacities are transferable and useful for both regional and multilateral cooperation (for example, national baselines of services liberalization as proposed by COMESA) and which are not (for example, time spent in meetings).

Index

For Product Safety Concerns and Information please contact our EU
representative GPSR@taylorandfrancis.com
Taylor & Francis Verlag GmbH, Kaufingerstraße 24, 80331 München, Germany